CRITICAL REALISM
IN CONTEMPORARY ART
AROUND ALLAN SEKULA'S PHOTOGRAPHY

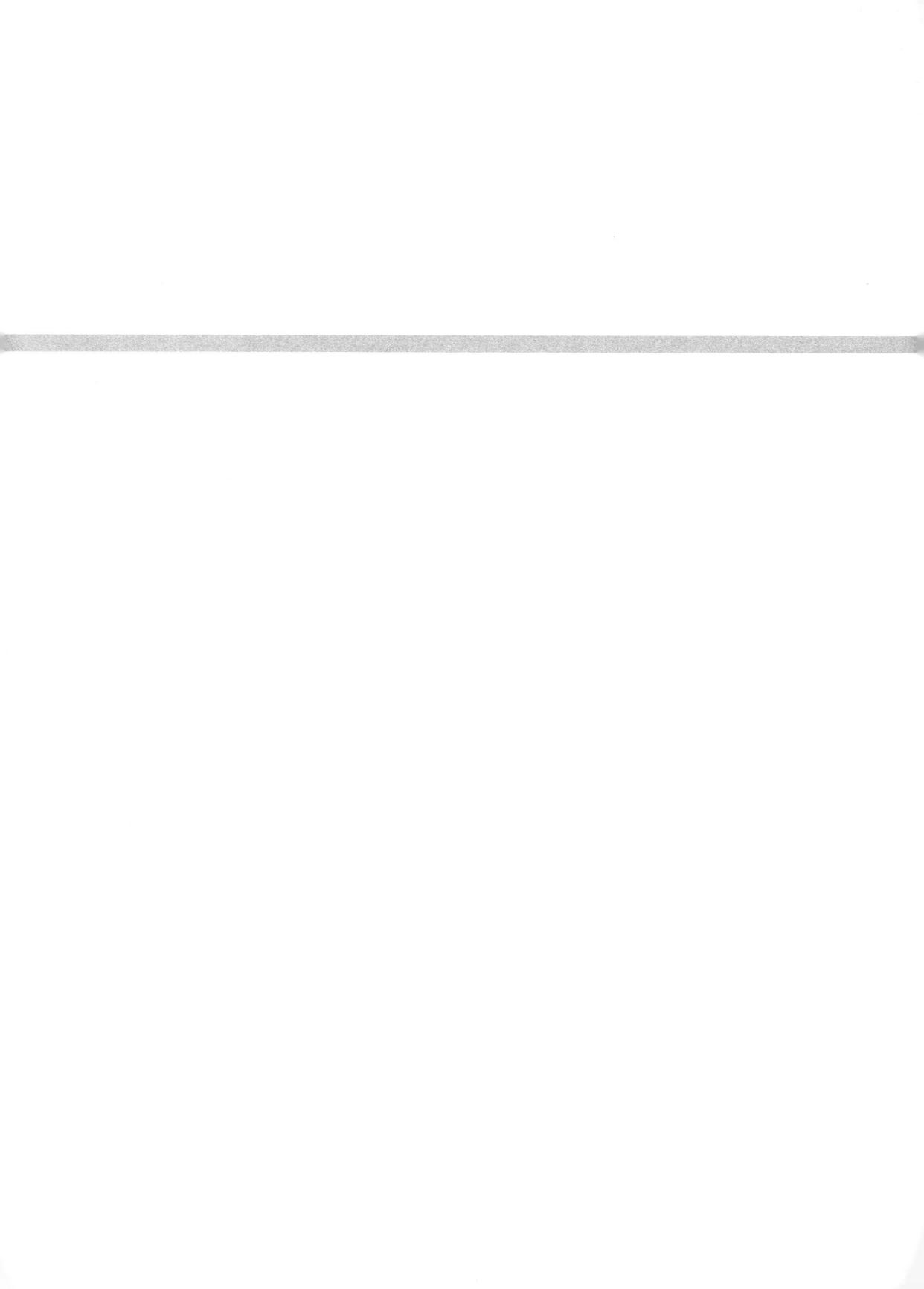

JAN BAETENS AND HILDE VAN GELDER (EDS)

CRITICAL REALISM
IN CONTEMPORARY ART

AROUND ALLAN SEKULA'S PHOTOGRAPHY

CONTENTS

INTRODUCTION

A NOTE ON CRITICAL REALISM TODAY

Hilde Van Gelder & Jan Baetens

20th-Century art, both in its modernist and postmodernist or –if one prefers– in its avant-garde or post-avant-garde paradigms, is at odds with realism, at least with the term. Realism seems incompatible with the basic features of what creative work and thinking in art is supposed to achieve: a distance toward reality itself, which art is not supposed to reproduce but to contest, to transform, and to supersede. Realism appears to go against the grain of a contemporary refusal of the canonical ways of presenting and representing (perspective in painting, narrative in literature, melody in music, and so on). Art should be a constant challenge to explore the boundaries of the not yet known and realism does not seem to serve this project. Realism, therefore, is often relegated to the museum of –in the eyes of current thinking– pre-modern styles and devices, safely locked in the toolbox of 19th-Century art history.

Yet modern societies are always divided. It should therefore not come as a surprise that 20th-Century art has been marked by a strong current or undercurrent of realism. Some avant-garde and modernist authors have deliberately claimed their commitment to reality, whereas certain postmodernist authors and artists have been trying to catch the 'signs of the times'. Moreover it is not exaggerated to argue that, probably under the double pressure of formalist exhaustion on the one hand (since the late 1960s, roughly speaking) and the explosion of virtual disembodiment of culture on the other hand (more or less since the last decade), realism is making a solid comeback, both in the art world and in society at large.

It is however mistaken to infer from the persistence of a word –'realism'– that it is one and the same thing or practice that bridges the gap between traditional and modern art (provided of course one accepts the dichotomy between tradition and modernity, but that is another story). The very notion of realism has indeed been radically redefined, in verbal as well as in visual frameworks or environments. One might say, although this is an oversimplification, that the concept of realism has undergone a series of dramatic changes.

First of all, technically or formally speaking, realism is no longer restricted to the implicit connotation of 'photographic realism': the 19th-Century model of detail realism as the production of a mechanical replica, no longer holds, either in literature, or in the visual arts. On the contrary, for those eager to maintain a realist stance in art today, realism is never simply reproductive (mimesis), but productive: it is the invention of new ways of representing the real, which always takes the risk of appearing utterly unrealistic, until these new styles become hegemonic, then stereotyped, and finally… unrealistic once again. Second, the notion of realism has shifted from the art-object to the attitude of the reader or the spectator, for whom a work appears to be realist if it reflects their ways of seeing and thinking reality, instead of directly reflecting reality itself. Third, realism itself is no longer a period label; it has itself been historicized, so that we have, instead of one realism, a full-fledged history of variegated and competing meanings, interpretations and assessments of the concept of realism. It is of course in this perspective that one has to examine the notion of 'critical realism'.

One of those who coined the concept was Georg Lukács, in his perhaps quixotic attempts to save realism from the attacks of the avant-garde. For Lukács, art *is*, i.e. *ought to be* realistic, many modernisms falling prey to shallow and hollow formalisms which often reflect reactionary politics. This is an argument that has become rather widespread in post World War II attacks on interwar modernism as well as from the artistic anti-model of socialist realism. For Lukács, art cannot –nor should it– be separated from a class perspective and therefore socialist realism may not be wrong in se.

But there were other uses of the term 'critical realism' and therefore other meanings. One of the major challenges of the concept is of course the difficulty –some might say the impossibility– of combining the adjective 'critical' and the noun 'realism'. For 'critical' is, in art theory, so strongly determined by the influence of the Frankfurt School and its 'critical philosophy', that it is not easy to reconcile the basic stance of transparency supposed by most types of realism with the Frankfurters' modernism and the violent anti-realism it implies. Theodor Adorno's art theory, for instance, is impregnated with the idea of negativity and anti-representation, not to speak of the conflict between the mostly democratic tendencies of realism and the Frankfurters' elitism, which discards all realism as vulgar populism. Critical realism, which is today often closer to the pole of the 'critical' than to the pole of 'realism', continues to be linked to avant-garde, formalism, iconoclasm, and the two traditions rarely meet. Engaged literature and art have been using rather formulaic devices for many years. In their most radical form, they simply do not care about forms, for art being seen as just one more type of political action is not something that should be assessed on aesthetic or formal grounds. Seen from this perspective the meaning of a form is measured by its political impact, i.e. its capacity to generate social change. On the contrary innovative literature or art tends to be discarded and debunked as fetishistic, anti-social and even anti-democratic.

It has been the merit of some 'enlightened' contemporary artists to bridge the gap between both worlds and to maintain the stance of commitment in art forms that do not accept the necessity of using and reusing too well-known forms in order to achieve a well inclined and broad audience, while being applauded at the same time for reasons which might be called politically correct. Allan Sekula's work is one of the most salient of such projects. His work features a number of characteristics whose combination makes it unique: Sekula's iconography rediscovers and reinvents the theme of labor, which had become completely outdated and artistically impossible after socialist realism. His photos, on the edge between art and documentary, and thus creating a kind of proto-documentary, reflect on the possibilities for the visual arts today to deliver an "act of criticism", as his fellow-American artist Martha Rosler has named it. The oeuvre of Allan Sekula, internationally known as one of the most prominent artists engaged in this debate, allows us to discuss the ways art can be critical about contemporary social questions without succumbing to a plain or overtly partial political statement. What comes to the fore as crucial in order for artistic images to avoid the trap of the slogan or propaganda, is the way they succeed in employing their metaphorical potential.

Critical realism, as we understand it, is a practice, a research method rather than an artistic style. It is a way of seeking to understand the social reality by critically 'making notes' of it. The visual comments artists such as Allan Sekula communicate to their public, are inscriptions and traces of the reality surrounding us, dialectically generated through the paradoxes of that reality and as such reflecting its contradictions. They bring questions to the foreground, without offering readymade answers, well aware as they are that clear answers are not to be found anyway. Yet, as scratches of reality, Sekula's photographs and films leave their traces in our minds. They encourage, yes, even force reflection, and through that, slow changes can probably become a reality, certainly at the level of the individual.

Photography –for many different reasons but especially because of its causal relationship to reality (its indexicality)– today appears as the best instrument to realize those ambitions, as many of the contributors to this book have asserted. Even after the so-called digital revolution, the photo is a material, tangible form of communication between the image and the reality it visually displays. The photo digs its critical potential out of this privileged relationship to reality; it really has something to say about it because it arises out of it. In this the strength and potential of photography is situated today. Photography, when conceived in this way, testifies to an attitude, an artistic way of approaching reality, whereby the artwork is not only the result of a committed process of investigation but also an actual, personally experienced record of it. In this search for the deliverance of visual information about the reality surrounding us, photography does appear to be a medium. Medium here is no longer to be understood in modernist, autonomist terms of self-definition but rather in terms of a method that researches reality rather than aspiring to reinvent an updated realist style. What the method does, is not trying to find its own very essence, but rather its boundaries and limits as a technique that aspires to do as best as possible what it can do: analytically and critically reflect on the reality it aspires to fathom.

Thanks to Sekula's work, realism has become once again critical (which it had been in the very beginning of the concept: in the 18th Century, realism meant social critique and satire), without resigning the experimental aspects of the creative process. The very method of the work enables it to link its realist content with all the questions that proved so crucial for 20th-Century avant-garde: the dialogue with an active audience, the limits of a medium, the social impact of art, the very distinction –and even more the very refusal of the distinction– between art and life.

1 _ CRITICAL REALISM

THEORY AND PRACTICE

1 _ REALISM AND THE DIGITAL IMAGE

W.J.T. Mitchell

"The currency of the great bank of nature has left the gold standard: images are no longer guaranteed as visual truth –or even as signifiers with stable meaning and value– and we endlessly print more of them." (Mitchell, 1992: 57)

One of the most consistent commonplaces about the nature of digital photography (and digital imagery more generally) is that the old claim of photographic images to represent the world faithfully, naturally, and accurately has been undermined by digitization. We are told that traditional chemical based photography had an indexical relation to the referent; it was physically compelled to form an image by the light rays emanating from the subject. This image or likeness was thus doubly referential, a double copy in that it was both an impression or trace, on the one hand, and a copy or analogon on the other. Both index and icon, it provided a kind of double entry bookkeeping of the real. Like the fossil trace, the shadow, or the mirror reflection in a still lake, traditional photography was a natural sign. It carried a certificate of realism with it as part of its fundamental ontology. Of course one could, as Mark Hansen notes, recognize that "the specter of manipulation has always haunted the photographic image", but insist that this is "the exception rather than the rule" (Hansen, 2004: 94). As William J. Mitchell argues, "reworking of photographic images is technically difficult, time-consuming, and outside the mainstream of photographic practice" (Mitchell, 1992: 7). With Photoshop, presumably, reworking or 'doctoring' photographs becomes technically easy, quick, and quite ordinary.

I remember a game that my father used to play with family photographs. It involved lining up my sisters and me behind him on a hillside, and my mother photographing us with the illusion that we were tiny pygmies standing on his outstretched hands. The photograph itself was not manipulated in the darkroom, but the pro-filmic event was staged for it and staged in such a way that it took advantage of the mechanical automatism of the camera lens (its perspectival design) to produce an illusion.

When Kaiser Wilhelm came to Palestine in the first decade of the 20th Century, he met with Theodore Herzl and a photo opportunity was staged to show them together in order to symbolize

European support for the Zionist project in Palestine. Unfortunately, when the photographs were developed, it turned out that the Kaiser and Herzl never actually appeared together in a single shot. So, the pictures went back to the darkroom and a famous photo of Herzl and the Kaiser together was fabricated. Was this photograph lying, given that the two men did actually meet? Was this an unusual occurrence? Was it technically difficult or time-consuming? Was it outside the mainstream? What would happen if a politically loaded photo fabrication like this was produced today in Photoshop? Would it be taken as authentic or would the 'specter of manipulation' automatically hover over it, by virtue of its digital character? The Herzl-Kaiser fabrication was not concealed; it was visually imperceptible (except to expert eyes) but it was widely known that the photograph had been manipulated. Would a digital trick of this sort have been more or less obvious? Or is it the imperceptibility of the 'specter of manipulation' that casts doubt on *all* digital photographs? In that case, of course, we would be back to square one. If all digital photographs are equally suspect, merely by virtue of their being digital, then none of them can be trusted –or distrusted– any more than any other.

I use Photoshop once a year to fabricate an illusion for my family's annual Christmas card. Once I tried to shrink my wife and kids down to little Munchkins and put them on the parapet of one of my sandcastles, with me at full size, looming above them like a Leviathan. Needless to say, this picture did not meet with the approval of the wife and kids; it exists now only in a fading print and a digital archive. Is this a rare or exceptional practice? Was it technically difficult or outside normal professional practice? My ordinary use of Photoshop is actually just the opposite in purpose: it is what is called the 'optimization' of images for whatever purpose they are going to serve –crunching them down for screening or transmitting over the internet, fattening them up in '.tiff format' to produce highly saturated color prints. In other words, I manipulate almost all the digital images that come into my computer, not in order to fake or fabricate anything, but to enhance their functionality in playing roles, very like traditional lantern slides or photographic prints. And in fact, I am barely competent at all these practices. People often complain that my PowerPoint presentations employ low-quality, low resolution images snatched from the Internet. And my answer is: "this is a kind of realism". Why should I try to simulate the color saturation and focus of a lantern slide, when in fact I am not showing lantern slides, but digital projections at 72 dpi? If realism means anything, surely it means candor about the nature of one's images.

The famous *Life Magazine* photo of Lee Harvey Oswald holding the rifle that killed Kennedy is probably a fake. What difference does it make that this was a chemical based photograph and not a digital photograph?

All these examples are mobilized, clearly, to undercut or at least complicate the prevailing myth that digital photography has a different ontology from chemical based photography, that this ontology dictates a different relation to the referent, one based in information, coding, and signage (the symbolic realm) rather than the iconic and indexical realms of the older photography. These examples also help us to question whether this very dubious 'ontology' (which isolates the 'being' of photography from the social world in which it operates and reifies a single aspect of its technical processes) has any fixed relation to issues such as authenticity and fakery or 'manipulated' and 'natural' images.[1] It seems clear that the authenticity, truth value, authority, legitimacy of photographs (as well as their aesthetic value, their sentimental character, their popularity, etc) is quite independent of their character as 'digital' or 'chemical analog' productions. The notion that the digital character of an image has a *necessary* relation to the meaning of that image, its effects on the senses, and its impact on the body or the mind of the spectator, is one of the great myths of our time. It is based on a fallacy of misplaced concreteness, a kind of vulgar technical determinism that thinks the ontology of a medium is adequately given by an account of its materiality and its technical-semiotic character.

I prefer Raymond Williams' account of media as "material social practices" (Williams, 1977) that involve skills, traditions, genres, conventions, habits, and automatisms, as well as materials and techniques. And (though this will take time to develop) I want to argue that the myth of digital photography has things exactly upside down. Instead of making photography less credible, less legitimate, digitization has produced a general 'optimization' of photographic culture, one in which better and better simulations of the best effects of realism and informational richness in traditional photography have become possible. My inkjet printer can now produce 8 by 10s with glorious color, something that was a rare and exceptional experience in the old days. If we are looking for a 'tendency' in the coming of digital photography, it is toward 'deep copies' that contain much more information about the original than we will ever need and 'super copies' that can be improved, enhanced, and (yes) manipulated –but not in order to fake anything, rather to produce the most well-focused, evenly lit image possible, in other words, to produce something like a professional quality photograph of the old style. We mustn't forget Marshall McLuhan's admonition, that one of the first effects of a new medium is simply the simulation and replacement of an older medium (McLuhan, 1994: 18). What is digital photography doing to the senses, the body, the referent, the sign, the image, much less that ever-vanishing entity known as 'the Real'? This ought to be at least a question to be asked and answered by some empirical particulars, not a transcendental deduction from a thin description of the bare technical facts about the digitization of images.

In saying this, of course, I don't mean to suggest that digitization has made no difference to photography or to image-making and circulation more generally. It's just that this difference has to be understood as a complex shift in many layers of photographic and image-culture, one that involves popular as well as professional, political, and scientific uses of automated image-production, and that is linked to modes of production more generally –i.e., new ways of making a living (or not) and of reproducing life itself. My argument is against the reduction of digital photography to a bare material and technical essence, "grounding it", as William Mitchell puts it, in "fundamental physical characteristics" (Mitchell, 1992: 4), rather than social practices and uses. I will be using Mitchell's discussion of digital photography throughout this essay as my principal example, simply because his book, *The Reconfigured Eye: Visual Truth in the Post-Photographic Era*, is so often cited as the principal authority and the 'classic' statement of this argument.[2]

The main use of digital photography has been (aside from simulating the effects of chemical based photography for amateur users) a deepening of the referent, not its disappearance. This point is demonstrated by Mitchell's own frequent recourse to techno-scientific examples such as the "spacecraft imaging" that makes it possible to take a "perspective view" of a volcanic landscape on Venus (Mitchell, 1992: fig. 2.1: 10). In this case, digital imaging enhances one of the most venerable aims of 'classic' or 'realist' photography, namely the revelation of realities that are inaccessible to the naked eye. Does anyone seriously argue that the digitization of x-ray images or magnetic resonance imaging compromise the 'adherence of the referent' to these images (Mitchell, 1992: 26)?

Of course, the kinds of manipulation and artifice that were already possible in traditional photographic practice become even easier in the digital darkroom. Photoshop is packed with magical tools for distortion, enhancement, cutting and pasting, re-sizing, cropping, and optimizing. But despite the hand-wringing over the coming inability "[to] distinguish between a genuine image and one that has been manipulated" (NY Times photography critic, see Mitchell, 1992: 17), the actual professional use of digital photography in the news media has revealed remarkably few attempts to fabricate false or misleading images. The very fact that cutting and pasting is so easy has, in fact, had just the opposite effect on professional practices and the National Press Photographer's Association has gone out of its way to warn against the use of digital technology to "create lies" (Mitchell, 1992: 16). As for the distinction between a 'genuine' and a 'manipulated' image, this is a paranoiac fantasy, since every photograph that was made in the traditional way was also a product of manipulation in the sense of technical, material standards, and decisions about what to shoot, at what settings and how to develop and print it. The concept of the 'genuine' image as a natural, unmanipulated entity is an ideological phantasm.

Again, none of this disputes the fact that the camera can be used to lie or that photographs can be manipulated to deceive. It is only to insist that the invention of digital imaging does not, by itself, render this capability the key to some essentialized ontology of the digital photograph. If ontology is the study of being, then we must not forget that ontology of photography should focus on its being *in the world*, not in some reductive characterization of its essence.

Mitchell makes a great deal of the de-realizing image practices that were first tried out in the first Gulf War, where "laser-guided bombs had nose-cone video cameras" and "pilots and tank commanders became cyborgs inseparable from elaborate visual prostheses that enabled them to see ghostly-green, digitally enhanced images of darkened battlefields" (Mitchell, 1992: 13). What he fails to note, however, is that these ghostly-green images permitted actual human beings to see what would have otherwise been invisible. There is a kind of paradox here in the relation of the image technology to the referent: what was dark is illuminated, what could not be seen becomes available to sight. The "de-realization" is only with reference to something like natural human night-vision, which would have seen nothing.[3] So, is this a loss of reality or a gain? My sense is that it is both and any attempt to confine ourselves to one side of the equation will miss the whole point of this kind of image technology as a worldly practice.

In that same Gulf War, Mitchell complains that

> "there was no Matthew Brady to show us the bodies on the ground, no Robert Capa to confront us with the human reality of a bullet through the head. Instead, the folks back home were fed carefully selected, electronically captured, sometimes digitally processed images of distant and impersonal destruction. Slaughter became a video game: death imitated art." (Mitchell, 1992: 13)

Of course, at the level of fact this statement is remarkably selective. There actually *were* real-time images of Iraqi bodies beamed by satellite from Baghdad after a U.S. 'smart bomb' destroyed what turned out to be a civilian structure. There *were* photographs (probably not digital) made of the trail of destruction left by the retreating Iraqi army massacred in a 'turkey shoot' by American bombs and rockets (though their circulation, along with images of U.S. servicemen's coffins, was suppressed).[4] If there was no Robert Capa, there was Peter Arnett on hand to verify the authenticity of the images of dead Iraqi civilians. And one wonders what Mitchell would make of the role of digital photography and video in the current U.S. war in Iraq.[5] The famous Abu Ghraib photos were all digitally produced. One of the most notorious of them (the stack of naked Iraqi men) was used as a screen-saver image on a computer at Abu Ghraib prison. The digitization of the photos had, so far as I can tell, absolutely no effect on their reception as authentic, realistic depictions of what was going on inside that prison, revealing as well the peculiar attitudes of sadistic enjoyment that characterized the American presence in front of, as well as behind the camera. Like the American lynching photographs of the early 20th Century, these images were revelations of a structural, social, and political reality that would have remained, but for their existence, at the level of rumor and verbal report. Of course, these images *could* have been manipulated and fabricated to convey false information. And many of them were quite visibly manipulated to erase the faces of the Iraqi victims. An entire internet industry of fake, staged Abu Ghraib photographs sprang up in the wake of the authentic images, especially in the period between May 2004 and February 2006, when the full archive was kept secret by the Pentagon despite a number of court rulings demanding their release. But these images were faked in the pro-filmic scenario, not in the digital processing of them. Their inauthenticity had exactly nothing to do with their status as digital images.

My point, however, is not that digitization is irrelevant, but that its relevance needs to be specified. In the case of the Abu Ghraib photos, the main relevance of digitization is not 'adherence to the referent' (which is almost always, in any case, established by documentation and testimonial credentials outside the image itself), but *circulation and dissemination*. If the Abu Ghraib photos had been chemically based, it would have been very difficult for them to circulate in the way they did. They could not have been copied so readily, or transmitted world-wide by e-mail, or posted on websites (not unless they had been scanned and digitized, that is). If Abu Ghraib did not have its heroic star photo-journalists to provide a human perspective, it had something perhaps even more striking and disturbing: a revelation of the inner workings of American military prisons, the Gulag outside the law that the Bush administration has been creating, and an insight into a different use of photography as an instrument of torture. Above all, the Abu Ghraib photos demonstrated a new role for photography's 'being in the world' made possible by digitization. They showed the way in which the rapid, virulent circulation of digitized images gives them a kind of uncontrollable vitality, an ability to migrate across borders, to escape containment and quarantine, to 'break out' of whatever boundaries have been established for their control. At a time when actual human bodies are being more and more fenced in by actual and virtual borders, fences, check-points, and security walls, when those same bodies are subjected to increasingly intensive and intrusive surveillance, the digital image can sometimes operate as a kind of 'wild gas' that escapes these restrictions.

It is not 'adherence to the referent' that is endangered by digital imaging then, so much as the adherence to a controlling intention in the production of the photographs. Certainly, the intention of the Abu Ghraib photographers was *not* exactly 'realized' by their digital circulation. Their intentions (which still remain somewhat obscure) were more along the lines of creating trophies of sadistic domination in a context where the American inability to contain the Iraqi insurgency was already becoming evident; and to humiliate the subjects of the photographs, perhaps even using them as blackmail to coerce Iraqis to work against the insurgency for U.S. intelligence (see Seymour Hersh's speculations on this point: Hersh, 2004). Both these intentions were frustrated or turned against the producers of the photographs. Their 'trophies' became exhibit A in the indictment of the 'few bad apples' that were punished for the 'abuses'. And far from helping to get information about the Iraqi insurgency, the photographs actually fueled the resistance and served as instruments of recruitment for the insurgency, and for world-wide terrorist networks.

What can we say then, about the actual, as opposed to the mythical meaning of the technical revolution in digital imaging? Are all the intelligent commentators simply mistaken in their portrayals of chemical photography as inherently realistic and the digital image as inherently open to manipulation and deceit, de-realization, disembodiment, and de-humanization? I think it is more complicated than a simple mistake, and that these sorts of mythic narratives of loss of authenticity and human meaning need to be stirred into whatever mixture of elements comprises the ontology of photographic images, their 'being in the world' of politics, techno-science, and everyday life. The very fact that these stories are somehow compelling, that they become classic or commonplace, is a part (but not the whole) of the ontology of the image. I want to conclude then, by widening the horizon of inquiry beyond photographic images to two more general domains: 1) the level of the 'codes' that underlie claims about referentiality and significance in images, especially the opposition between the digital and the analog image; 2) the analogy between images and life-forms that is drastically enhanced by the quantitative increase in production, reproduction, and circulation of images in the digital world.

William J. Mitchell's distinction between digital and analog codes is a convenient place to start:

> "The basic technical distinction between analog (continuous) and digital (discrete) representations is crucial here. Rolling down a ramp is continuous motion, but walking down stairs is a sequence of discrete steps —so you can count the number of steps, but not the number of levels on the ramp. A clock with a spring mechanism that smoothly rotates the hands provides an analog representation of the passage of time, but an electronic watch that displays a succession of numerals provides a digital representation." (Mitchell, 1992: 4)

While this illustration might seem compelling at first, it quickly deconstructs itself. Rolling down a ramp may be continuous motion, but one *can* in fact count the number of rolls. Or, if the metaphor is made consistent, one can walk down a ramp and count the number of steps one takes. As for walking down stairs: yes, one can count the stairs, but one may *experience* that descent (as my lively nieces and nephews routinely demonstrate) as a kind of flight or free fall. There is a real difference then, between digital and analog representation, but it is a highly labile and flexible difference, a dialectical relationship, not a rigid binary opposition. It is not, most important, an ontological difference, but a difference in representation and perception. The same thing can be scanned, mapped, depicted, described, and assessed –in a word, represented– in a digital or analog format. The stairs can be given analog representation; the ramp can be digitized.

More important, the two forms of representation are mutually definitive and complementary. The idea of isolating one of them as somehow self-sufficient is a myth (which is why the very idea of a 'digital culture' strikes me as such a slovenly and misleading shorthand, even while I recognize the inevitability of its deployment). The analog only has the meaning it does in contrast to some specifiable notion of the digital and vice versa. And the mutual, reversible translation between the two formats is essential to their practical usages. Digital sound recording, for instance, does not produce a digital output. The analog signal returns the moment when the recording is actually played on speakers driven by an amplifier. Throughout the 20th Century chemical based newspaper photographs were routinely digitized, long before the invention of computers, at the moment of their printing. Examine any older newspaper photo with a magnifying glass and you will find that it is composed of a grid of Ben Day dots, pixels before the pixel. It was the human eye that 'resolved' the digitized grid into an analog representation. If digitization is (as Mitchell suggests) a matter of "discrete steps", then everything, from mosaic tile to pointillist painting, is already digitized. Chemical based photography itself had to contend with a digital level known as 'grain' at the heart of its own processes. Anyone who has seen Antonioni's classic film *Blow-Up* is aware that, at high levels of magnification and enlargement, chemical based photographic prints dissolve into an abstract *mélange* of black and white specks.

A better guide to the relation of digital and analog is provided by Nelson Goodman, who insists that we specify the kinds of digits and marks being differentiated, and the codes that are governing their combination (Goodman, 1976: 159-163). The digital/analog relation varies, for instance, depending on what sorts of digits or 'discrete elements' are being employed. Letters of the Latin alphabet and Greek numerals are already digital in the sense of being 'discrete'. Black and white tiles assembled to produce a geometric figure that seems alternately to recede and advance are digital elements that are received as analog in perception. A geometric curve that descends the y-axis and extends infinitely along the x-axis is an analog depiction that can be expressed digitally in the expression $y = 1/x$. And sometimes, a system of representation can be a compromise between a precise digital quantification and a rather vague, qualitative assessment. Is the specification of shoe sizes as 8, 9, 10, or 11 a 'digital' representation, in contrast to T-shirt sizes defined by 'Small, Medium and Large'? Digitization need not, in other words, involve binary number systems (1 and 0). It need not even involve numbers at all, but can occur whenever a limited number of unambiguous characters (e.g. red, yellow, green) are deployed to signal unambiguous meanings (e.g. stop, caution, go).

I like to illustrate the dialectical character of the digital/analog difference by referring to Chuck Close's paintings, which simulate the look of the digital grid or screen of depiction, but then treats the individual 'pixels' or discrete units as objects of individual painterly operations, as if each pixel were a miniature abstract painting. Or, if a more widely known example is desired, consider two scenes from that universal cultural referent, the film *The Matrix*. In one scene a character named appropriately 'Cipher' is watching a computer screen that is awash with a stream of alphanumeric characters. When he is asked what he's looking at, he says it is the Miss Universe contest and that he is so familiar with the code that it has become transparent to him. He sees right through the numbers and letters to the analog images they represent (just as we 'see through' the Ben Day dots on a newspaper photo to the analog images they transmit). The other scene is the moment of revelation of the 'digital reality' that underlies the analog 'surface' or 'illusion' constructed for human beings by the Matrix. When Neo has his moment of revelation, he suddenly sees the deadly Agents of the Matrix as what they 'really are' –nothing but streams of alphanumeric characters in a virtual space. But at the very moment of this revelation we also see that the ghost of the analog is returning and the shapes of the Agents' bodies are clearly outlined amidst the flow of numbers and letters that lie 'behind' their corporeal illusion. When sophisticated commentators tell you (as they routinely do) that the 'analog' era is behind us, that digitization has destroyed photography, digital video has destroyed film, and that the image itself has been eliminated by digitization, ask them what they make of this scene. If the Desert of the Real is, in fact, just numbers, then we can take some comfort in the fact that Plato already made this point over two thousand years ago and he still thought the only moral to be drawn from it was that we had to go on living in this world of shadows, illusions, and images –in short, in the world of the analog.[6]

But still, the mythmakers are not completely mistaken about the digital image. Digitization makes an enormous difference to the role of images in culture, politics and everyday life, but those differences cannot simply be 'read off' their material or technical features. One would expect, for instance, that since digital images can be duplicated with a simple set of keystrokes, that the world would be flooded with more copies of these pictures than ever. But my own experience is just the reverse. Digital images (private, amateur pictures, that is) tend to languish unseen on the hard drives of computers in much the same way that 35 mm slides used to remain hidden away in storage boxes or carousels. Printing a digital photograph requires a new set of habits. Should one drop off the memory card at the drugstore the way one did with a film canister? Or should one first optimize and edit them in Photoshop, then copy them to a CD Rom, and then take them to the drugstore? Should one buy a photo printer and do them at home, a process that looks simple until you try formatting the images for smaller sizes like 4 by 6"? Should you send them in to an on-line service and wait for the prints to arrive in the mail?

Notice that the problem here is not that it is difficult to produce a set of prints in the traditional way, but that there are too many choices of how to do it. The simplest one, dropping off the memory card (or sending them into an online service) is made complicated by the fact that one knows that it would not be difficult to do this just a little better by taking a bit more time to optimize the images. But who has time? And who has time even to think about choices like these? My answer, which I suspect is typical, is to defer these decisions for another time, leaving the family photos safely (one hopes) in the digital archives.

Digital photographs have a different life-cycle from chemical based photos. They do not necessarily circulate in printed form, but remain in a mainly subterranean realm, unseen and mostly forgotten, but (thanks to a variety of search mechanisms) available for retrieval much more quickly than printed photos. Although it is tempting to call this a 'de-materialization' of the image, since it only exists as a data file on a disk somewhere, the fact is that this is also a material existence, occupying a real place, and it is subject to material decay just as surely as traditional photographs. William Mitchell claims that a traditional photograph "is fossilized light" (Mitchell, 1992: 24) and if this metaphor makes sense, it means that digital photographs are simply the instruments of a more far-reaching paleontology of the image.

Another implication of the fossil metaphor is that images are like dead, dormant, or even extinct life forms that can be brought back to life by being brought back into the light –printed, projected, or screened. And this, I think, is one of the key frameworks for thinking about the larger cultural context of the digital image. These images have achieved technical perfection in the same period that an entirely different class of images has been subjected to an analogous process. I'm thinking here of the reproduction of organisms, biological life-forms, by the process of cloning. Clones are a living, organic version of the digital image, involving a similar relation between an underlying genetic code and a visible, bodily, analog manifestation. And much of the anxiety about digital imaging echoes the common phobias about cloning: both processes are accused of replacing a 'natural' process with one involving artificial manipulation; both are accused of producing endless copies that threaten the identity of the individual specimen. As Mitchell puts it: "a digital image that is a thousand generations away from the original is indistinguishable in quality from any one of its progenitors" (Mitchell, 1992: 6).[7] The metaphor of 'generations' and 'progenitors' makes clear the biological figure of the perfect, artificial double or twin, in contrast to traditional copying processes which always involve loss of detail and natural decay. There is a kind of horrific immortality about the digital image, whether photographic or organismic. And this may explain why the descriptions of them so often resort to biological metaphors, as if we were beset by a 'plague' of images, self-generating, virulent entities that threaten, not just traditional photography, but traditional forms of life itself (for more on the subject of the "life of images", see Mitchell, 2005).

One of the most fundamental consequences of the more virulent and volatile 'life', produced by the digitization of images, is an erosion of the boundaries between the private and public, amateur and professional circulation of photographs.[8] The digital image is not merely a matter of taking a picture with a digital camera and storing it on a disk or printing it out. It is also a matter of circulating it on the internet via e-mail and 'photoblogs'. Family albums are now easily transformed into public exhibitions and even secret photographs (again, Abu Ghraib is the conspicuous example) can easily circulate globally once they break out of their quarantine.

What does all this say, finally, about the problem of realism in photography or in images much more generally? It obviously all depends on what you think that counts as realism in representation. I think it means that we must untether the problem of realism from the ontology of the medium. Despite Susan Sontag's passionate arguments, there is nothing automatic about realism in photography, nothing encoded in the ontology of the photograph that makes it 'adhere to the referent'. And realism can be, in any event, many other things besides 'adherence to the referent'. For one thing, the referent of a photograph has to be stipulated. Is a photograph of my Aunt Mary referring to her, to her dress, or to her expression on this particular day and the meaning of an occasion? Is it realistic if she puts on her Sunday best to be photographed, so that this image shows her in a way that was somewhat exceptional? And would discussions of the value or quality of this picture be likely to focus on the question of its realism at all? Or would they focus on whether she looked pretty in this picture, looked her best and what a special day this was? My sense is that in ordinary family photographs realism is very low on the totem pole of evaluative criteria.

Realism is not 'built in' to the ontology of any medium as such. Cinematic realism reveals this perhaps most vividly, since it is a very special project within a medium that, if it has a built-in tendency, would tend toward fantasy and spectacle, not the faithful portrayal of ordinary life. Most people take photographs in order to idealize and commemorate, not to realistically portray something. As for what realism 'really is', this is a subject that would take up a lot more space than I have here (but see Mitchell, 1994: 345-362). One can make a photograph that 'adheres to the referent' in a quite literal way by producing a direct transfer contact print, but this guarantees nothing about its realism. Socialist realism, as we know, was anything but. It was a contrived process of ideological idealization of a projected, hoped-for reality, but (as Lukács pointed out) it was not the same thing as what he called "critical realism", a project of objective, historically informed representation built upon an independent point of view 'outside' of socialism, a view which necessarily identifies the critical realist as someone who occupies a middle, perhaps even bourgeois, class position (Lukács, 1971: 93-135). Literary realism, as Northrop Frye pointed out long ago in a similar vein (Frye, 1957), involves the representation of ordinary people in a 'middling' situation, between the Aristotelian categories of 'high' subject matter (tragedy and romance) and 'low' (comic characters and incidents). 'Social realism' of the sort practiced by Allan Sekula, tends to fuse Lukács' 'critical realism' with an emphasis on conditions of labor and an interest in exposing to photographic view a world that is overlooked or generally hidden away from public view —all this, however, in tension with his photographs' artistic status, their character as highly crafted and often beautiful objects.

As an example, consider Sekula's photograph of a displaced wrench on page 16 of his photo essay *Fish Story* (Sekula, 1995: 16). The photograph exemplifies social realism in that it does not stand alone, but is part of a whole world that is documented in loving detail, both in other photographs and the accompanying text. It satisfies Frye's notion of low mimetic realism in its emphasis on the world of masculine labor. It is 'critical realism' in Lukács's sense, in that it is the sort of image that would only occur to an outsider to the world Sekula is documenting. It is safe to say that no sailor on board of a container vessel would be likely to regard this as a picture worth taking. It would be 'overlooked' and invisible, not only to the outside world, but to the insiders as well. But in addition to all this, it is an extraordinarily beautiful and haunting image as well, one that I have never forgotten since the first time I picked up this book. Why? First, it satisfies many of the aesthetic criteria of abstract formalism with its simple, bold, geometric composition and its defiance of perspectival depth in favor of a flatness to the picture plane that would have pleased a Clement Greenberg. This flatness is coupled with a high resolution and high color saturation as well as attention to the materiality of rusting metal, and the sheer beauty of those materials when they are isolated as a graphic specimen in a high-gloss representation (if photography has an automatism, it is as much a tendency to aestheticize and beautify as much as it is to 'adhere to a referent'). And finally, what is the 'referent' of this photograph? Is it the wrench or the ghostly trace of its displacement that appears just to the right of it? Whatever else this picture refers to, it clearly refers to the very issue we have been pondering, namely the 'adherence of an image to its referent'. The ghostly trace of the displaced wrench is a kind of natural contact print, traced in the medium of rusting metal, very like those solar prints I used to make of leaves on paper in elementary school science classes. One would like to know whether the artist displaced the wrench himself or simply found it this way. Neither answer would lower my high estimation of the picture, though I suspect that Sekula might, as a matter of a certain realist principle, not have moved the wrench.[9] Either way, the photograph satisfies another condition of modernist aesthetics and that is the revelation of self-consciousness and self-reference in the work of art. It would make no difference to *this* meaning of the image if it turned out that it was made with a digital camera or were projected as a digital slide.

And then, finally, there is scientific realism, which carefully defines its notion of truth, correspondence, adequation, and information, and which (given its quantitative basis) is deeply in love with the precision of digital imaging. Scientific realism, however, is generally at odds with common sense realism, which tends to content itself with the realm of analog information, with dense, qualitative impressions filled with random, unsystematized detail. Scientific realism, in fact, usually begins by taking issue with common sense and showing us something that we couldn't see with the naked eye. That is why, obviously, photography (both chemical and digital) plays both sides of the fence with regard to the debate between science and common sense, verifiable truths and the idealizations of desire. And that is why I come to rest, finally, with philosophical realism (as distinct from nominalism). The view that abstract, ideational entities are 'real entities' in the real world –more real, in fact, than our confused repertoire of sense impressions and opinions. Truth, Justice, Being, and 'the Real' itself (along with geometric concepts such as the circle, the square, and the triangle) are, for the philosophical realist, the foundations of the real world. But the realism that would get at them is not uniquely tethered to any particular medium or its putative 'ontology'. They are themselves the foundations of ontology and the media – verbal or visual, material or immaterial– are simply poor instruments for representing them. That is why realism is a project for photography, not something that belongs to it by nature.

[1] As William J. Mitchell puts it: "the difference is grounded in the fundamental physical characteristics that have logical and cultural consequences" (Mitchell, 1992: 4).

[2] This may be an appropriate place to state for the record that William J. Mitchell, a distinguished professor of media studies at MIT, is not the same person as W. J. T. Mitchell, the obscure drudge who is the author of the present article. I

had considered entitling this article "Mitchell versus Mitchell".

[3] For a discussion of the claims of realism and illusionism in photography and image-making more generally, see my book, *Picture Theory* (1994), especially section IV, "Pictures and Power": 323-362.

[4] See my essay 'From CNN to JFK' on the media coverage of the first Gulf War (Mitchell, 1994: 397-416).

[5] It is worth noting that the presence of digital photography has had a major impact on the circulation of realistic images of the war in Iraq. No longer the exclusive purview of professional journalists, photo- and text-blogs from Iraqi civilians and American soldiers are flooding the internet. And the U.S. military mission has made it clear that notions of journalistic professional neutrality will not be honored in this war. The mandatory 'embedding' of journalists with military units and the confinement of journalists to military controlled compounds was only the first stage in the attempt at total media control. Direct violence and incarceration are also favored tactics: 67 journalists have been killed in the U.S. war in Iraq, in contrast to the 63 who were killed in ten years of reporting in Vietnam (www.Salon.com, accessed 30/08/2005).

[6] I recommend here Brian Massumi's superb essay 'On the Superiority of the Analog' (Massumi, 2002: 133-43).

[7] But see Lev Manovich's discussion of "Lossy compression" for a technical puncturing of this myth of the perfect copy (Manovich, 2001: 54). A similar problem occurs with the notion of a clone as a perfect copy. Actually, a clone is less similar to its donor or parent than an identical twin, because it has generally been gestated in a different womb and matures in a completely different environment, at least one generation after its ancestor. Neither clones nor digital photographs can be identical twins in this very fundamental sense.

[8] I am grateful to Allan Thomas for pointing this out.

[9] During the discussion at the Leuven Conference in September 2005 on 'Critical Realism' and the photography of Allan Sekula, it became clear that he had in fact moved the wrench, not to mention bringing in artificial light to enhance the photograph's color saturation.

Works Quoted

Frye, Northrop, *Anatomy of Criticism*, Princeton: Princeton University Press, 1957.

Goodman, Nelson, *Languages of Art*, Indianapolis: Hackett, 1976.

Hansen, Mark, *New Philosophy for New Media*, Cambridge (Mass.): MIT Press, 2004.

Hersh, Seymour, *Chain of Command: The Road from 9/11 to Abu Ghraib*, New York: Harper Collins, 2004.

Life Magazine, 21/02/1964: Photo of Lee Harvey Oswald.

Lukács, Georg, 'Critical Realism and Socialist Realism', in: Id., *Realism In Our Time: Literature and Class Struggle*, New York: Harper & Row, 1964: 93-135.

Manovich, Lev, *The Language of New Media*, Cambridge (Mass.): MIT Press, 2001.

Massumi, Brian, *Parables for the Virtual: Movement, Affect, Sensation*, Durham (N.C.): Duke University Press, 2002.

McLuhan, Marshall, *Understanding Media*, Cambridge (Mass.): MIT Press, 1994 (1964).

Mitchell, William J., *The Reconfigured Eye. Visual Truth In The Post-photographic Era*, Cambridge (Mass.)-London: MIT Press, 1992.

Mitchell, W. J. T., *Picture Theory. Essays on verbal and visual representation*, Chicago: University of Chicago Press, 1994.

Mitchell, W. J. T., *What Do Pictures Want? The Lives and Loves of Images*, Chicago: University of Chicago Press, 2005.

Sekula, Allan, *Fish Story*. Exhibition.Rotterdam. Witte de With Center for Contemporary Art. 21/10/1995, Düsseldorf: Richter Verlag, 1995.

Williams, Raymond, 'From Medium to Social Practice', in *Marxism and Literature*, Oxford: Oxford University Press, 1977: 158-164.

www.Salon.com, accessed 30/08/2005.

2_ LOOPS OF HISTORY

ALLAN SEKULA AND REPRESENTATIONS OF LABOR

Katarzyna Ruchel-Stockmans

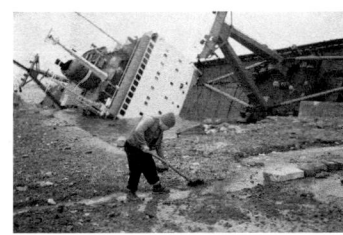

Fig.1 Allan Sekula, *Shipwreck and Worker* , from: *Titanic's Wake* (2001) (original in color).

In the well-known passage from *The Theses on the Philosophy of History* Walter Benjamin describes a scene in which the angel of history sees the past events as a series of catastrophes and piling debris. The angel wants to interfere, to help put everything back in order, but he cannot, for his wings are lifted above by a strong blast of wind from heaven. In *Shipwreck and worker* (2001) Allan Sekula has also captured an image of the angel of history, but this one is much less concerned by the disaster taking place in full view **[fig. 1].**[1] A ship is quietly sinking behind his back, unnoticed by the lonely figure holding a shovel, occupied with sweeping garbage and mud in front of him. This angel is more like the peasant from Bruegel's painting, *The Fall of Icarus*, says Sekula. Undisturbed by the tragedy of the falling Icarus, the peasant continues ploughing the field, just as the lonely worker continues shoveling. But if this worker is the angel of history, then his disinterestedness is ominous, for now nobody —since he was the last to do so— cares any longer about the impending disaster. This image, taken in Istanbul, constitutes a hidden kernel of the exhibition *Shipwreck and workers* by Allan Sekula, shown in Leuven, Belgium (2005). Although the photograph is absent from the exhibition itself, it nevertheless lies at its origin and forms its conceptual framework. First, it connects with it visibly through the title. Second, in the exhibition itself there are many workers in different photographs and the same shipwreck is shown, but in a triptych and without a single human presence. The photograph *Shipwreck and worker* is, in a sense, expanded onto the whole series.

The association with Walter Benjamin's figure of the angel of history made by Sekula is very revealing here. It grants us access to the most crucial feature of Sekula's project. By looking into historical images, like that of Bruegel and especially those of Constantin Meunier, Sekula attempts to re-conceptualize photography as a realist medium. Labeling his practice as 'critical realism' implies that the photographer investigates to what extent the medium can mirror reality and how much it constructs this reality. Therefore, his project consists also of rewriting the history of representation and the history of art —as the title of his well-known book puts it— against the grain. However, it is not only the history of visual culture that is at stake here. Sekula aims at re-writing social history in a much broader sense in order to critically rearrange the image that we might have of the contemporary world. His political stance is quite clear. Paraphrasing Victor Burgin's description of the 'politically 'left' photographer' one can say that Sekula "wants to help correct society's false picture of its actual conditions of existence" (Burgin, 1997: 77). His particular interest follows the representation of work and workers in their present-day situation, as he detects that in this sphere there is a conspicuous misrepresentation in the dominating discourse. But it would not quite be right to call Sekula a documentary photographer. Rather, he positions himself critically towards the tradition and current practice of documentary photography, using such different tools as critical theory, structuralism, photo-conceptualism and cinematic and literary sources. To achieve that, he engages in a dialogue with archival images of labor and politics hidden behind the representation of workers, not only by doing photography and film, but also by researching and analysing images in his essays. By returning to this conspicuously unpopular theme within the iconography of 'high arts' of the 21st Century, Sekula attempts to demonstrate that the widespread opinion about the disappearance of manual labor is far from being true. As Benjamin Buchloh noted, "the experience of production and condition of industrial labor have been banned by a massive representational prohibition from modernist visual culture" (Buchloh, 1997: 11).

Meeting Meunier

In his project in Leuven, Sekula wrested with the notion and the role of the monument to labor as it came to a stand in the late 19th-Century sculpture of the Belgian artist Constantin Meunier.[2] His photographs take on a double role played by the monumental sculpture from the 19th Century and by the street advertisements of the 20th Century. In the Spring of 2005, the city of Leuven saw his now well-known posters *Dear Bill Gates* in different locations throughout the town. Their repetitiveness resembled advertising strategies, but their content impeded any instant reading. Later the same year, the exhibition *Shipwreck and workers* opened in STUK Arts Centre, or to be precise, it overflowed through the walls of the center to the outside, from both entrances to the building, where huge panels with photographical diptychs and triptychs were hung. Again, the sheer size of the photographs made of them an intervention in the city space. The dialogical character of this exhibition, which was a response to a historical presentation of Meunier's sculpture, introduced a new, distinguished note in the work of Allan Sekula.

However, in order to see this recent project in an adequate perspective, it is necessary to have a glimpse of Sekula's earlier artistic activity. Along with such prominent figures as Martha Rosler, Sekula emerged in the late 70s as a conceptual artist and activist in San Diego. His first performances included, for instance, throwing stolen pieces of meat under the wheels of racing cars on a motorway. Only at a later stage did he take up photography, which appeared to be the medium best suited to registering the reality of working people and their powerlessness against the shifts of a more and more globalized economy. Above that, his use of photography was steered by his disinclination towards high genres of art. In America, abstract expressionism still reigned supreme, but –I'm paraphrasing Sekula here– what could it say about such crucial facts in the newest history as the Vietnam War (Sekula, 1984: IX)? Especially in the context of socialist realism, entangled as it was in the propaganda of the totalitarian powers of 20th-Century Europe, both painting and sculpture have manifested their defenselessness in the face of ideological exploitation.

Already in his early work, which was designed to be shown as a slide sequence, Sekula has shown interest in the representation of workers in a direct way. In his *Untitled Slide Sequence* (1972), he exhibited a number of photographs of workers leaving the aerospace factory after their dayshift. He has followed this interest ever since. In his other early work, *This Ain't China* (1974), another significant characteristic of his photographic practice becomes apparent, namely the inclination towards theatricality and overtly exaggerated staging. In that project, Sekula intended to document work in a restaurant where he had been employed. After realising that the owners would not allow photographing their business from the insider's perspective, Sekula decided to recreate the working conditions in the kitchen, staging it together with other employees who were dismissed from work shortly before. The apparent tension or even contradiction between these two projects, namely the propensity towards 'straight' photography of the *Untitled Slide Sequence* on the one hand, and overtly theatrical staging of *This Ain't China* on the other, remains central to Sekula's whole oeuvre.

In his colossal project, *Fish Story*, shown at the *Documenta XI* (2002), consisting of an exhibition and a book, he developed another crucial theme –that of the sea and the maritime world. The sea attracted him as a forgotten or obliterated space, which is nonetheless fundamental for the contemporary globalized economy. But it also turned out to be a powerful metaphor that helped him define the relations of late capitalism and observe the changing representational modes and

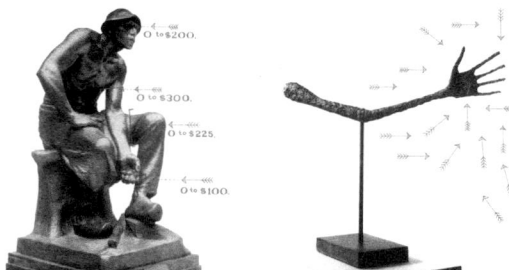

Fig.2 Allan Sekula, Montage of Constantin Meunier's *Puddler* (1893) as published in: Crystal Eastman, *Work Accidents and the Law*, 1910; and Alberto Giacometti's *Hand* (1947) as photographed by Mark Trivier, with arrows added by Allan Sekula (original in color).

attitudes towards maritime society. The photographic work was complemented by short texts explaining the context as well as essays, which dug deeper into the questions of literary and visual representations of the sea.

Imported Images

Invited to Leuven to reflect on Meunier as an exponent of 19th-Century social realism, Sekula chose to enter into a dialogue with his monumental work. It is important to mention Meunier's *opus magnum*, an impressive sculptural complex of the *Monument to Labor*, upon which the artist worked in Leuven, but which was never completed during his lifetime. Meunier waged a genuine revolution in the mode of representation of a manual worker, lifting this 'undignified' subject to a monumental position. His attitude and style did not bring him immediate recognition and even today he is a somewhat forgotten figure. One of the most well-known sculptural pieces belonging to the artist is the *Puddler*. This figure of a brawny and muscular worker, weakened by persistent fatigue, was also the first piece by Meunier that Sekula encountered during his research on the representation of work. Strangely enough, the book where the image was reproduced was not an art history survey. Meunier's *Puddler* was perhaps one of the first appropriated works of art. It appeared in a publication by the socialist activist Crystal Eastman entitled *Work Accidents and the Law* (1910) **[fig. 2].** Sekula re-appropriates the image from the book, placing it in the center of the Leuven exhibition, at the inner court of the arts center. Under the *Puddler*, he adds a photograph of another work of art, or rather a small fragment of it, namely a hand by Giacometti. A panel with a text appears next to the images, placing the word on the same level as the image and also making the two 'borrowed' pictures a clue to the whole group of photographs.

This double appropriation poignantly illustrates how the meaning of a photograph can shift. Even works of art dating from before the age of mechanical reproduction acquire the ambiguity that photography brings with itself, as John Berger observed regarding paintings: "in the age of pictorial reproduction the meaning of paintings is no longer attached to them; their meaning becomes transmittable: that is to say it becomes information of a sort, and, like all information, it is either put to use or ignored; information carries no special authority within itself " (Berger, 1973: 24). The benefits of reproduction and broad dissemination of works of art are accompanied by a faltering of the solidity of meaning of an image. Crystal Eastman re-contextualizes Meunier's monument to dignity of manual labor into an ironic illustration of meager compensations for work accidents. Arrows and numbers indicate the maximum compensation for the damage to an arm, a knee or the forehead. At the same time, her photomontage *avant-la-lettre* can call forth other visual associations. Allan Sekula writes that "her transformed Puddler is both St. Sebastian and a butcher's sectioned side of beef".[3] A slight alteration in the image places it within a different constellation of visual references.

By inserting under it another montage of Giacometti's hand with arrows, Sekula emphasizes the role of the hand as emblematic of manual labor (Sekula, 1996). The two hands meet above the formal and historical differences. Strangely enough, this encounter of a realist and a modernist sculpture resembles a Sots-art installation by Leonid Sokov entitled *Lenin and Giacometti* (1986)**,** on which the Socialist leader meets Giacometti's elongated figure. While Sokov intends to juxtapose the two modernisms from both sides of the Iron Curtain, Sekula projects Giacometti's existential sculpture onto its historical predecessor, from the period when realism was not yet tinted with the ideology of a totalitarian regime. He turns intentionally to this earlier form of 19th-Century realism. By re-appropriating the image of the *Puddler*, he turns his own exhibition of photographs of workers into a sort of anti-monument to labor. His pictures are also placed in the public space, outside of the institution and on prominent spots. Furthermore, they portray working people, though the medium has changed. It would be difficult, however, to call this project a monument, because the role of the image has changed significantly since the time of Meunier. This change is apparent, precisely at the point where the figure of Giacometti negotiates between the 19th-Century realism of Meunier and socialist realism of the Soviet monumental sculpture. The idea of monumentality itself became ambiguous. However, the urge to represent labor that drove Meunier and that made his art 'problematic' for the public of the time reappears in the artistic project of Sekula.

Archaic Work or Archives Rediscovered

As already mentioned above, Sekula committed several of his earlier projects to depicting people working in heavy industry, shipyards, or construction sites. *Shipwreck and workers* consists of a slightly different collection of portraits of workers. Among them are museum guards, a curator, grape harvesters, an oil deliveryman, a ship inspector, a logger, and even goldsmiths. There is something noticeably archaic about these professions. The oil deliveryman is shown next to the grape harvesters, connoting, according to the artist, a common source of the two symbolic substances –oil and wine– in the book of Genesis that opens the Bible. Some of the workers are shown during their normal activities; some are posing self-consciously for a portrait. This collection of individual and group portraits of working people strikingly resembles an early modern tradition of illuminated manuscripts illustrating professions. One particular example, the Balthasar Behem Codex from the beginning of the 16th Century (1505), shows similar scenes of workers in their environments, for example *The Potter* or the *Shoemaker's Workshop*. They too are occupied with their daily business, but nevertheless look at the spectator, as if willing to incite a dialogue. Strangely enough, the goldsmith's workshop in this codex is also shown through the window, which –although the technique and close-up differs– resembles Sekula's goldsmiths at work.

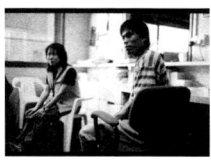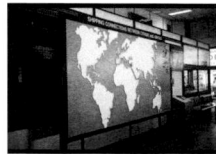

Fig.3 Allan Sekula, *Seafarers*, diptych, 2005 (original in color).

The reconnection with older modes of representation of labor is, in my view, not accidental; although I am not purporting that Sekula consciously referred to this or any other particular illuminated codex. The main difficulty of the contemporary images of the working class lies in the looming risk of falling into one or the other stereotyped representational style. The photographic tradition of sentimentalized and aestheticized labor, as it was propagated by the well-known exhibition, *The Family of Man* (1955), is often transported to a journalistic black-and-white style of photography. On the other hand, there is still a vivid visual memory of socialist realist grandiose representation of workers, which reminds one of the risks of false pretences and propagandistic misuse. Re-looping back to historical modes of representation is a means of escaping the contemporary dead-end situation of documentary photography.

Having said that these images often have archaic connotations, I would like to point out that the contemporary malaise of the post-industrial is not completely absent from this exhibition, but it became more concealed. A hint of this can be found in the photograph of the seafarers shown next to a map **[fig. 3]**, as well as in the two scenes with the ship inspector. These give a clue to the deplorable work conditions on ships and scarcity of control. The sweatshop became more inconspicuous or even invisible as it moved to the Third World countries. The symbol of this globalized industry in Sekula's imagery is the cargo container –an invention of the 50s that facilitated transportation of goods on a global scale. Sekula associates it with another emblematic form present in the iconography of late modernist art –a minimalist box. In the exhibition, *Shipwreck and workers*, the container-box resurfaces in a little diagram **[fig. 4]** illustrating the physical law defining the work input needed to shift an object up a hill. These discrete hints at the global economy and the sea as a metaphor of this economy refer to Sekula's earlier concerns and connect this exhibition with his previous projects.

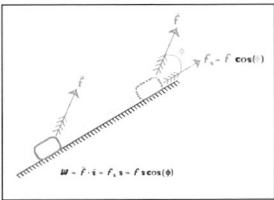

Fig.4 Allan Sekula, *Shipwreck and Workers* (Version II for Leuven), fragment of text panel (original in color).

Two Perspectives

The three photographs of the wrecked ship, which open the exhibition starting from the main entrance of STUK Arts Centre in Leuven, introduce a disquieting note in this discourse **[fig. 5]**. If the "Angel of History" in Benjamin's account was lifted up by a strong wind, the working Angel from the seminal Istanbul photograph by Sekula has already disappeared from the triptych. And even when he was still there, he was not really concerned with what was happening. Now that there is no one in the wake of the ship disaster, the story of the angel appears even more pessimistic than in Benjamin's recounting. There is, however, a contrast between this dim beginning and the relatively optimistic faces of the subjects in the portraits. The gloomy vision of the economic world –known already to those acquainted with Sekula's book and exhibition entitled *Dismal science*– is counterbalanced by the quiet and affirmative attitude of the photographed workers.

35

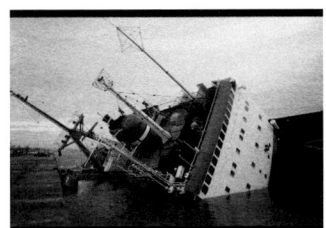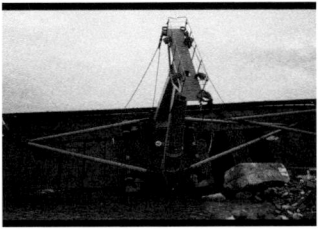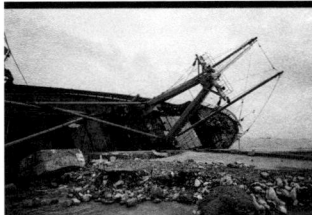

Fig.5 Allan Sekula, *Shipwreck*, triptych, 2005 (original in color).

This also relates to a contrast between a more global view of the present day reality and the singular lives of individual people. Both perspectives are present in Sekula's photographic and theoretical work, and they mark a clear difference between his project and that of, for instance, Andreas Gursky. Gursky is often described as the new painter of the post-modern life, photographing immense spaces of post-industrial cities, such as a stock exchange and an airport. In Gursky's pictures, human beings are always mere patches of color in a vast mosaic. His illustration of the work environment is highly aestheticized and –from Sekula's standpoint– obliterates the true working conditions of individuals. Sekula maintains the contrasts between panoramic views and frog-perspective frames in order to achieve a tension within his work. In *Fish Story*, this tension was built between panorama and detail –two opposing perspectives on the same reality. In the current project, he also contrasts different modes of photographing by grouping his pictures in diptychs and triptychs. The juxtaposition of the oil deliveryman and grape harvesters was already mentioned above. There are also two frames showing consecutive moments in a scene with a ship inspector and the captain, which create an almost cinematic sense of narrative **[fig. 6],** defying the ascendancy of the aesthetics of the 'decisive moment'. Two sets of triptychs of the sinking ship and the goldsmiths are shown contiguously to each other to create yet another tension. The shipwreck is shown in three frames revealing three different sections of the tilted deck. The whole looks like a displaced photomontage, which intensifies the nearly sublime feeling of destruction. The other triptych, showing Turkish goldsmiths at work, depicts a time sequence in still images, again calling to mind film stills **[fig. 7].**

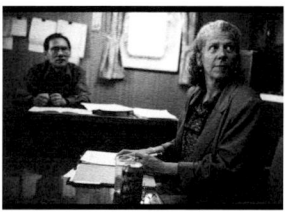 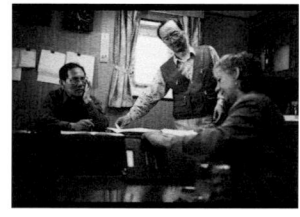

Fig.6 Allan Sekula, *Ship inspector and captain*, diptych, 2005 (original in color).

Document between Engagement and Aesthetization

Already in Meunier's time it was not clear how to interpret the new iconography of the working class. With all the respect and concern for the conditions of workers, Meunier did not intend to incite political action aimed at overthrowing the existing social order. But he was also aware, as Hilde Van Gelder points out, "of the fact that too stark a 'neutral' line of approach can easily tip over into an overly non-committal sensational reproduction of reality" (Van Gelder, 2005: 76). A similar dilemma is present in contemporary documentary practice. A too distanced look can easily lead to aestheticism and –paraphrasing Burgin– "the photographer's narcissistic display of concern for the poor" (Burgin, 1997: 74). Showing engagement with the situation of people, on the other hand, is being criticized for "having a ghoulish addiction to misery and, worse, profiting financially from the desperation of others" (Rosler, 2004: 212). These are the ethical concerns that stem from the choice of the socially informed subject matter. But they do not merely question the relevance of such iconography. Even when one agrees on the necessity of visualizing this subject matter, there remains a question of how to depict it correctly. As Adorno poignantly noticed: form is a "sedimentation of content" (Adorno, 1999: 139). It is in the form that Meunier's works gained their most lasting power. They can still speak to contemporary artists using different media. Meunier chose an image of a worker that is not bereft of dignity

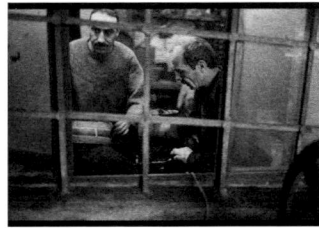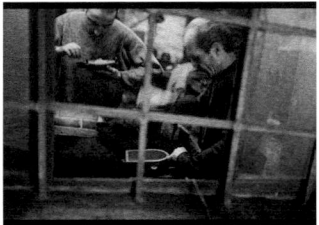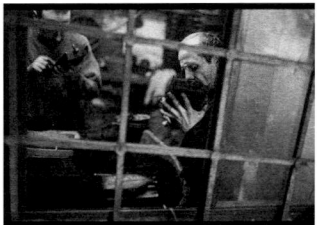

Fig.7 Allan Sekula, *Goldsmiths*, triptych, 2005 (original in color).

and at the same time remains accurate in showing the physical side of the manual chore. The encounter with Constantin Meunier allows Sekula to revisit the question of the monumentality of work –undoubtedly present in Meunier's sculpture– and the materiality of manual labor, so poignantly visible in the *Puddler*, whose exhaustion, sweat, and dirt are almost tangible in the bronze statue.

Sekula also deals with the question of the aesthetics of the photographic image. Against the Marxist objection towards the beautiful as a typically bourgeois category, Sekula creates work that is often visually attractive and riveting. By this, he seems to be reaffirming the thesis of Herbert Marcuse, who in Sekula's early student days was one of his teachers. Marcuse maintained that "the political potential of art lies only in its own aesthetic dimensions" (Becker, 1994: 120). Therefore, the impact an image can have is inextricably connected with its visual qualities. The aesthetic holds the knowledge about the subject matter and the ethical dimension of the work of art together, in a similar vein to Kant's architecture of human faculties. The aesthetic dimension, however, does not only encompass the category of the beautiful. The sublime is equally present, especially when the sea comes to the fore as the space of great risk. One can even find the borderline category of the abject (Kristeva, 1982) in Sekula's deferred views of slime from the oil spill in Galicia, shown in his newest film *The Lottery of the Sea* (2005) or in his previous occupation with severed fish heads in his film *Tsukiji* (2001).

The aesthetic references become much more visible to the learned viewer. The allusions to 20th-Century artworks, literature, and philosophy introduce a whole richness of the visual pleasure of looking. This might sound paradoxical, but the images Sekula is producing ask, or even require, to be filled in by text, film, and other images. To be sure, Sekula usually provides detailed information about his subjects, the situation they are in, and gives more general comments on the matter. But the information never takes the form of a caption attached to the image, which would distract the spectator from a direct encounter with the picture. The captions are usually listed at the end of a show or –as in the case of the Leuven exhibition– under the text on one of the panels.

According to the old distinction of Marshal McLuhan between hot and cold media, photography is said to be a hot medium giving a high definition of data and thus requiring little participation from the side of the spectator. Then Sekula's project might be seen as putting photography into a refrigerator. His images begin to work when they are considered together with the research results of the artist and when they are confronted with past and present models of the representation of work, like that of Meunier's. This makes Sekula's work immune to what Adorno despised as "culinary consumption of art" (Adorno, 1999: 92), but at the same time it places a great constrain on the spectator, demanding a much higher involvement from his/her side. Sekula's recent work still resembles what he once called a "disassembled movie" (Buchloh, 2003: 25) in which still images have to be pieced together with text and sound. Even in his films this rule seems to be valid.

Sekula's project of critical realism is based on Bertolt Brecht's seminal concern about the invisibility of the real relations of production and power. As Brecht says: "a photograph of the Krupp works or the A.E.G. tells us next to nothing about these institutions" (Benjamin, 1979: 255). As such, it has to be anchored in the right context and thereby invested with meaning. Sekula's proposition for the contemporary representation of labor encompasses photographic sequences and series accompanied by considerable doses of research. This includes, besides theoretical, social, and political investigations, an effort to interpret the different styles and conventions of representation from the past. Documentary thus appears to Sekula as a platform for critique. To use his favorite visual metaphor, one can say that documentary is like a ship which, as an extension of land in the vastness of the sea, offers a "heterotopic" (Foucault, 1986) space from which all other spaces can be called into question. This endeavor, however, raises some objections. The learned photographer asks for an equally learned and attentive spectator. There are multiple layers of meaning to be discovered and reassembled by a willing recipient. If he or she does not meet up to these requirements, the photographs of Sekula might start to live up to their own 'afterlife' in entirely different contexts. In that case, we will not learn anything more about the Krupp works or the A.E.G factory.

I mentioned earlier the significant presence of archaic elements in Sekula's recent photographs, such as the oil and wine symbols or ancient professions. There is one more way in which Sekula's project appears –without any negative connotations– as archaic. His urge to search for meanings is conveyed to the spectator, who is asked to make an attempt to decipher the multi-layered context. Only in the continuous effort of gathering visual data and textual references in the process of incessant friction between images and words can the meaning be incited in the viewer.

[1] The photograph belongs to the series *Titanic's Wake* (2001).

[2] To celebrate the centenary of the death of this social realist sculptor and painter, the city and museum of Leuven, in collaboration with the Lieven Gevaert Research Centre For Photography and Visual Studies, invited contemporary artists to reflect on the actuality and relevance of Meunier's oeuvre.

[3] Quotation from the text by Sekula included in his exhibition Shipwreck and Workers. Version II for Leuven (2005)

Works Quoted

Adorno, Theodor, *Aesthetic Theory*, trans. Hullot-Kentor, Robert, London: The Athlone Press, 1999.

Becker, Carol, 'Herbert Marcuse and the Subversive Potential of Art', in: Id. (ed.), *Subversive imagination: Artists, Society, and Social Responsibility*, New York: Routlege, 1994: 113-129.

Benjamin, Walter, *One-way Street and other writings*, trans. Jephcott, E., London: NLB, 1979.

Berger, John, Blomberg, Sven & Fox, Chris, *Ways of Seeing: Based on Television Series with John Berger*, New York: Viking Press, 1973.

Buchloh, Benjamin, 'Allan Sekula: Photography between Discourse and Document', in: Id., Sekula, Allan & Gierstberg, Frits (ed.), *Dead Letter Office*, Rotterdam: Nederlands Foto Instituut, 1997: 10-26.

Buchloh, Benjamin, 'Conversation between Allan Sekula and Benjamin H.D. Buchloh', in: Sekula, A. & Breitweiser, S. (ed.), *Performance Under Working Conditions*, Vienna: Generali Foundation, 2003: 21-52.

Burgin, Victor, 'Art, Common Sense and Photography', in: Evans, J. (ed.), *The Cameraworks Essays. Context and Meaning in Photography*, London: Rivers Oram Press, 1997.

Foucault, Michel, 'Of Other Spaces', in: *Diacritics*, no. 16, Spring, 1986: 22-27.

Giacometti, Alberto, *La main*, 1947. Photo Mark Trivier, in: *Alberto Giacometti*, Bazel: Editions Beyeler, 1991.

Kristeva, Julia, *Powers of Horror: An Essay on Abjection*, trans. Roudiez, Leon S., New York: Columbia University Press, 1982.

Rosler, Martha, 'Post-Documentary, Post-Photography?', in: Id., *Decoys and Disruptions: Selected Writings 1975-2001* (October Books), Cambridge (Mass.): MIT Press, 2004: 207-244.

Sekula, Allan, 'An Eternal Esthetics of Laborious Gestures', in: Choinière, F., *Portrait d'un malentendu. Chroniques photographiques récentes*, Montreal: Dazibao, 1996: 27-36.

Sekula, Allan & Buchloh, Benjamin (ed.), *Photography Against the Grain: Essays and Photoworks 1973-1983*, Halifax: Nova Scotia, 1984.

Van Gelder, Hilde, "Social Realism' Then and Now. Constantin Meunier and Allan Sekula', in: Id. (ed.), Constantin Meunier. A Dialogue with Allan Sekula (Lieven Gevaert Series, vol.2, 2005: 71-91.

3_ CRITICAL REALISM

TEXT, CONTEXT AND TIME

David Green

Questions of how we understand and experience photography in terms of time never seem very far away in any discussion of the medium. Indeed, many of the most influential theoretical accounts that we have of the photographic image seem ultimately to hinge upon the analysis of its peculiar temporalities. Depending from which direction we approach the subject, however, we find that we can pose different kinds of questions as to the significance of photography's relationship to time. Recently rethinking the temporal nature of the photograph for myself has been the result of the convergence of two sets of interests.

The first of these relates to a preoccupation amongst some contemporary video artists with exploring aspects of the stillness of the image and its duration in time in a medium that we take to be primarily orientated to quite distinct, indeed contrary, aesthetic possibilities. There may be a number of reasons why artists might choose to use a medium of the moving image in a manner that initially seems counterintuitive. Certainly one such reason for the contemporary video artist, as well as for those artists who turned to the use of film in the 1960s, would be as a means of distinguishing their practice from the dominant conventions that govern the employment of the medium elsewhere and to ends other than those of art. If there remains any critical purchase in the modernist tenet of the exploration of the medium as being of value in itself (and I believe there is) then –in the case of video art– this might paradoxically involve the need to look beyond the medium rather than in to it. Compelled by circumstances in which what might be regarded as the essential properties or norms of the medium are by and large defined by its uses in the culture industry, video artists have had recourse to strategies that explore the interface of the medium with that of another. An engagement in the work of video artists with the near or absolute stasis and pure duration of the image is one such manoeuvre, staging as it obviously does the intimate conjuncture of video and photography (Green, 2004).

It is true that the doctrine of medium specificity and the modernist desire for the self-sufficiency of different artistic mediums is from the outset extremely problematic. Inasmuch as that which is deemed to be intrinsic and exclusive to a given medium is arrived through its differentiation from other mediums, any notion of autonomy is logically compromised. If what constitutes a medium is defined by means of reflection upon other mediums in which it is in relation, then any Greenbergian pursuit of the 'purity' of medium through a reflexive process of 'self-definition' is a non-starter. Yet if such an economy of negation automatically and always leads to the return of that which is excluded or suppressed as a ghostly 'other', the situation as regards those mediums that share properties or effects that appear as central to both, then the problems are of a different order. In such circumstances what then is taken to be that which distinguishes one medium from another takes on extraordinary, perhaps inordinate, importance. Such is the case of the relationship of photography and video (and, needless to say, film) and the different temporality that is thought particular to each.

We owe to Lessing's famous essay *Laocoön*, published in 1766, the idea of a fundamental distinction between the 'arts of space' and the 'arts of time'. Unlike poetry, which was intrinsically suited to relaying events 'which succeed each other in time', the visual and plastic arts of painting and sculpture, he argued, were bound by their inability to represent 'actions'. Whilst not entirely devoid of the possibility of narrativity (hence the well-known concept of the 'pregnant moment' that Lessing introduces as a kind of hinge between past, present and future) the task of the painter or sculptor was to be directed towards the representation of the human body in repose. Stillness, therefore, was both the limitation of painting but also its advantage over poetry. It's a moot point as to whether photography can simply be directly integrated into Lessing's arguments concerning the visual arts or whether it constitutes a qualitatively different notion of stasis. There is a sense, when reading the very earliest accounts of the new medium, that it constituted a radically different conception and experience of stillness and time as compared to the existing forms of art, including those of painting and sculpture.

The principal reason for this, I think, lies with photography's indexical nature, which is the second of my reasons for revisiting the issue of its relationship with time. Discussions of the photograph as indexical sign are now commonplace and it is widely recognized that the unique status of the photographic image lies with the fact that it exists by virtue of being directly connected to what it represents. Tethered to the material existence of things and touched by reality, the photograph testifies to the actual presence of an object before the camera and herein resides its unparalleled authority and power as a means of visual representation. Equally important, however, to an understanding of the photograph as index, is that it also embodies the moment of its making. Inverting the usual relationship of cause and effect, its temporal vector of the photograph is always retrospective. The logic of the photographic index is thus predicated upon its own historicity in a way that is not true for other kinds of images and in this it brings into existence a radically novel conception of time into the domain of pictoriality. We might say that photographs fix time rather than merely stilling time.

The dual aspect of the photographic index –its power as testament to the putative presence of an object or event and its being a record of its logical absence– constitute the paradox that lies at the crux of the medium. This paradox involves, according to Roland Barthes, an unprecedented type of perception and mode of consciousness. As he argues, the reality that the photograph offers is nothing as simple as "the *being-there* of the thing" but "an awareness of its *having-been-there*" (Barthes, 1977: 44). Thus, the photographic index has to be thought of in terms of the co-ordinates of both its spatial and temporal dimensions. Specifically, as Barthes states: "What we have is a new space-time category: spatial immediacy and temporal anteriority, the photograph being an illogical conjunction between the *here-now* and the *there-then*" (*Ibid.*).

What is rarely acknowledged is that Barthes' extremely influential account of the peculiar nature of photographic indexicality (though it is never named as such) and its complex reorientation of the space-time relations of the image is conducted in direct dialogue with the medium of film. Introduced first of all in *The Rhetoric of the Image* and later reformulated in the more phenomenological language of *Camera Lucida*, Barthes' attempts to find a way in which to describe the distinctive temporality of the photograph is consistently framed by references to cinema. Indeed it is clear that for Barthes it is only through the comparative distinction with the moving image that photography finds its inimitable identity. In *The Rhetoric of the Image*, immediately following his description of the photograph as "an illogical conjunction between the *here-now* and the *there-then*" he goes on to argue that

> "the photograph must be related to a pure spectatorial consciousness and not to the more projective, more 'magical' fictional consciousness on which film by and large depends. This would lend authority to the view that the distinction between film and photograph is not a simple difference of degree but a radical opposition. Film can no

longer be seen as animated photographs: the *having-been-there* gives way before a *being-there* of the thing…" (Id.: 45)

Barthes is not alone in seeing the comparison of photography and film as central to an understanding of both. As with others before him, the differences between the two mediums appear as stark and absolute: on the one hand we have movement that not only is present but also lends to the image a 'presence' that is associated with life, and, on the other hand, we have a moment frozen in time and an immobility that is lodged within an ever-receding past that can only testify to an absence that ultimately carries with it the spectre of death (Green, 2006).

It would seem that the two routes by which I had initially pursued independently the question of photography's relationship to time have led me to a place were a number of issues become inseparable. If any consideration of the indexicality of the photography cannot be thought outside of the particular temporal character of the image, equally the temporal character of the photograph appears inextricably bound into its differential relationship to the mediums of film and video. The potential field of enquiry opened up here is clearly vast. However, my purpose in making these extended preliminary remarks is to draw attention to a number of issues that, I think, have an important bearing upon the discussion of what we might understand by the term 'critical realism'. In what follows I hope to indicate how the question of photography's relationship to time, and thereby its relationship to notions of history and memory, have been important to any practice of critical realism, even if they have not always been foregrounded.

I will begin with a thought from Susan Sontag:

> "Through photographs, the world becomes a series of unrelated, free-standing particles; and history, past and present, a set of anecdotes and fait divers. The camera makes reality atomic, manageable and opaque. It is a view of the world that denies interconnectedness, continuity, but which confers on each moment the character of a mystery." (Sontag 1977: 22-23)

In an essay written in response to the publication of Sontag's *On Photography*, John Berger seizes on this notion of the photograph as being both a spatial and temporal fragment. Acknowledging its indexical character —"a photograph is not a rendering, an imitation or interpretation of its subject, but an actual trace of it"– Berger directly links this unique capacity of photography, compared to the visual media that preceded it, to the fact that the object or event pictured is thereby 'fixed' and removed from the flow of time (Berger, 1980: 50). Whilst this might suggest an analogy with the faculty of memory, Berger notes that "[…] unlike memory, photographs themselves do not preserve meaning. They offer appearances –with all the credibility and gravity we normally lend to appearances– prised away from their meaning" (Id.: 51). The fate of the photographic meaning, however, depends upon the uses to which it is put. For the 'private' photograph, the personal snapshots that make up the family album, meaning is redeemable since the image belongs to a continuing context in which "the photograph is a m[e]mento from a life being lived" (Id.: 52). By contrast, the 'public' photograph offers appearances as "information severed from direct lived experience" (Ibid.). If the mass of photographic images in circulation in contemporary culture have any connection to the faculty of human memory, "it is to the memory of an unknowable and total stranger" (Ibid.).

Yet whilst Berger (again following Sontag) sees photography as contributing to the diminishment of the functions of memory in the modern world, it is possible to envisage an 'alternative photography' based upon practices which would seek "to incorporate photography into social and political memory, instead of using it as a substitute which encourages the atrophy of memory" (Id.: 58). The principle requirement of such an alternative photographic practice would be that it followed the 'laws of memory' and that would require the creation of a 'context' for the individual image.

> "Such a context replaces the photograph in time –not its own original time for that is impossible– but in narrated time. Narrated time becomes historic time when it is assumed by social memory and social action. The constructed narrative time needs to respect the process of memory which it hopes to stimulate. There is never a single approach to something remembered. The remembered is not like a terminus of a line. Numerous approaches or stimuli converge upon it and lead to it. Words, comparisons, signs need to create a context for a printed photograph in a comparable way; that is to say, they must mark and leave open diverse approaches. A radial system has to be constructed around the photograph so that it may be seen in terms which are simultaneously personal, political, economic, dramatic, everyday and historic." (Id.: 63)

Neither the emphasis that Berger places upon the idea of the photograph as a spatial and temporal fragment nor his advocacy of a strategy of creating a inter-textual context as a means of combating this were particularly original. Most notably both Walter Benjamin and Siegfried Kracauer had in the early 20th Century seized upon the notion of the photograph as fragment, though each reached different conclusions as to the prospects of reconstituting mnemonic experience from amidst the ruins that photography had created. It was Benjamin, quoting Brecht, who gave us one of the clearest formulations of the idea that photography preserved appearance at the cost of meaning.

> "As Brecht says: the situation is complicated by the fact that less than ever does the mere reflection of reality reveal anything about reality. A photograph of the Krupps works or the AEG tells us next to nothing about these institutions. Actual reality has slipped into the functional. The reification of human relations –the factory, say– means that they are no longer explicit. So something must in fact be *built up*, something artificial, posed." (Benjamin, 1979: 255)

The capacity of photography to reduce the social, economic, political and historical complexities of the world to a series of atomized and discontinuous images was something which Benjamin saw as progressively more likely as the result of technological developments that made it easier for the camera to seize the instantaneous moment. Most importantly, however, the photograph as a singular dislocated instant, violently wrenched from the flow of time, registered its psychical effects. The increasing mobility of the camera, Benjamin notes, made it "readier than ever to capture fleeting and secret moments whose images paralyse the associative mechanisms in the beholder" (Id.: 256). In other words, photography's fissuring of time and its reduction of the world to a collection of physically discrete and historically dislocated images left the subject bereft of the possibility of constructing for them a meaningful context in terms that might be both personal and political. Hence Benjamin's recommendation of the necessity of the caption that accompanies the photograph and "whereby photography turns all life's relationships into literature" (*Ibid.*). Benjamin's recognition, that the meaning of the photograph was never singular, immutable or intrinsic led him on several occasions to urge for the use of the written caption to accompany the image in order to "rescue it from the ravages of modishness and confer on it a revolutionary use value" (Benjamin, 1973: 95). The use of words, together with the techniques of photomontage, were the principal strategies whereby the single photographic image could be both physically and semantically re-contextualized. In accordance with the task of the contemporary allegorist such methods set out to revitalize the mute fragment, to release it from its exclusive association with that which is past and to set it to work in accordance with the needs of the present.

In the 1970s the revival of interest in Benjamin's essays on photography meshed with the growing influence of semiotics (including most prominently the writings of Roland Barthes) to provide an important platform for the political critique of the dominant modes of contemporary photographic practice. The principal targets were, on the one hand, the formalism that underpinned most fine art photography at the time, and on the other hand, a tradition of social documentary photography that remained wedded to the notion of the transparency of the photographic image to what it represents. It was, of course, in direct opposition to the idea of the photograph as a direct transcription of reality as revelatory of some kind of social truth that the practices of 'critical realism' emerged: the primary distinguishing factor of the latter lying in the belief that the photograph constructs the real rather than representing it. Without wishing to gloss over the complexities of such a debate (either then or now) it is, I think, important to recognize that in the shift from "the representation of politics" to "the politics of representation" (as Victor Burgin once succinctly described it (Burgin, 1986: 39)) critical realism necessarily involves some measure of self-reflexivity as regards the medium or mediums that it puts to use. However, it is significant that the photographic-based practices that emerged in the 1970s –that we might align with the term critical realism– did so in a way that highlighted 'inter-medial' concerns. It would seem that if photography itself was to be subject to interrogation in terms of 'the politics of representation' it was to be either through forms that explored the relationships between image and text or that used multiple photographs in series or sequence. Either route abandoned the identification of photography with the autonomous single image, as a spatial and temporal fragment, in favor of strategies that opened out a different set of narrative possibilities for the image and that questioned the dominant conception of the temporality of the photograph.

In broad terms this was also a shift from thinking about the photograph primarily in terms of the moment of its production, whereby meaning would always be constituted and understood as belonging to the past, to a way of thinking about the photograph as encountered at the moment of its reception and to the significance of the image as one encountered through a process of reading that takes place in the present. Perhaps emphasis should be placed here on the notion of 'reading' since it was primarily through the use of new modes of image-text work which challenged the traditional demarcation of the literary and the visual (and the different conception of time associated with each as derived from Lessing), that photographic practices of the 1970s predominantly explored the possibilities of narrative form. Nonetheless, what appears equally important in retrospect was the employment of the means of the distributive spatialization of photography in the repetitive forms of seriality that constitute the distinctive temporality of the archive. Together, both literary and the archival modalities dramatically refigured the arena of photographic representation bringing into play an entirely different understanding of the photograph's relationship to time.

More recently, and as a direct consequence of technological developments that have eroded the boundaries between the still and the moving image, the question of the temporality of the photograph has once more been brought into prominence. Moreover, in the work of some contemporary artists that operates within the interstices of photography and video, we are once more confronted by those issues that have been central to a definition of critical realism and which I have briefly outlined here. As a way of bringing together some of these issues, I want to consider a recent work by Fiona Tan, entitled *Countenance* (2002). Some background to this work is necessary.

Tan's starting point for *Countenance* was August Sander's photographic survey of the German nation –*Citizens of the Twentieth Century*– begun in 1910, published in partial form as *Antlitz der Zeit* in 1929, and left unfinished at his death in 1964. Sander's project is one of the most extensive and ambitious attempts to unite photography and scientific positivism to produce an archive of photographic portraits to be read as empirical evidence of social, physiognomic and psychological typologies. In 1925 Sander explained his methods and intent in the following terms:

> "Pure photography allows us to create portraits that render their subjects with absolute truth, truth both physical and psychological. That is the principle which provided my starting point, once I had said to myself that if we can create portraits of subjects that are true, we thereby in effect create a mirror of the times in which those subjects live… In order to create a representative glimpse of the present age and of our German people, I have collected these photographs into various portfolios, starting with the peasant and ending up with representatives of the intellectual aristocracy. This is then paralleled with an album which traces the evolution of the village to modern urban concentrations. By using absolute photography to establish a record of both of the various social classes and of their environments, I hope to give a faithful picture of the psychology of our age and our people." (Lemagny & Rouillé, 1987: 142-43)

Whilst shortly after its publication *Antlitz der Zeit* received the unreserved approval of Walter Benjamin, more recent critical writings on Sander's project have been less than positive as regards its ideological and political ramifications. Allan Sekula, amongst others, has been scathing of Sander's belief in photography as a 'universal language' and his faith in the idea that visual appearance constituted a form of truth. Yet, the real danger, according to Sekula, is that such naive belief in photography's objectivity and neutrality serves to obscure a deeper problem. This is that Sander's project is directly implicated in the instrumental mechanisms of social power and political domination which are implicit in the historical functions of the archive and taxonomic forms of knowledge which, "as modes of administration [...] subject social life to an institutionalized scientific expertise" (Sekula, 1981: 19). The problems are not merely methodological, however. Sander's project is also deeply enmeshed in the logic of the photographic portraiture as established in the preceding century and its consolidation of a hegemonic model of individual identity entirely consistent with the ideologies of bourgeois subjectivity. As Sekula argues, the presentation of the bourgeois self, a function that photography inherits from painting, went hand in hand with an entirely new role which was "to establish and delimit the terrain of the Other, to define both the generalized look –the typology– and the contingent instance of deviance and social pathology" (Id., 1986: 7). Portrait photography thus constituted a dual system of representation "capable of functioning both *honorifically* and *repressively*" (Id.: 6). Together, these two complementary and interdependent forms of portraiture operated as a generalized and inclusive photographic archive of individuals and implicit in the function of such an archive was the belief in forms of social, if not always, biological determinism. More recent writings on Sander have sought to shift a reading of his work away from within a general account of the photographic archive to a more complex analysis that acknowledges its historical specificity (Jones, 2000; Baker, 1996). Even so, the politics of Sander's project, according to such accounts, still remains highly ambivalent.

Tan's *Countenance* can be taken, I would suggest, as a contribution to these debates on Sander's work. Certainly, she is not unaware of the pitfalls posed by modelling the work directly on that of Sander's archival project. This much is certain from the evidence of the first of the two rooms that comprise the video installation. On a small screen a sequence of head and shoulder portrait shots are projected. The first of these is different from the rest –consisting of a woman facing the camera at an oblique angle rather than directly and the image is held there for longer than those that follow. We are led to believe that this is a self-portrait, since it precedes the start of a voice-over monologue that refers to the making of the work that we are viewing. In the form of a diaristic narrative Tan refers to herself as an outsider 'set adrift' in a place she does not know. "Do I look better at someone's face in a foreign city?", she asks. Gradually the project on which she settles and which we are now witness to is introduced: "I gather impressions and snapshots like an amateur biologist in the 19th Century would catch butterflies. Type. Archetype. Stereotype". Yet, any pretensions to scientific objectivity are soon abandoned: "all my attempts at systematical order must be arbitrary; idiosyncratic" she later notes. Sander's notion of using, what he called "exact photography" to obtain "an absolutely faithful historical picture of our time", is referenced and then refuted when Tan asks "Could I possibly collect, collate a time in history?" only to conclude that such an attempt would be "doomed to fail".

In the second room of the installation three large screens carry full length and approximately life size portraits of individual figures, pairs of figures or larger groups. The conventions of the genre are those set by Sander, as too –to a large degree– is the classification and ordering of these images into particular sets. There are three main sections: "Social Constellations", "Working People" and "Miscellaneous". Each section is further subdivided. In the section "Working People", for example, Tan begins with the sub-category "Farmers" (as of course did Sander) to be followed by "Worker", further subdivided into "Factory Worker", "Unskilled Worker", "Self employed" and so on. But it would be useless to seek logic here. The sub-categories of "Curator" and "Artist" are placed not amongst the "Working People" but in "Miscellaneous" alongside the unemployed, the beggars, and the homeless. Following the lines of the children's nursery rhyme, the butcher and the baker are indeed followed by the candle(stick) maker but also –it must be added– the futon maker as well. We should not begrudge Tan this slightly whimsical element because overall the highly idiosyncratic nature of her typologies only serves to underline a far more complex agenda.

If *Countenance* observes some of the protocols of a taxonomic method only to cast doubt and uncertainty upon it, so it would appear that a positivist philosophy of visual representation, that is the basis of Sander's work, is also rendered problematic. The key to this lies with the first-person narrative voice of the artist herself, which grounds the visual document not only in the realm of the subjective but in a hesitant and unsure subjectivity at that. More importantly, however, what this first-person narrative does is to shift the basis of our spectatorship, in as much as the tendency to internalize the spoken word has the effect of binding the viewer into a certain kind of relationship to the image. Tan's encounter becomes our own as we confront those she has photographed and who now meet our gaze.

Drawing on Volosinov's theories of 'reported speech' Steve Edwards has argued that it is possible to discern in some of Sander's images the evidence of a dialogic process, one in which those who are photographed find a 'voice' (Edwards, 1990). Rather than assuming that what subtends the relationship of the photographer (and hence the eventual viewer of the photograph) to those who are photographed is the power of the gaze to fix the subject as object, Edwards suggests we must consider Sander's subjects as possessing a capacity to author themselves. The photographic portrait might therefore be seen as a space of negotiation between viewer and viewed, a space of inter-subjectivity. Seen in these terms, the distinction between the 'subject body' and the 'object body' may not always be clear. Commenting on once having his photograph taken, Roland Barthes observed that "I am neither subject [n]or object, but a subject who feels he is becoming an object" (Barthes, 1981: 14). It is interesting that Barthes describes being photographed in terms of 'becoming', as a process that exists in time, indeed a process that takes time. If this 'becoming' cannot be equated with the split-second when the photograph is taken it can, I think, be related to the act of preparing to be photographed which precedes it. When we present ourselves to the camera we are aware of the need to make ourselves into a picture, to pose ourselves in a manner which mimics the stasis of the photograph itself. The act of being photographed elicits a particular process of self-presentation. We might even say that after photography subjectivity is performed differently, mediated by a sense of the moment when the camera shutter is open.

This brings us to what is the most obvious difference between Tan's *Countenance* and Sander's *Citizens*. Tan takes on all of the conventions of the genre of portrait photography used by Sander including most importantly the act of posing, but leaves us without the resolution of the subject's performance for the camera as an arrested image. The pose here is something that takes place over time, but unlike the photograph it is characterized by its ongoing presentness. Thus Joanna Lowry has argued that unlike the 'stilled surface' of Sander's photographs which "provide a site for the fixing of a semiotic of the subject", turning it "into a text that could be read" (Lowry, 2006: 73), Tan's images

> "disrupt the implicit dynamic of power that normally allows the spectator to look at the subject and that gives the former the advantage of time being on their side. For a brief moment these figures seem to look back and to share in a kind of performed duration; they are not simply framed and distanced –their bodies reach out beyond the space of the screen and are briefly intertwined, locked in an engagement with the spectator in the lived moment." (*Ibid.*)

As Lowry makes clear, what is at issue in *Countenance* are the complex relationships between our notions of the self, both of our selves and other selves, and the technologies of visual representation. What is important in this work is how the question of the subject's presence in relationship to the spectator is changed by the framing of the encounter in time: that is by the introduction of an experience of duration. In Tan's filmed portraits we are made aware, as Walter Benjamin once observed of the procedures of early portrait photography which "taught the models to live inside rather than outside of the moment", of the subject 'growing' into the picture (Benjamin, 1979: 245). It is a process which is not without ambivalence since what we are witness to is a negotiated process of the presentation of the self to another –hence all those slight adjustments of posture and expression of Tan's subjects as they face the camera.

The encounter between viewer and viewed that is staged within Tan's work takes place as a kind of shared presence of self and other. This spatial presence is, of course, inextricably linked in this case to the temporality of a continuous present that is the time of video. It is the experience of duration, the sense of an ongoing present, with which *Countenance* endows the 'photographic' portrait that constitutes its primary effect, which is that of stilling time and thereby opening out time to a distinctive kind of mnemonic experience. If *Countenance* explicitly references Sander's project, it implicitly connects a sequence of historical events that span the past, beginning with the publication of *Antlitz der Zeit* in 1929 and of dates –1933, 1945, 1989– that mark out a historical narrative between then and now.

Walter Benjamin saw photography as a potential means of rescuing moments of historical contingency from oblivion. But that task could not be accomplished if the past was conceived of as something to which we are compelled to return, to reconstruct it "as it really was". On the contrary, the task was to realize that if any knowledge of the past is to be had, it already exists in the present. In the moment of remembering, past and present intersect and lose their exclusivity. It is a moot point whether the predominant ways in which photography continues to be understood, and which primarily binds the photographic image to a moment that has been, can operate in a politics of the present in the way that Benjamin envisaged it might.

As I have noted earlier in this essay, it has been commonplace to think of photography in terms of the idea of fragmentation and that through photography the world becomes a series of discontinuous temporal and spatial events. The extension of this idea is that photography –whether understood as symptom or cause– is also tethered to the increasing sense of the fragmentation of social relationships and that it carries with it the intimation of the loss of authentic subjective experience. It is perhaps for such reasons that much of the writing about the photograph is elegiac and melancholic, fixated upon the stasis of the image as a signifier of loss. It is also perhaps for such reasons that the photographic portrait has occupied a place of peculiar importance in theorising the photographic image. It would be foolish to suggest that somehow, through the technologies of the moving image, we are able to fully restore social connectedness, to rescue a sense of identity from the depths of a collective anomie that is said to be the mark of the world in which we live. But if we do accept that the technologies of film and video have reconfigured our understanding of the relationship between subjective experience and space and time, then a work such as *Countenance* offers us some clues as to what this might mean.

Works Quoted

Baker, George, 'Photography between Narrativity and Stasis: August Sander, Degeneration and the Decay of the Portrait', in: *October*, no. 76, Spring, 1996: 73-113.

Barthes, Roland, 'The Rhetoric of the Image', in: Id., *Image, Music, Text*, trans. Stephen Heath, London: Fontana, 1977: 32-51.

Barthes, Roland, *Camera Lucida: Reflections on Photography*, trans. Richard Howard, New York: Hill and Wang, 1981: 14.

Benjamin, Walter, 'A Small History of Photography', in: Id., *One-Way Street and Other Writings*, trans. Jephcott, E. & Shorter, K., London: Verso, 1979: 240-257.

Benjamin, Walter. 'The Author as Producer' in: *Understanding Brecht*, London: New Left Books, 1973, 85-103.

Berger, John, 'Uses of Photography', in: *About Looking*, London: Writers and Readers, 1980: 48-63.

Burgin, Victor, 'The Absence of Presence: Conceptualism and Postmodernisms', in: *The End of Art Theory*, London: Macmillan, 1986.

Edwards, Steve, 'The Machine's Dialogue', in: *Oxford Art Journal*, vol. 13, no. 1, 1990: 63-76.

Green, David, 'Marking Time: Photography, Film and the Temporalities of the Image', in Id. & Lowry, J. (eds), *Stillness and Time: Photography and the Moving Image*, Brighton: Photoworks/Photoforum, 2006: 9-21.

Green, David, 'The Visibility of Time', in: Gaensheimer, S. (ed.) *et al.*, *David Claerbout*, München: Lenbachhaus-W. König, 2004: 19-43.

Jones, Andy, 'Reading August Sander's Archive', in: *Oxford Art Journal*, vol. 23, no. 1, 2000: 3-21.

Lemagny, Jean-Claude & Rouillé, André (eds), *A History of Photography: Social and Cultural Perspectives*, trans. Lloyd, J., Cambridge: Cambridge University Press, 1987: 142-43.

Lowry, Joanna, 'Portraits, Still Portraits and the Accounts of the Soul', in: David Green & Id. (eds), *Stillness and Time: Photography and the Moving Image*, Brighton: Photoworks/Photoforum, 2006: 65-78.

Sekula, Allan, 'The Body in the Archive', in: *October*, no. 39, Winter, 1986: 3-64.

Sekula, Allan, 'The Traffic in Photographs', in: *Art Journal*, Spring, 1981: 15-25.

Sontag, Susan, *On Photography*, London: Allen Lane, 1977.

2 _ CRITICAL REALISM

PHOTOGRAPHY AND OTHER ARTS

1 _ DEPICTING THE CONTEMPORARY ARTIST'S STUDIO
FOUR EARLY WORKS BY BIK VAN DER POL
Wouter Davidts

In his story *Le Chef d'oeuvre inconnu* from 1832, Balzac introduces us to Master Frenhofer, an elderly painter who mysteriously keeps his studio hermetically closed. For several years, he has been working on a portrait of a woman that is to be his ultimate masterpiece. Due to his forced isolation, however, he is unable to finish it. In his desperation, Frenhofer believes that a bit of 'reality' might help and that he needs a 'model'. His painter friend Nicolas Poussin offers him his beloved Gillette, a ravishing beauty, on condition that he and François Porbus are allowed to enter. Frenhofer is persuaded, lets them in, and shows them his work. Instead of the marvelous apparition they were expecting according to Frenhofer's description, however, Poussin and Porbus see only a formless cloud and chaotic scrawls of color on the canvas. Rather tactlessly, Poussin lets slip to Pourbus that Frenhofer will have to admit, sooner or later, that there is nothing on his canvas. Frenhofer does not survive this merciless exposure and desecration of his personality as an artist and of his work; the following night he burns all his paintings and dies.

In Balzac's dramatic tale the modern artist's studio is depicted as a highly mythical and auratic space and place. *L'atelier d'artiste* is a private and fixed milieu where the monastic artist creates his masterpieces, safely secluded from the world. The studio stands in for the new social reality that artists face in modernity. The studio 'mediates' the loss of place and destination suffered by art in modernity, and acts as a counterbalance to the new 'public' platform (Reijnders, 2001: 17-20; Bätschmann, 1993: 97-108). Whereas since the 19th Century, the museum, both as institution and as building, has been the paramount place for the *public presentation* of art, the artist's studio is considered the unique place of its *private production*. Art originates in the studio. That is why the studios of the great icons of modern art still hold such an appeal. In the famous pictures of such renowned photographers as Alexander Liberman, Michel Peppiat or Brassai, the studio emerges as an almost 'impossible' place, an inaccessible place where such a thing as authenticity is of high importance. The studio is depicted as a place of transformation, where art and life intermingle, producing new things. Often the studio emerges as if it resides in a timeless limbo; there are no clocks or other devices that refer to the daily progression of time; it almost seems to detach itself from the demands, laws and regularities of modern life.

Due to their mythical status, many artist's studios have been carefully preserved in their original state after the artist's death, such as the studios of Claude Monet, Jackson Pollock or Man Ray, while others have been meticulously reconstructed in a different place, such as those of Francis Bacon, Giorgio Morandi, and Constantin Brancusi. In contrast to Balzac's sinister tale, these projects are often the source of rather amusing stories. In the case of Man Ray's Paris studio, his widow Juliet safeguarded her husband's studio after his death in 1976. During the next twenty-four years, Juliet saw it as her responsibility to keep the space clean and tidy, maintaining the space as Man Ray left it when he died. During all those years, the space looked the same, as if the 'master' could return at any moment, reducing the space to its mere image. In 1990 she moved back to the US with the heartbreaking statement: "Après moi la poussière".

Another fairly popular operation of recent years is that of meticulous reconstruction, no longer on the original location, but *elsewhere*. Probably the most famous examples of this procedure of geographical relocation are the studio's of Francis Bacon, Giorgio Morandi, and Constantin Brancusi. They all have been painstakingly rebuilt on a different spot, even a different city.

In Brancusi's case, this was even arranged by the artist himself. In his will, Brancusi stipulated that this studio was to be conserved in its entirety after his death. Around the middle of the 1950s, Brancusi became aware that his true masterpiece was his studio. Since then, he refused to show his work elsewhere and devoted himself to perfecting and rearranging the collection of his works in his studio, creating his very own *Gesamtkunstwerk*. Thus, Brancusi not only prevented the dispersal of his works and the subsequent speculation, but also guaranteed that every visitor would enjoy a viewpoint similar to his own during the production process. Today, Brancusi's studio and all its contents no longer reside on their original location, the barracks at 11, Impasse Ronsin, but occupy an elegant pavilion designed by Renzo Piano, on the square in front of Centre Pompidou (for the eventful history that led up to this removal, see: Tabart, 1997). The studio has been pared down to merely an interior, observable all round through glass walls. The outer architecture has been peeled off. The everyday environment of the studio, represented by the workbench, the chisels and hammers, and the record player, has congealed into anecdotal scenery, a charming simulacrum, a pleasant reminder of a work process long past.

Similar operations were performed on the studios of Francis Bacon and Giorgio Morandi. The former being relocated from 7 Reece Mews, South Kensington to the Hugh Lane Museum in Dublin, the latter from the Via Fondazza in Bologna to the Palazzo Accursio, the city hall and museum. In both cases, the exterior architecture was peeled off, reducing the studios to merely their contents and all the multifarious objects and paraphernalia. The architectural frame –and thus constitution– of the studio is reduced to an interior, an inner space that solely wants to be looked at. The studio space is frozen into an image, albeit a three-dimensional one. They act as an art historical 'period room', an artistic diorama merely lacking a 'stuffed' version of the artist.

But upon visiting these 'reconstructions', we face the question of what we are actually looking at: the 'real studio' or merely a fancy simulacrum? Secondly, the question arises what these –in the case of Bacon– titanic operations actually yield. Do these 'interiors' really tell us something, besides offering a truthful image of the former studio? Do they have any documentary value or are they mere artful artefacts, satisfying our persistent need to peek inside the artist's "magic chamber" –to use Michel Peppiat's description of the studio? What critical or theoretical insights do we actually gain from these reconstructions and especially from the historical reality of these studios, and if possible, the contemporary reality of the artist's studio?

In the story of Frenhofer, the space of the studio appears not only as a space of seclusion, but first and foremost as a space of *imagination*. Because the studio is resolutely closed off from the outside world, reality can only be 'imagined' inside it. In the studio, every representation of the world has to be born from the artist's personal inspiration. And that is why Frenhofer's fate is so tragic: he has none. To counteract this condition, Daniel Buren rejects the studio in his polemical article of 1971 '*Fonction de l'atelier*'. In Buren's view, the fact that studio art is conceived and made beforehand, it can never engage in a significant and 'true' relationship with the site where it ends up and where it will be exhibited. The studio is the space par excellence to produce place-less art: "the studio is a boutique for the *prêt-à-porter à exposer*" (Buren, 1991: 195-204; Davidts, 2005: 40-52). Consistent with his views, Buren exchanged his studio for an office five years previously and abandoned his painterly work in favor of *in situ* practice. He reduced his visual toolkit to a set of instructions –the systematic use of a pattern of vertical stripes, alternating white and colored, 8.7 centimeters wide– which he applies in every place his work is shown. Buren's works no longer originate in his imagination and they do not deal with any theme. Instead, they use their context as both model and medium. Buren has developed a practice that *relates* directly to a specific site. His studio is no longer a fixed workplace, but a movable spatial condition, an artistic work situation. This does not mean that Buren's *studio* is nonexistent, empty, or fictitious, however. It has simply been 'interiorized'. The artist 'embodies' and 'inhabits' it in person: "*Mon atelier, en fait, est le lieu où je me trouve*" (Buren, 1991: Id.). His studio installs itself, as it were, within every institutional context where he starts to work.[1]

Since Buren and contemporaries, such as Robert Smithson and Robert Morris –generally considered as the main protagonists of the so-called post-studio era– announced the end of the

57

studio, it has lost its natural role and mythic status (Jones, 1996). But does this, however, mean that the artist's studio or the artistic workplace in general has become obsolete ever since? It remains surprising that the critical reading of the institutional regime and its paradigmatic spaces –studio, gallery, museum and collector's house– by such artists as Buren, Smithson and many of their contemporaries, amounted to a radical elimination of only the studio –the single space we nowadays determine by the prefix 'post'. Has the studio turned out to be the privileged dupe of the neo-avant-garde's urge to destroy at least one component of the institutional nexus? Or is the announcement of its end merely a product of the inexorable desire of art criticism and theory to come up with sweeping labels, alongside those other famous passings, such as the author and the original, etc?

It is a truism that, in the current post-studio era, artist celebrities spend more time in airplanes than in their studios, if they have one at all. Many of them will list multiple cities when asked where they 'live and work'. A contemporary star like Rikrit Tirivanija undeniably steals the show. Tirivanija was born in Buenos Aires, Argentina, but lives and works in New York, Berlin and Thailand; an almost superhuman enterprise. Artists have never been as mobile as today and the same applies to their studios. The art world has become an ever-growing network of exhibition spaces and events, but also of temporary workplaces and 'residencies' where artists stay and work for a shorter or longer period. Both the pioneers and the latest generation of 'site-specificity' are nomads who fly around the world and intervene in different places, institutions, and cities, according to their own artistic idiom or 'practice'. Most contemporary art is no longer produced on a single spot, but on multiple locations and within a network of artistic, institutional, and socio-political 'actors' (Gielen, 2003). But does this mean that –within this social and institutional reality– the artist's studio as a location and as a space can no longer be distinguished, let alone defined? Has it lost its validity? Is there still such a thing as an artistic workplace? And if so, how can it be defined in conceptual terms? Now that art and artists are continually 'on tour', the studio has become a camp that is constantly being struck and set up again. Doesn't that mean we always arrive on the scene too late? Does that imply that we can merely rely on entire or partial reconstructions? Is there an image that critically corresponds to the artist's studio's current reality, one that surmounts the traditional and auratic figure?

A sequence of early works by the Dutch artists Liesbeth Bik and Jos Van der Pol offers a series of particular and stimulating views on the nature and identity of the contemporary artist's studio. The first work they execute as a twosome, in 1995, consists of a detailed copy of the kitchen of Jos Van der Pol's living space, entitled *The Kitchen Piece*. Together with Peter Fillingham, they built an exact replica of the kitchen at the other end of the room, including all the cupboards, appliances, and contents. Fillingham is the first artist who 'resided' in Duende, the artists' initiative that was set up by Liesbeth Bik and Jos Van der Pol, together with a few artist friends in 1984, and that has been housed in an old school building in the Rotterdam Crooswijk district since 1994.[2] Duende contains about 45 artist studios and guest rooms. *The Kitchen Piece* is an '*homage*' to the kitchen of Jos Van der Pol (Interview Bik Van der Pol, 2004). That kitchen is located in the attic of the Duende building and functioned from the start as the epicenter of the life and work of the three artists. The kitchen and not their studio was the place where they held their discussions, made their plans, cooked their meals, and threw their parties. *The Kitchen Piece* is the first in a series of reconstructions. After the kitchen, they built replicas of the shower of their curator friend Arno Van Roosmaelen (*The Shower Piece*), the bookshop of the London ICA (*The Bookshop Piece*), and the original gallery of the notorious gallery keeper Konrad Fischer (*Proposition For Reclaiming a Space*). At first sight, there does not seem to be any obvious logic behind this series of replicas. It appears to be a fragmentary collection of both programmatically and geographically miscellaneous spaces. But above all, why are the works that kick off the artistic collaboration between Liesbeth Bik and Jos Van der Pol, all 'reconstructions'?

When Bik Van der Pol –the name the artists have used consistently ever since they started working together– describe their own artistic activities, they use a terminology that incontrovertibly places them in the critical tradition of site-specific and post-studio art on the one hand, and in the contemporary trend of collaborative and relational art on the other. They have an 'artistic practice' that deliberately interacts with the outside world via all sorts of 'projects': "Our projects engage with functionality, usability and site sensitivity, concerned with interaction at an institutional and intimate, local level, aiming to improve situations, add what is missing, highlight what is in the dark and to open rather than close. Our working method is based on co-operation and we use this as a platform for various kinds of communicative activities" (http://www.bikvanderpol.net; Bik & Van der Pol, 2001). Each work starts with an investigation of the framework in which it will present itself. It sets up its own performative platform and engages in a dialogue with the context, whether that context is New York, Utrecht, Stockholm, or Terassa. Fully in keeping with the logic of the artist as a 'networked interventionist', Bik Van der Pol, just like Buren, have said goodbye to their studio. In the early years of their career, both Liesbeth Bik and Jos Van der Pol made classical studio art. They made paintings and sculptures, respectively. But their first joint work, *The Kitchen Piece*, says Liesbeth Bik in an interview, allows her and Jos Van der Pol to dispose of that 'studio past': "The copy of Jos' kitchen in *The Kitchen Piece* was, initially, our answer to the limitations. Our collaboration started really playful and critical, but constructive. And it was impossible, after taking this road, for us to go back to the individual way of working, to our former studio practice" (Interview Bik Van der Pol). *The Kitchen Piece* constitutes a critical departure from their former activities. Just like Frenhofer, Liesbeth Bik and Jos Van der Pol were fundamentally dissatisfied with their achievements in the studio. They no longer experienced the seclusion as productive. But unlike Frenhofer, they did not bring a 'live model' into the studio. They wanted to enter into contact with the world outside, with other artists, and with curators and critics. Nor did they simply abolish the studio, like Buren. Instead, for their first 'model', they took the workplace itself, or at least, their 'new' workplace: the kitchen.

Immediately hereafter, their own studios became the location for the next reconstruction, that of the shower of the curator Arno Van Roosmalen. Together with Jeanne Van Heeswijck and Hans Snoeck, their neighbors in the Duende complex, Bik Van der Pol started the project *REST* in 1995. Like-minded curators and theoreticians were invited to reside and work in the living rooms and workplaces of the four artist hosts. Van Roosmalen was the first resident. For a period of three weeks he studied, experienced, and described a personal selection of artworks, texts, and music. However, the space that Van Roosmalen finds the most beneficial to reflection is his shower. It is the epicenter of his intellectual labor. To make the curator feel comfortable and to offer him a fitting 'workplace', the artists made an exact and fully operational reconstruction of the shower at his own home, placed on a pedestal. In 1996, this was followed by the temporary, but, again, exact and completely functional replica of the bookshop of the London ICA in an exhibition space of the Rotterdam museum Boijmans van Beuningen. In those days, Bik Van der Pol spent a lot of their time in London and the ICA bookshop was one of their favorite hangouts. They enriched the Dutch museum with a bookshop stocked with books and magazines on art criticism and art theory that were hard to find in Rotterdam and were certainly not sold by the real bookshop of the Boijmans. In 1997, they made the last reconstruction in the series: a copy of the first gallery opened by Konrad Fischer in the 1960s on Neubruckstrasse in Düsseldorf. Fischer, a former artist, created his gallery by putting a glass wall with doors in the two open sides of a passage underneath a block of buildings. In the space thus created, Fischer started showing art, pursuing one of the most influential and progressive gallery policies that existed in the post-war avant-garde. Many protagonists of European and American minimal, conceptual, and post-minimal art were given a platform there. Bik Van der Pol applied the same 'demarcation principle' to a passage underneath a building in Norwich, in the UK. Strangely enough, this work was not called *Gallery Piece*, but received the programmatic title *Proposition for Reclaiming a Space*. Fischer's gallery, one of the mythical places of the post-war art canon, originated in the simple gesture of occupying an intermediate or residual space and transforming it into an exhibition venue.

On closer inspection, then, it becomes clear what unites the four reconstructions: a delayed departure from the studio. The first reconstruction in the series, *The Kitchen Piece*, is not nostalgic, but forward-looking. With this work, Bik Van der Pol do not remember the past, but put it behind them. Together with the successive reconstructions of the shower, the bookshop, and the gallery, it marks out the itinerary along which both artists 'settle' with their studio past. Bit by bit, they take their leave of the traditional concept of the studio as an exotic locus and literal embodiment of their authorship, inspiration, and genius. It is a process of purification that enables them to come to terms with their studio past, to become confident about leaving their individual studios, and eventually, to identify with the post-studio condition. In this process, the studio is neither renounced nor abolished. Instead, it is replaced. With their series of reconstructions, Bik Van der Pol distinguish themselves within the rich tradition of representations of the artistic workplace, going from the classic genre of the self-portrait in the studio in painting and photography to the many replicas, scale models, copies, and complete or partial reconstructions of studios that have been showing up in gallery spaces in recent years, such as Ross Sinclair's *Studio Real Life* (De Appel, 1995), Rirkrit Tirivanija's *Tomorrow is Another Day* (Kölnischer Kunstverein, 1996), or Paul Mc Carthy's *The Box* (Hauser & Wirth, 1999). In the four works by Bik Van der Pol, the studio itself is neither represented, nor recreated. They reconstruct merely the peripheral places of the artistic production process and allow its actual center to appear as empty. The artistic practice of Bik Van der Pol no longer has a center. They work in so many different places and with so many people that the studio itself has fallen vacant. It has not disappeared, but it remains unoccupied as it is impracticable. Even when they receive a residency in another city, say Bik Van der Pol, they experience the studio space as inadequate: "For example, the one year we visited 'P.S. 1' in New York, there was a moment we said: what are we doing here? We were in this empty studio and there was no base like the situation we had here in Rotterdam, a situation that we partly created ourselves. But then, after a few months, we felt we wanted to make the city of New York into our local place; if we were going to live there for one year or longer, then we better make it our city, even if it is big and there is a lot happening" (*Ibid.*). Here, Bik Van der Pol point to the paradoxical nature of a guest studio in a foreign city. Artists not only arrive in an empty studio, but also in a city where they are strangers, where they have neither a social nor a professional network. This leaves only two possible options: either they stay inside and rely on their imagination or go out and embrace the city. Bik Van der Pol went for the second option and, together with a few other artists, started the project *Nomads & Residents*, in which people of various backgrounds who were 'passing by' in New York were invited to reside, talk, and 'work' at their place and on other locations in the city.[3]

Bik Van der Pol do not experience the fact that their studio is empty as tragic in any way. They know they need reality and must consequently 'go out'. But they realize only too well that this does not mean they are leaving the studio behind. To 'work', you always need a place. Every artistic intervention requires a 'residency' of some duration, whether short or long. And it can be done in places of very different description and program: you can work in a kitchen, a shower, a bookshop, or an art gallery. And that is precisely what the works of Bik Van der Pol are driving at. Each and every one of them is a partial embodiment and a peripheral manifestation of the contemporary artist's studio. *The Kitchen Piece* tells us that the contemporary studio has evolved from an isolated to a socially conditioned space. An artist can generate artistic energy on his own, but interaction with others works best. However, that does not prevent the workplace –as we are shown by *The Shower Piece*– from being, invariably, 'personal' and subject to a semi-private regime. Then again, *The Bookshop Piece* illustrates the undeniably discursive nature of every workplace. An art practice does not develop in a vacuum, but manifests itself in the theoretical framework of the art world, as well as in the socio-political milieu of our contemporary society. With the introduction of an existing bookshop into a museum, Bik Van der Pol stress the necessary presence of this broader context in the museum, albeit in published form. The museum is not merely a place to 'see' artworks, but first and foremost to 'study' them. *Proposition for Reclaiming a Space*, in its turn, points to the artists' responsibility to create their own 'context' –of both production and presentation– and to take control. They can no longer work complacently in the studio and "sadly wait for the moment of fame".[4] A figure like Konrad Fischer represents the attitude of self-empowerment, the consciousness that artists no longer need to depend entirely on others to give their work a public platform.

For Bik Van der Pol, the secrecy of the studio is no longer something to fight for, let alone to die for. Following Buren, Bik Van der Pol demonstrate that art is about more than delivering masterpieces, and that it mainly involves negotiation. These days, it is no longer possible to pin down or define such a thing as an artistic workplace. It can only be 'circumscribed'. The contemporary studio –to use Robert Smithson's characterization of his own works– is "fugitive".[5] It constantly navigates between social, personal, discursive, and institutional actors and places. But that doesn't lessen –as Bik Van der Pol's erratic series expresses– the intellectual and artistic challenge to come up with a material appearance that critically attunes itself to the contemporary –socio-economic and cultural-political– conditions of artistic reality after all. Most likely, architecture might turn out as an appropriate medium every now and then.

[1] Whereas an artist such as Marcel Broodthaers transformed his studio into a museum in 1968, upon opening the first department of Musée d'Art Moderne (the Département des Aigles / Section XIXème siècle) in the Rue de la Pépinière 30 in Brussels, Buren converts the museum into his studio. While the mobile studio of Buren appears as empty and fictitious as Broodthaers' mobile museum, they share the same critical agenda. By doubling studio with museum or vice versa, both center on the distinct role and place they occupy in the institutionalized art world since the 19th Century. Both are essential parts of the commercial art system.

[2] The artists' initiative Duende started in 1984 in a building on the western outskirts of Rotterdam. After 10 years,

Duende had to leave this building. Since April 1994, Duende has been housed in the Crooswijk building, where it has been able to grow from about 15 studios to 45.

[3] http://www.nomadsresidents.org. 'Nomads & Residents' (N&R) was not limited to 'P.S. 1', but was held in a different space in the city each time, such as Apex Art, Art in General, Location 1, Swiss Institute, Whitney Museum, etc. These institutions were approached with the request to use their space for one evening for N&R. That way, the various participants (initiators, speakers, and public) got to know the city from different angles.

[4] 'Interview with Bik & Van der Pol', art. cit. In fact, this ambition was realized by Bik and Van der Pol themselves when they started up the artists' initiative Duende. In the middle of the 1980s, there was not much going on in Rotterdam in the field of contemporary art, and there were very few artists' studios. Consequently, artists started to organize themselves and create their own platforms for production and presentation. In the process, Duende developed from a collection of studios into a buzzing platform with both permanent and guest studios that were also used for exhibitions, lectures, and debates.

[5] Smithson, Robert, 'Interview with Robert Smithson (1970)', in: Id. & Flam, J. D. (ed.), *Robert Smithson: The Collected Writings* (The Documents of Twentieth Century Art), Berkeley: University of California Press, 1996: 240: "My objects are constantly moving into another area. There is no way of isolating them –they are fugitive".

Works Quoted

Bätschmann, Oskar, *The Artist in the Modern World. A Conflict Between Market and Self-Expression,* Cologne: DuMont Buchverlag, 1997: 93-108.

Bik, Liesbeth & Van Der Pol, Jos, *Absolut Stockholm*, Stockholm: Moderna Museet, 2001.

Buren, Daniel, 'Fonction de l'Atelier' (1971), in: Id. & Poinsot, J.-M. (eds), *Daniel Buren. Les Écrits (1965-1990). Tome I: 1965-1976*, Bordeaux: CAPC Musée d'art contemporain de Bordeaux, 1991: 195-204.

Davidts, Wouter, 'Das Atelier ist immer woanders. Über ein Paradox in Daniel Burens Praxis des in situ', in: *Kritische Berichte*, vol. 33, no. 3, 2005: 40-52.

Gielen, Pascal, *Kunst in Netwerken*, Heverlee: Lannoo Campus, 2003

http://bikvanderpol.net

'Interview with Bik Van der Pol', in: *Open Issues*, no. 1, 2004.

Jones, Caroline A., *Machine in the Studio. Constructing the Postwar American Artist*, Chicago-London: The University of Chicago Press, 1996.

Reijnders, Frank, 'De tussenkomst van het atelier', in: *De Witte Raaf* , no. 94, November, 2001: 17-20.

Smithson, Robert, 'Interview with Robert Smithson (1970)', in: Id. & Flam, J. D. (ed.), *Robert Smithson: The Collected Writings* (The Documents of Twentieth Century Art), Berkeley: University of California Press, 1996

Tabart, Marielle (ed.), *L'atelier Brancusi*, Paris: Éditions du Center Georges Pompidou, 1997.

2_ PAINTING THROUGH PHOTOGRAPHY

CRITICAL REFLECTIONS ON THE WORK OF LUC TUYMANS, DIRK BRAECKMAN AND ANNE-MIE VAN KERCKHOVEN FROM THE EARLY 1990S

Liesbeth Decan

Quite a lot has been written about Dirk Braeckman (b.1958), Anne-Mie van Kerckhoven (b.1951), and especially Luc Tuymans (b.1958). Their works have been analyzed from the perspectives of art history, philosophy, politics, and sociology. The most important, most self-evident ideas have been expressed and it seems as if only relatively small nuances can open up innovative and new perspectives. As such, it is neither my ambition nor my intention to shed new light on their individual work or to defend a kind of eclectic and summarized vision. Rather, I would like to situate the work of these three artists in the wider artistic context of the late 80s and early 90s, by presenting them side by side. The central question is how the use of certain artistic media –understood as instruments and carriers– plays a crucial role in the presentation of what can be called a 'critical-realist' content.

The work of Tuymans, Braeckman, and van Kerckhoven emerged in the 80s and started to take a prominent place in the Belgian art scene in the early 90s. Their work, having come to full fruition, attained international recognition from the mid-90s onwards. Their oeuvres emerged in an international artistic climate in which neo-expressionism was in its final years of full bloom. Especially in Germany, artists like Georg Baselitz (one of the key figures in this movement) propounded –in a strongly regressive way– painting as the center of visual culture, totally ignoring and even denouncing the impact that other, new media (such as photography) had had during the preceding decades. The communication of historical or political topics from the work of art to the viewer was not important to these artists, but rather they were engaged with the establishment of a national artistic practice in which the artist loudly vents their emotions by means of excessively moving lines and expressive, often sultry colors. In general, it mainly involved strictly individual, emotional expressions, leaving little room for a larger social discourse (Buchloh, 1981: 61-68; Lucie-Smith, 1995: 173; Foster *et al.*, 2004: 612).

I argue that the work of Tuymans, Braeckman, and van Kerckhoven can be seen as a certain reaction against the rather conservative, regressive art of neo-expressionism. To this they offer a forceful answer through images with multiple layers of meaning. Their aim is not only to research the possibilities of the medium that is used ('medium' as in the meaning of instrument and carrier), but also to succeed in realizing a 'critical-realist' content.

Luc Tuymans' Photographic Paintings

The paintings of Luc Tuymans have been described by himself as 'authentic forgery'. As such, he clearly indicates that absolute originality of a work of art does not exist, yet at the same time he suggests that recycling existing material does not necessarily have to be viewed as regressive (Van Gelder, 2004: 288). The working method of Luc Tuymans is a complex one, that not only involves taking photographs (mostly Polaroids), but also includes the use of scale-models, aquarelles, film stills, and photocopies. The last step, however, before the painting process is, in most cases, a Polaroid (or a combination of several Polaroids) (Decan, 2006: 4-5). This way it can be assumed that Tuymans uses photographic materials as a starting point for his painting. He translates reality through the use of photographic images into painting, and it is in this translation/transformation that I search for the substrate of the critical-realist content in his work.

I would like to introduce a small selection of his works, made from the mid-80s to the mid-90s —the period I am interested in for this paper. I will frame these works by proposing two 'themes'. The first concerns the representation of political-historical topics and the second involves the notion of the uncanny or *das Unheimliche*. The latter notion recalls the words of Emma Dexter, who mentioned the concept of the uncanny in her text for the catalogue of Tuymans' exhibition at the Tate Modern in London and K21 in Düsseldorf in 2004 (Dexter, 2004: 24-26).

The first painting is *Gas Chamber* (1986). The image itself is fairly abstract: there is the suggestion of a room with a doorway, architectural shadows, and a number of unspecified black details. When we look at the title, though, the room that was at first hard to identify, becomes frighteningly real: we are looking at a gas chamber. The literature on this painting explains that it was based on a photo taken at Auschwitz.

When Tuymans represents this charged political-historical theme, he is confronting the concept of remembrance (an idea developed by Ulrich Loock in his 1996 essay: 42-44). He tries to reflect the horror linked with the holocaust, but irrevocably his work tackles its unimaginable aspect. He is looking for a language to say the unspeakable, represent the unthinkable, but only succeeds in finding hints that *might* get through to the intended meaning. The representation lacks referential and symbolic force.

When we analyse work dating just ten years later, though, we notice that this indexical, iconic, and symbolic function of the image, which Loock focuses on, *is* present. I am referring here to the *Heimat* series, painted in 1995, that includes the painting *Yser-Tower*, an abstract, but clearly recognizable image of the monument erected in memory of the Flemish soldiers who fell in the First World War, and also *The Flag*, a fairly abstract, yet recognizable representation of the symbolic Flemish Lion. In both paintings, the dull, faded colors suggest the present-day transformation of these once idealistic nationalist symbols into the insignia of an extreme-right ideology.

Although these images are not based on photographs of immediate reality, but on Polaroid photos of representations of reality (a watercolor and a miniature building made by the artist himself), it seems as if their photographic (indexical) identity determines the recognition of the (socially critical) content. The intermediate step of the photograph constitutes an effective method to both analyze and observe a certain reality and to communicate a message about that reality to the viewer (Van Gelder, 2001b: 174).

Painting often lacks the immediacy of a photograph, yet on the other hand, an all too literal representation of the subject (e.g. a documentary photo), in many cases proves fatal for the stimulation of reflection in the viewer. The 'intermediate phase' of the photograph as a source of 'factual' information is as crucial as the act of painting itself. Between the photographic and the pictorial a 'meaning vacuum' emerges that offers room for reflection.

In summary, it seems that Tuymans first looks for a solution to the problem of the impossibility of representing a strongly charged subject in the abstraction of that subject (as seen in *Gas Chamber*). But the readability of the work remains problematic. When paintings acknowledge their photographic character more strongly, as is the case in the *Heimat* series, and also later in *Mwana Kitoko* (an ensemble around the theme of Belgian colonialism, presented by Tuymans at the 2001 Venice Biennial), their meaning emerges more clearly. The photographic element functions as a more direct link to a (recognizable) reality and appears to have an important influence on the communicative power of the work. The integration (to a greater or lesser degree) of the photographic medium within the art of painting allows the painter (again, to a greater or lesser degree) to overcome the impossibility of representation. The painting thus functions as an image that does not deny the forgery or failure of its own representation, but actually highlights it —now it is strangely freed from the impossibility of representation and creates the possibility to reflect critically on what the viewer sees and remembers. In this way, Tuymans appears to tackle the still successful neo-expressionism twice: first of all in the unvarnished use of photographic materials and second in the stunning stillness of the composition, created by a pictorial abstraction and the application of a very thin layer of paint.

An image that also belongs to the *Heimat* series, *Flemish Village* (1995), leads me to my second theme. The blind walls, the apparently closed windows and doors, the white facades that are brilliant in the sunshine against a dark grey sky, and the deserted street of this polder village have something eerie about them. Something does not fit in the peaceful atmosphere associated with these places. This image is not calm, but threatening —a threat of what the viewer does not (or cannot) see.

About three years earlier, Tuymans painted *Silent Music* (1992): a partial view of an interior, which —taking into account the soft pastels, the railings on the bed, and the little chair in the foreground— probably represents a nursery. But here, too, the striking emptiness is eerie. What ordinarily evokes cheerfulness or endearment radiates a deathly atmosphere.

This uncomfortable feeling (that also emerges in his work of the 80s) can be described as 'the uncanny', a term that Emma Dexter in her analysis of Tuymans' work borrowed from Freud, and that has to be located in the unsettling 'meeting' between '*das Heimliche*' (the ordinary, the homely, the familiar, the friendly) and '*das Unheimliche*' (the unfamiliar, the strange, the frightening). In this way, what at first appears as normal, somehow becomes strange —a process that Freud explains by 'the return of the repressed' (Dexter, 2004: 24; Freud, 1983: 183).

How does Tuymans create this feeling? 'Emptiness' and the resulting 'silence' probably constitute the main strategies, next to the use of such motifs as eyes, mirrors, shadows, doubles, dolls, mannequins, and models, in addition to his exhibition practice where he juxtaposes, "[…] works that reference some of the most horrific or dramatic events in recent history [with] those that are based upon objects or interiors of extreme banality and anonymity", as Dexter rightly states (Dexter, 2004: 25). But to my mind there is another aspect that plays a role. If we look at other works that evoke this feeling, like *Silence* (1991) or *Body* (1990), then it is striking that they are all characterized by a 'photographic view'. *Silence*, for instance, consists of a child's head that has been solarized, and *Body* shows a close-up of a doll's body. I propose that this photographic fragmentation has an undeniable influence on the *unheimlich* content of the image. The precise cuts and extreme close-ups upset the viewer, as do the striking use of colors (often due to the specific tones of the Polaroid) and the evocation of emptiness. The content of the painted image is not only defined by these (formalistic) photographic techniques, but it is also the nature of photography that serves as a witness to something 'that has been' and thus indicates death

(Barthes, 1980: 120). This concept of death is revealed in its immobility and silence, and therefore explains the uncanny feeling in Tuymans' paintings.

Dirk Braeckman's Pictorial Photographs

Considering the theme of *das Unheimliche*, I would like to discuss the work of the photographer Dirk Braeckman. A comparison of his *B.L.-N.Y.-94* **[fig. 8]** with Tuymans' *Blacklight* **[fig. 9]** struck me with how both artists, at the same time (both works were created in 1994) show a 'common sensitivity'. These are two predominantly dark images. The center of each image

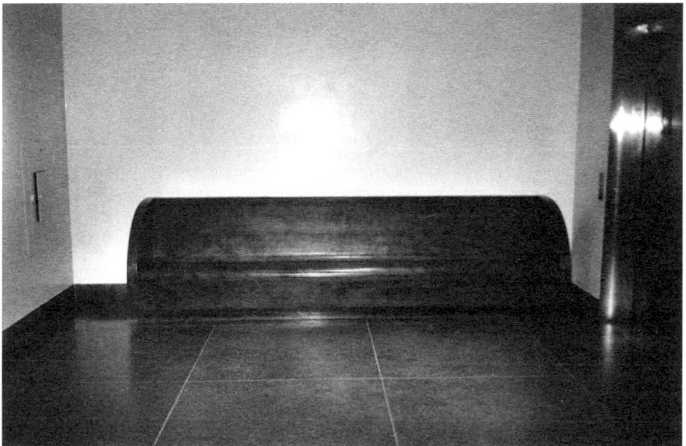

Fig.8 Dirk Braeckman, *B.L.-N.Y.-94* (1994) - Courtesy Zeno X Gallery, Antwerp (original in color).

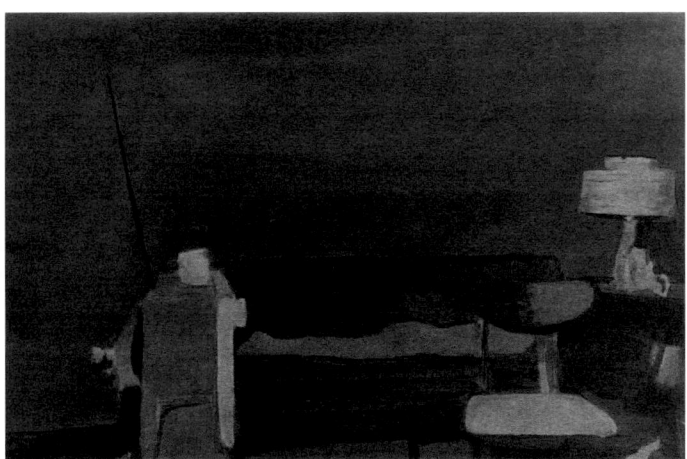

Fig.9 Luc Tuymans, *Blacklight* (1994) - Courtesy Zeno X Gallery, Antwerp (original in color).

is a long couch and on the right a relatively small, yet distinctive lighting effect is created (in Tuymans' image a small atmospheric light, while Braeckman utilizes the bright reflection of a flash of light).

Both works are also characterized by a fundamental emptiness, which aided by a quite ingenious lighting effect, generates a feeling of uneasiness. In Tuymans' image, there are more objects: the couch serves as a place to read (a book is seen beside the reading lamp) or to lie back in front of the television set. These 'props' give the interior a warmer feeling, a more personal touch, and as such also a more anecdotal content. The extreme emptiness and sterility of Braeckman's image, on the other hand, produce a horrific chill, enhanced by the gleaming touches of light. This use of lighting has a different effect than the dull light in the painting of Tuymans, whose specific shades are due to the fact that it was based upon a black-and-white photograph, illuminated by a blacklight, to which the title of the piece refers (Conversation with Luc Tuymans, Antwerp, November 2005). We are not in private quarters, but in an impersonal, (semi-)public transit room: a hall with an elevator (seen on the right), and a couch, which at most, serves as a short-term 'waiting spot'. Next to Braeckman's highly unfriendly image, Tuymans' painting comes across as fairly cosy; though, this homey feeling immediately disappears when we realize that there is a dead body on the couch! The crime scene police photograph, on which the painting is based, brings the private into the public, since an intimate situation evolved into a very public police case. More than ever the notion of *das Unheimliche*, as something 'homely' that has become 'un-homely', is present. The pleasant feeling of intimacy is marred because something hidden came to the surface. Here, the double meaning of *heimlich* as both domestic/familiar/intimate and hidden/secret/clandestine/furtive comes to the fore (Masschelein, 2003: [1-2]; Freud, 1983: 160, 162, 164).

Although the 'plain' image of Braeckman gives the viewer less clues to the grim content than the painting by Tuymans, the photographic image –from its indexical identity– refers to reality more than the painting. No doubt, the photograph is more real for us and as such even spookier. *Das Unheimliche* that is communicated in the photograph becomes part of *our* world in a more immediate manner. It reminds us of places we have been ourselves and again evokes the unease we felt there. As the photographer indicated himself, his photos function as images of crime scenes in which the crime itself is absent (Debate between Dirk Braeckman and Erik Eelbode, University of Leuven, March 3rd, 2004). Braeckman's remark can now be easily confirmed by the striking resemblance between his image and Tuymans' *Blacklight*, which *is* the image of a crime scene.

Yet, the large format in which Braeckman presents his photos and the dark veil that hangs over his pictures, partially obscuring them, do soften the images. These particularly pictorial qualities distinguish the photo from a purely documentary image, which shows us *that* room with *that* couch and *that* elevator. The scope of the image is much wider than that. Braeckman's interiors are always very specific, yet go beyond the particular. This can be confirmed by the difficult, cryptic titles: plain 'codes' that allow the photographer to organize his archive, but do not reveal any (anecdotal) information. By means of strategies taken from painting, Braeckman diminishes the individuality of photography by representing something universal instead of the instantaneous. In doing so, he seems to reveal something about the present-day human condition, about an urge for perfection and cleanliness, which is overshadowed, though, by a lethal boredom, an unbearable void. Yet, the pictorial aspect of his oeuvre also ensures that these strongly charged images never tend towards *morbid pessimism* (hopeless negativity). Braeckman himself stated in an interview with Erik Eelbode that there is always a certain lightness in his images: "[…] sometimes I try to charge my images to such an extent, go to such extreme lengths in that darkness that everything starts to topple and is relativized" (Eelbode, 1998: n.p.).

In this manner, Braeckman's work –just like that of Luc Tuymans– could be understood as metonymic. Characterized by an emptiness and an 'anti-(neo)-expressionist' stillness that leads to a strong 'internalization', their work displays the political-historical and more present-day social topics in an indirect, non-literal way that pushes the viewer back to their own opinion regarding the subject on view. In the case of Tuymans, this 'internalization' is generated by the painterly abstraction and the stunning use of color originating from the Polaroid photographs, whereas with Dirk Braeckman it is obtained by the pictorial dark veil that makes the pictures go beyond the particular to something more universal.

The aspect of painting was already present, more literally, in Braeckman's earlier work –namely his portraits and self-portraits of the 80s. The nervous strokes on the figures' bodies were made by brushing the image with developing fluid. The painting effect that these brushstrokes create brings about a 'veil' that makes the image surpass the particular. Indeed, the identity of the people portrayed is never revealed. The work shows a strong autobiographical undercurrent, yet simultaneously reveals something about a reality more open to objectification. The visual hiss caused by the strokes constitutes an appeal to the viewer to meditate on the nuances of the portrait of that specific person, yet in the end something larger (such as the human condition) is reached. As such, the interaction between the photographic and the pictorial is –just like with Tuymans, but in reverse– of invaluable importance for communicating the content of the image. The interaction between both media produces a 'relativization' of the critical-realistic content of the photo that prevents the 'overwhelmed' viewer from giving up immediately. Once again, in the meeting between the photographic and the pictorial, a vacuum opens that invites reflection.

Anne-Mie van Kerckhoven's Pictorial and Photo-based Computer Images

The mixing of different media and its consequences for the content of the work are of equally crucial importance in the art of Anne-Mie van Kerckhoven. Since the 80s she has been involved in drawing, painting, video, and computer art. Yet her approach to these media is not conventional –drawings are scanned into the computer and printed; the printouts are hung on the wall like paintings; plastic, not canvas, is the basis for her paintings, which in turn appear in animation films.

A case in point is the series *De Loreley*, realized between 1987 and 1990. For three years, van Kerckhoven painted on Perspex portraits of friends, acquaintances, and family members who happened to visit her. Every 'visitor' had to pose for two hours, looking her straight in the eye. In order to structure or limit the whole process, she gave every person who posed a stanza from the 19th-Century poem *Die Loreley* by Heinrich Heine. The artist describes it as "[…] a poem [about] melancholy and inescapability, fate in its most fatal form" (www.clubmoral.com/amvk/Loreley/index.html). The complete six-stanza poem was handed out nine times, resulting in a series of 54 portraits. This structural 'limitation' offered her the possibility, to link a present-day conclusion with Heine's words, through the connection with a personal portrait. To this conclusion, she tries to break the suffocating melancholy by reducing fate and death to 'mere' expressions/manifestations of Love (www.clubmoral.com/amvk/Loreley/index.html - Conversation with Anne-Mie van Kerckhoven, August 2005).

The portraits, however, were never made to be shown or sold as such. They functioned as instruments in a highly personal examination of how she saw those people, how she experienced their presence, in order to analyse herself through them. In this light, it is logical that the portraits were not considered 'finished products', but were further integrated into a computer animation. In this second stage within the artistic process, we discover van Kerckhoven's absolute faith in the multi-reproducibility of the image, which in a further development of Walter Benjamin's idea, she not only wants to see realized in photography, but also in other 'media'. Fundamentally opposed to the then flourishing neo-expressionism, she was not interested in the uniqueness and the accompanying market value of the work of art, but rather in the possibility of distribution. In 1981, with this idea in mind, she founded, in co-operation with her life partner and artist Danny Devos, the periodical *Club Moral*. This periodical was a forum for radical, unconventional forms of art, which rebelled against what they saw as an art world that had become very materialistic (Conversation with Anne-Mie van Kerckhoven, August 2005).

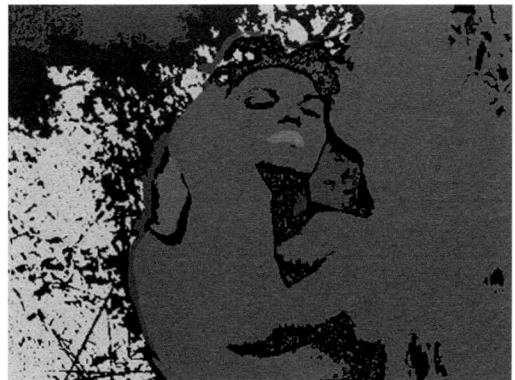

Fig. 10 Anne-Mie van Kerckhoven, *Logical reasoning (eroticized concepts nr. 02). HeadNurse Project* (1996)
- Courtesy Zeno X Gallery, Antwerp (original in color).

Now, I would like to examine van Kerckhoven's *HeadNurse Project*, which started in 1995 and remains an ongoing venture. In this complex project, van Kerckhoven repeatedly uses pornographic images of women in order to analyse the still prevalent sexual and social roles of women **[fig. 10]**. The artist functions as 'the head nurse', and therefore provides the viewer with 'mental massages' (Van de Sompel, 2005: 27). Through a complex processing of different media, and consequently in the perception of the viewer, she transforms the image of women as willing objects of desire into a representation of women as powerful subjects. She therefore undercuts the notion of the uncanny that turns intimacy inside out and displays it in the public space, typical of pornographic images (Luyckx, 1999: 110; Van Gelder, 2001a: 4-6).

It seems as if during the 80s in a work like *De Loreley*, which is somewhat separate from her participation in the often provocative artistic performances and political actions of *Club Moral*, van Kerckhoven develops from painting a personal imagery, in which she conducts some multi-layered research of her own perception of the world. Later on –as observed in the excessive *HeadNurse Project*– she uses photographic material as one of the starting points and gives her images a more externally communicated tone of social criticism.

Conclusion

In this concise presentation concerning the work of Luc Tuymans, Dirk Braeckman, and Anne-Mie van Kerckhoven, I have attempted to shed some light on how these artists –each along their own individual path– have offered a clear response to neo-expressionism. During the late 80s and the first half of the 90s, all three artists achieved a visual discourse that clearly differs from the regressive and emotional use of the medium of painting. By means of painting based on photos (in the case of Luc Tuymans), photography with subtle pictorial dimensions (as with Dirk Braeckman), or multimedia art in which computer images are generated through photographic and painting materials (as with Anne-Mie van Kerckhoven), each artist managed to develop a highly topical imagery, transcending personal mythology. These works are clearly embedded in a present-day society with its political-sociological past and present. In their technical materiality and the highly layered content of their work, the viewer can always identify a kind of 'internalization' of reality, which pushes them back to their own vision with respect to the subject on display. This metonymic power, characteristic of the three oeuvres presented here, offers an opportunity for critical reflection.

Works Quoted

Barthes, Roland, *La chambre claire. Note sur la photographie*, Paris: Gallimard-Le Seuil, 1980.

Buchloh, Benjamin H. D., 'Figures of Authority, Ciphers of Regression. Notes on the Return of Representation in European Painting', in: *October*, no. 16, 1981: 39-68.

Decan, Liesbeth, 'Voor-beelden. Over de polaroidschetsen van Luc Tuymans', in: *FotoMuseum Magazine*, no. 34, 2006: 4-9.

Dexter, Emma, 'The Interconnectedness of All Things: Between History, Still Life and the Uncanny', in: Id. & Heynen, J. (eds), *Luc Tuymans*, exhib. cat., London: Tate Modern Gallery (& Düsseldorf: K21), 2004: 16-27.

Eelbode, Erik, [Interview with Dirk Braeckman], in: *zZ(t). Dirk Braeckman*, Gent: Ludion, 1998: n.p.

Foster, Hal *et al.*, *Art since 1900. Modernism, Antimodernism, Postmodernism*, New York: Thames & Hudson, 2004.

Freud, Sigmund, 'Het 'Unheimliche' (1919)', in: *Sigmund Freud. Nederlandse editie* (Cultuur en Religie, vol. 2), Amsterdam: Boom, 1983: 153-196.

Loock, Ulrich, 'On layers of sign-relations, in the light of mechanically reproduced pictures, from ten years of exhibitions', in: *Luc Tuymans*, revised edition, London: Phaidon Press, 2003: 33-93.

Lucie-Smith, Edward, *Artoday*, London: Phaidon Press, 1995.

Luyckx, Filip, 'Van Pin-Ups tot Betekenismachines', in: *Anne-Mie Van Kerckhoven. Beauty, Therapeutic Use of*, exhib. cat., Antwerp: Museum voor Hedendaagse Kunst, 1999: 102-112.

Masschelein, Anneleen, 'A Homeless Concept. Shapes of the Uncanny in Twentieth-Century Theory and Culture', in: Masschelein, A. (ed.), *Image [&] Narrative*, no. 5, January, 2003: [1-10].

Van de Sompel, Ronald, 'De omkering van de verleiding. Het HeadNurse Project van AMVK'-'The Inversion of Seduction. AMVK's HeadNurse Project', in: Van Rossem, P. (ed.), *Anne-Mie van Kerckhoven. The HeadNurse-Files*, Aachen: Neuer Aachener Kunstverein - Bern: Kunsthalle Bern - Antwerp: objectif_exhibitions, 2005: 27-29.

Van Gelder, Hilde, 'AMVK's braindrain: de transformatie van het burgerlijke naar het begeerlijke'-'AMVK's Brain Drain: The Transformation from the Bourgeois into the Desirable', in: *Tijdschrift Sint-Lukasgalerij Brussel*, no. 3, 2001a: 4-11.

Van Gelder, Hilde, 'Een kritische boodschap over de dagelijkse realiteit: fotografie tussen poëzie en politiek / A Critical Message on Everyday Reality: Photography between Poetry and Politics', in: *A-Prior*, no. 5, 2001b: 170-189.

Van Gelder, Hilde, 'Luc Tuymans: de werkelijkheid schilderkunstig 'structureren'', in: Vlieghe, H., Stroo, C. & Van Gelder, H., *Vlaamse Meesters. Zes eeuwen schilderkunst*, Leuven: Davidsfonds, 2004: 288-291.

3_ PHOTOGRAPHY

SEEING TIME / EXPERIENCING TIME

Maarten Vanvolsem

In this contribution I would like to question the photographic image's relation to reality and how it conveys a message to a society. Part of photography's relation with the world is its curious relation to time. What is the relation of the image to time? Do photographic images have a time component? Can they convey an event or duration? Is a photograph even capable of telling something about time? I think photography rather than only being part of the category of still images, can be part of the category of images that give us a sensation of movement and time, a category of images that reflect the dynamism of time. In this sense, those images are a reflection on how we see the world. This idea came to me first and foremost in my own practice as a photographer. I hope to demonstrate that photography, as a medium, is able to engage time in ways we might not have thought possible. More and more artists working with photography try to get rid of the snapshot or time-freezing tradition in photography (Celant, 1998: 11) and look for ways to engage time in their work in one way or another: Joachim Bonnemaison, Simon Read, Stephen Lawson, Jonathan Shaw and Sam Taylor-Wood to name just a few. I would like to present an extreme case, in which in the relation to the work an experience of time arises.

Strip Technique

The technique that is the subject of this paper is the strip or slit technique.[1] This technique, rather than exposing frames in their whole one at a time, can be seen as a scanning technique. The photosensitive material is exposed by a narrow slit which, compared to the photosensitive material, is in motion. This means that either the slit moves past the fixed film or the film moves past a fixed slit. Although the slit is typically 1.6 mm wide for panoramic photography, it is less than 1 mm for the cameras I built myself. This technique was first used in panorama photography and is almost as old as photography itself. The panorama camera designed by Joseph Puchberger used the strip technique to cover a 150° arc. For his design he was granted a patent in 1843 (McBride, 1994). Other cameras that operate with this system are: aerial continuous strip-cameras as used for photogrammetry (1915), rollout or peripheral cameras (+/- 1900), and the photo finish camera (1937).

All those cameras use a shutter technique that builds the image in time. As such, the images are compositions made by a moving film/slit and a moving camera/object. There is no click of a closing shutter, only the 'dzzzz' of a revolving film/camera. Due to the narrow slit and the movement of the film, the exposure time of each point on the film can be very short. The overall time to expose the image or actually to compose the image, has no direct relation to this fractional exposure time; rather, it is dependent on the size of the actual image. Here, contrary to Philippe Dubois' belief (Dubois, 1983), the exposure of the photosensitive material is not achieved in a split-second and all at once. The photographic image is built in time and new elements are added on to the film during the movement of the film and the camera. The composition is the result of a cameraman who operates the film and the camera movement simultaneously.

An Image that is not Still

A lot has been written on the impossibility of perceiving a work of art in an a-temporal fashion. In 1951 Pierre Francastel wrote: "Neither do we see the world nor art in a glance, we itemize" (Francastel, 1977: 58; my translation). With his writings Francastel criticizes the doctrine of the central perspective as promoted by Alberti. In doing so, he rejects the idea of photography as a superior form of art to painting, as in photography the unity of time and space, and so its representation of reality, would not necessarily be much better. In his writing on painting and time, Bernard Lamblin makes a similar remark. Although even more than Francastel, he emphasizes the fact that an image can only be read in time. "The perception of a painting requires time: to realize the integration of all stimuli that are coming from the unremittingly stimulated retina, the eyes have to move over the surface of the canvas in all directions" (Lamblin 1981: 48; my translation). Earlier, in the summer of 1949, Etienne Souriau's article 'Time in the Plastic Arts' appeared in the *Journal of Aesthetics and Art Criticism*. As we learn from Hilde Van Gelder, Souriau's article reacts against the "rather banal description of the plastic arts as arts of space" (Van Gelder, 2000: 49). And he insists that each visual work of art is inhabited by a temporal dimension. "It is only by dangerous abstraction, favored by certain habits of teaching or of technical thought, against which we must react […] that one can conceive of a work of art as a totality seen in a single flash" (Souriau, 1949: 295). This 'reading' of an image, a term used in a similar way by Ernst Gombrich in 'Moment and Movement in Art' (1964) and by Danièle Méaux in *La Photographie et le temps* (1997), is very important for the strip image. This 'reading' is a fluent movement from a beginning to an endpoint. This means there is a direction, there is movement, and there is the generation of meaning because one moment is followed by the next. It is the action of going through and taking into consideration the order of the elements seen. The panorama paintings were, from the very beginning, described as an experience of walking along. Often they were constructed so the spectator could only view the panorama when walking through the pavilion.

> "The person situated inside the panorama was forced to move in a circulating fashion parallel to the screen, since the only *fixed point* conceivable, the center of the observation platform, was occupied by the entranceway. The observer was obliged to adopt a mode of reception in which he views the landscape while moving around." (Maekawa, 1999)

Primitive wall drawings and the hieroglyphs or Maya pottery are another example, although they might be considered as language rather than pictures. But there is also the "continuous narrative" as used in painting from the 14th, 15th, and 16th Century.[2] The continuous narrative is a method that combines more than one moment from a story in a single painting. As we learn from Jocelyn Penny Small and Ranunccio Bianchi Bandinelli, it is a term not at all restricted to Medieval or Renaissance painting and was first proposed by France Wickhoff in 1895 (Small, 1999). Most definitions of the term have been made in a context of ancient and early Christian art. Bianchi Bandinelli defined it as a compositional technique "presenting the various episodes of a single narrative against the same background and, in effect, uniting them in the same composition, the same figures always being repeated for each episode" (Bianchi Bandinelli, 1955: 149). As Bianchi Bandinelli notes, the key figure in the tale is repeated twice or more in one coherent space. Within the picture the different episodes of the tale are not physically separated. *Saint John the Baptist retiring to the desert*, a painting by Giovanni di Paolo (ca. 1453, 311 x 388 mm, London, National Gallery) is an example of this well documented technique. The Bayeux tapestry (ca. 1075) is another example, although exceptional, because of its immense length (more than 70 meter). Later, in the 17th Century, the complementary method was used. Here different actions appear simultaneously in one painting. To understand the painting one has to look first at one part before continuing to the next part. In the East there is a long tradition of scroll painting that dates back to as early as the 10th Century. The oldest are the horizontal scrolls. They were never meant to be looked at in their entirety.

"The hand-scroll is never shown throughout its whole length, nor is it displayed in a room as decoration. [...] At the proper occasion [...], the scrolls are brought out to be unrolled on a desk or a table, never more than two feet or so at the time, and enjoyed as a progression while the painting is revealed foot by foot." (Laurence Sickman in *The Art Council of Great Britain*, 1965: 8)

In a more recent period, around 1919, Hans Richter and Viking Eggeling experimented with long panorama or scroll sized abstract painting. They wanted to get rid of the ideas of the expressionists' tradition and were looking for a logical and completely objective way of painting according to strict principles. Via an interest in music and the Chinese language, they started to create their own universal language. The results were scroll paintings, *Rhytmus 23* (1923) to name one, from which Hans Richter tells: "Forms painted on scrolls would be animated by the eye –the eye, instead of being a passive receptor, is compelled to move over the extended surface of the canvas [...]" (Joray, 1965: 6).

All of these examples concern paintings rather than photographs, but according to Bernard Lamblin this tendency to scan an image is not cultural but psycho-physiological. It does not only apply to panorama size or long paintings, but to all paintings (Lamblin, 1981: 124). And as it is not culturally defined, there is no reason to think the two-dimensional surface of the photographic image would be read differently. Therefore, it is reasonable to state that the same innate reflexes are guiding the eyes when looking at a photograph, certainly when it comes to the stretched size the strip images allow us to make. With ratios varying from 1/4 up to 1/25, it is hard to imagine one not trying to slide the gaze over the image. The photographs are too wide to be seen as one. Either you can see the strip as one, but then you have to withdraw from it to such an extent that nothing is left of the image but a surface with colors, or you come close enough to see some picture details, but then only a small part of the image is visible without moving one's head. Of course these movements are not predetermined, but they are evoked by the image. This, Souriau says, is one of the differences between music or film and a picture. However, it does not mean a picture lacks the ability of imposing this temporal reading. "The movement of the eye, in a picture, is doubtless not forced or determined, but it can be directed, by virtue of a kind of gentle and firm influence without which the composition of a picture would be unintelligible" (Souriau, 1949: 296).

The Image as a Score

A. Perspective

Not merely the size of the image will lead to scanning with the eyes; also other elements in the image promote a temporal reading of the image. In the strip images there is first of all the continuous variable perspective. Due to the movement of the lens and continuous movement of the exposed film, as mentioned before, a fleeting vanishing point rather than a fixed one is created. *Maastricht 2* (Vanvolsem 2002, Lambda-print, 350 mm x 2000 mm) **[fig. 11]** can serve as an example. In a photographic image, made with a classic shutter, the central perspective can operate as a framework to which we can hold on. It gives stability to an image, unless extreme vanishing points are used like the bird's-eye view or cod's-eye view. The incessant changing vanishing point of the strip image doesn't give the eye this stability. On the contrary, a vanishing line is created that grabs our attention and guides us through the image. In *Maastricht 2* the horizon line makes a sinusoidal curve that fades to the right of the image. This fluent movement of the horizon line, created with the camera during the exposure of the film, grabs the eye of the viewer and guides him through the image. Also in Bonnemaison's *Les coquelicots* (1982) a fluent horizon line enhanced by the gentle waves promotes the sliding of the eye trough the image from left to right. Sometimes we try to hold on to a detail, but these attempts are foredoomed to failure as the ever changing vanishing point drags us further. As a result, the strip image becomes a dynamic image. It's an image that does not allow the eye to rest or be passive in its perception. Hans Richter was quite right when for his scroll paintings he said: "the eye […] is compelled to move over the extended surface" (Joray, 1965: 6). The same can be said for the strip images. In the composed or nowadays digitally stitched panorama images we do not seem to get this dynamic effect. This is due to the working of the central perspective. Our eye is drawn to the center of each individual print and hops from one center to the next. This is most obvious in 360° panorama's composed of only a few images. It is also what makes the QuickTime VR simulation so strange to look at.[3] What we encounter in those panorama constructions are wall-like objects with depictions on it that first cut into the imagined space and then all of a sudden pivot at a corner and almost slam into your face before rolling away at the opposite side of the frame.

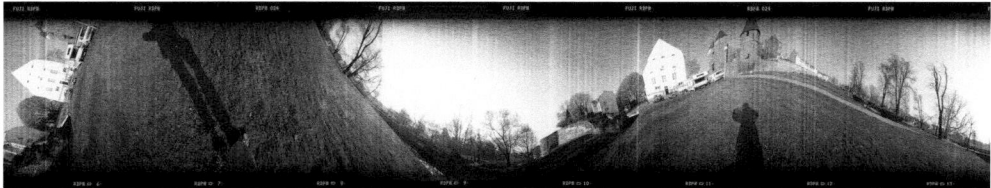

Fig.11 Maarten Vanvolsem, *Maastricht 2* (detail), 2002 (original in color).

B. Rhythm

Another element that promotes the reading of the images is the creation of rhythms. Those rhythms can be the result of the vertical exposure lines that are often apparent in the image and the repetition of depicted objects. That there is the creation of rhythm by the vertical exposure lines speaks for itself and does not need further explanation. They function like bars in a score. They represent the natural way in which we divide a linear, temporal flow. A certain level of control over the appearance of those lines exists in the image. Their appearance is due to the way the film is pulled through the camera and the dimensions of the exposure strip. But the differences between a night shot made with a manual camera in combination with the extreme slow movement of the film (one rotation takes 20 seconds), as can be seen in *Wave Length* (Vanvolsem 2002, transparency slide, 60 mm x 1600 mm) and an automatic film transport in *Maastricht 2*, is apparent. The repetition of depicted objects is the result of a more than 360° rotation with the camera during the exposure of the film. These repeated elements operate as landmarks on the image. They are a kind of main theme of the image. They are the big movements within the image. The spectator will go from one to the next in big strides to hold on just a little longer to those landmarks before continuing to the following. It is also those repeated objects that will make the spectator go back and retrace the previous. In this sense, they have a double function. First of all, they are slowing down the reading pace and secondly they are a kind of repeat mark, starting back from the last theme. In a first reading of the image the in-between substructures are looked at with less attention. They do not consist of a strong enough entity to catch the attention. They operate as a transit between the main themes of the image.

C. Sharpness

The differences in sharpness along the image will cause different reading speeds. This is because sharp or blurred parts of the image offer a different kind of information. The spectator's eye is accelerated at every change from sharp to blurred and decelerated when going from blurred to sharp. These differences in reading speed can really be felt. Contrary to one's intuition, the blurred parts do not reflect the camera's or the film's acceleration. In fact, this kind of blur is the result of slowness. Only when there is a perfect equilibrium between the speed with which the film is pulled behind the exposure strip, the movement of the camera, and the movement of the depicted space, is a sharp image possible. Then, the blurred image parts are the result of a slow or still camera compared to film and space. Nevertheless, in the image they have the function of speed since we have learned by convention that fast moving objects or parts of objects are depicted as blurred. Similar observations have been described by Ptolemy in the 2nd Century, referring to the invisibility of the spokes of a rapidly turning wheel, and by Leonardo da Vinci who writes: "actual motion made with rapid impetus will never obstruct from the eye the object which is behind the body that is moving" (Sturgis, 2000: 43). However, it was not until the 17th Century that Western painters first painted objects in motion as blurred (Id.: 44). Photography will enhance this tradition. Due to the lack on light sensitivity moving objects could not leave a trace on the photographic image. As light sensitivity of the photographic film increased, more and more could be seen of the moving objects. In specialist literature the word 'speed' is used to indicate the sensitivity of the film. When the light sensitivity of the film increases, the speed of the film increases. With the reduction in exposure time, fast moving objects could be depicted as sharp. Strip images, in a certain sense, will reverse this logic. When in the Palestine campaign the R.A.F. was looking for a system to make low altitude reconnaissance photographs, they were confronted with too slow exposure time compared to a too fast moving aeroplane. The strip technique could solve the problem, as the movement of the plane to the ground that caused the 'motion blur' was compensated with the movement of the film during exposure (Howard, 1970). A similar reasoning is done in sports photography when with the classic shutter camera the athlete, cyclist, horse or car is moving too fast to 'freeze' this on the film. The photographer then moves the camera along at the same speed of the moving object during the exposure. As a result, the background is blurred and stretched to a line pattern. The moving object on the contrary is depicted as sharp because it was perceived as 'still' in front of the panning camera.

The three elements just discussed (reading, rhythm, and sharpness) are quite similar to how the temporal dimension is seen in music. Souriau names them as follows: "The three chief classifications of aesthetic facts relative to musical time concern (a) its dimensional extent (b) its structure, notably in the form of rhythm (c) its agogic (tempo or speed) variations" (Souriau, 1949: 300). To Souriau those elements play an important role in the appreciation of most works of art. No wonder those qualities have also been attributed to scroll paintings. "Long scrolls […] organize the dimension of time, […] in the form of sequentially changing tempi, analogous to a musical score" (Sickman in *The Art Council*, 1965: 19). And as we have seen, they play an important role in the perception of strip images.

Time and the Strip Image

Much has been written on time and its relation to photographic images. However in *La Photographie et le Temps, le déroulement temporel dans l'image photographique*, Danièle Méaux seems to be right in remarking that all these writings are only looking to this relation from one point of view (Méaux, 1997: 23-33). But as Jean Molino (Molino, 1978: 47) noted for music and thus for photography, there are three important dimensions that should be considered: the poetic, the aesthetic, and the neutral. For photography Méaux translates this to "*le photographique*" or the photographic (the process or the work of an author as revealed in the picture), the interpretation of a reader and "*le photographié*" or the photographed (the world as it appears in the photograph) (Méaux, 1997: 9). I would like to argue that through a combination of those three dimensions in the strip technique something new will come out, beyond the mere communication of the existence or passing of time. I'm convinced that it is possible to make images that make us experience time.

As we are here interested in the experience of time, we are not so much interested in the depicted object that is seen as moving or that incorporates time. For example, the famous photograph *Place de l'Europe* taken near the Saint-Lazare station (Paris, 1932) by Henri Cartier-Bresson, shows us a man who jumps. We can also see his reflection in the puddle he is trying to avoid with his effort. So, his gestures, arms in the air and legs spread open, and his reflection that tells us he is not touching ground, show us this man is in an impossible position. He cannot be like that in the world for long. Although, without doubt this image is referring to a movement, to what was before and what will be after the moment presented to us in the image, this movement, the time flux presented, is entirely part of the subject depicted. We, as spectators, are passive onlookers. To Méaux all the different ways the image can convey time as duration are linked to its indexical character and our encyclopaedic memory. "The indexical nature of the image, which is known by the spectator, tends to inscribe the depicted scene in a temporal flow […]" (Id.: 37; my translation). This is the 'snapshot' quality of the image. It is the photographic image selected from the flow of time. I would like to call this the filmic time of the photographic image. It is linked to the object, depicted as if this was something in the real world we are looking at. We, as spectators, are passive, just like in the movies. As spectators, we are not part of this kind of images; they happen to us, even if we are not sure about what has been depicted or what the previous and next step of the object will be. When it comes to movement and time, they only belong to the depicted object and not to us looking at the photograph. Of course the role of the spectator is not really passive. The images that are needed to 'see' the movement of the depicted object have to be imagined so the movie of the event can start. Based on our encyclopaedic memory we generate a movie from one still and see the movement by virtue of the imagined movie. In this notion of photography, when looking at a depiction of a single space, we also see a single moment in time. I'm not dealing with this filmic time in my pictures. Also part of this kind of time are images that convey to a more general scenario known by the spectator. Known rituals or natural time cycles are part of this category.

What Méaux sees as the interpretation of the reader, should in the case of strip photography be translated into what we earlier called the reading of the image, where the sharp and blurred parts of the image get the meaning of accelerated space for instance, or when the image refers to the time needed to discover the depicted space in real life, which is the case for panorama photography. I will discuss it in combination with Méaux's third category which consists of the making of the image, i.e. the artist's work as revealed in the image, or as Méaux called it "*le photographique*". Once the spectator comes close to the image, he spontaneously tries to figure out what is happening. It takes the spectator by surprise. The strip images clearly are not family snapshots. Something strange is happening with the depicted space. Objects, a hill, a flower, a characteristic tree seem to come back twice or more, but not quite in the same position or seen from the same point of view. They are not copies of each other, are they? The spectator will start to investigate the depicted space and will realize it is not a one-view or central-perspective image. For the panorama images of Joachim Bonnemaison, Méaux describes it thus: "Even if the spectator does not know the recording technique, he will automatically understand the making of the image needed a duration" (Id.: 163; my translation). Even if the technique is not known? Of course! It doesn't matter whether the image is made with a panning camera lens, a moving camera, or even if it is clearly made out of a set snapshot. The view is larger than the eye's view and does not correspond to the snapshot. In that sense, there is no fundamental difference between a stitched panorama and one of Bonnemaison's panoptics (Bonnemaison *et al.*, 1989: 18).

The difference will be found on a more subtle level, namely which kind of movement or speed is conveyed. In his deciphering of the depicted space, the spectator will try to recompose the different positions of the camera. It is the creative process, the making of the image that is reflected. For the stitched images and the collages, the changes between different positions in the image will be abrupt. The reconstructed space will consist of a few distinct spaces. For the strip images, the reconstructed space will be a smooth changing space, a continuous reshaping of the same space. What happens is a constant re-matching of the eye's view of the world to the camera's view. As such, the image rather than referring to an existing object refers to the camera's movement. Then, the image is the evocation of the performance of making the image. But rather than being a document that shows a moment from the performance, we can now recreate the movements of the performance in reading the image. So, it is not that we can see the performance developing in front of us. We re-live it through the image. It is in this re-living that we feel the flux of time. Here the recreation of the image takes over from the interest in the depiction. The curvilinear perspective reflects the movement and it is out of the active reading of the photograph that the awareness of time arises. It seems that what Souriau called the intrinsic time of the work of art became prominently visible in these photographs. In his article 'Time in the Plastic Arts', he compares the musical execution to the experience of viewing a work of art and he writes:

"One must see in the same way the movement of the spectator around the statue or the architectural monument as a plastic or view-absorbing execution, which unfolds in order the various aspects which are held within the physical frame, and which are the aesthetic reason for that frame as it was planned." (Souriau, 1949: 295)

When the film transport is done by hand, with, as a result, an uneven exposure of the film, the image surface can get a curtain-like look. The uneven exposure results in a vibrating surface. It creates a surface with an artificial shadow pattern that is very similar to the effect of light that shines on a curtain. It is artificial because it has nothing to do with the light intensity in front of the camera or the shadow play of the depicted scenery. It is the result of playing with the shutter of the camera during the exposure of the film. As often in photography the process is of controlled randomness. It is controlled in so far it is possible to make smooth images if the exposure strip is enlarged and, even more important, the film transport is operated at an even pace. As we move the film by hand, the amount of irregularities can be altered. But it is a random event in the sense that a perfect match of the pattern with the depicted, this means a 100% prefigured one, is only possible in a theoretical model. The texture of the film that seems to appear is the result of playing with the shutter of the camera during the exposure of the film. In the creation of this vibrating surface the vertical lines become more dominant and a greater emphasis is put on the rhythms in the image.

But the strip images mainly attract attention because of their size. This size is the result of the exposure technique: a narrow strip fixed in the camera behind the lens and in front of a moving film. As a result, the length of the image can be as long as the initial light sensitive film with which the camera is loaded. In my case, I use the 220 film, which is a medium format photo film. This film has a usable length of 1630 mm. With a slide adaptation on the camera even longer films could be loaded and cine film would be a possibility.

Due to its size, the spectator has to move around to get some grip on the image. This moving is not only a moving along the image, it is also going to and moving away from it. In so doing, two things happen: there is the constant struggle to get hold of the image, to oversee it as one, and there is an attempt to get the finest detail out of it and detect the slightest movement of the camera. To have an overview on the image we have to move away from it, stand back. But with this retreating we are loosing the detailed view. This also means a loss of information. The only thing that will be left is an overall sloping perspective line, sometimes enhanced by a clear or rolling horizon. In this reading of the image (going from one to the next) and in the relation between the detailed and the whole of the image, a dynamic image appears. This process in painting has once again been described by Hans Richter: "I had arrived at a kind of dynamic expression. The sensation lies in the stimulus which the remembering eye receives by carrying its attention from one detail, phase or sequence to another" (Richter & Gray, 1971: 114). In bringing the overall image together with the recollection of the detailed, different overall movements and paces will become visible. Behind every vertical line in the image a 3D space is hidden. The image as a whole represents a N-dimensional space in time. While a snapshot can be seen as 2D representation of the Cartesian space at a fixed moment in time, the strip image can be seen as a 2D representation of an ever-changing flux shown through an nD space. Those spaces cannot be seen, they can only be imagined. They are curled up behind every vertical line. In going through the image, changes over time can be felt.

The dynamism of the image lies in the ever-changing relation from one element to the next and the previous in the reading of the image. This is enhanced by the texture of the strip images from which, due to the working of the remembering eye, the experience of time erupts. In general, we seem to be occupied with the depicted image, what we see in the image rather than the image as we see it. This physical relation with the image nevertheless is part of the complex relation of the three components together: the image with its physical dimensions, an active spectator as reader, and the photographic that reveals the composition as a score. I have only focused on the tension between the reader/spectator and the strip image as a photographic image, a tension from which an experience of time arises. Of course this is only one aspect of the much more complex relation between the three components.

[1] Andrew Davidhazy has been publishing on the technical aspects of the strip since the late 1960s. Most of his articles can be found on his website: http://www.rit.edu/~andpph/articles.html (accessed 12/2005).

[2] In footnote 13 of the text *Telling Time*, Alexander Sturgis mentions the rather confusing use of the term "continuous narrative", as "different writers have used different terms to describe the same narrative technique and, more confusingly, used the same term to describe different techniques" (Sturgis, 2000: 68). For a recent elaborated publication on the subject see: Andrews 1995.

[3] QuickTime VR is a program that stitches series of single framed photographic images to a flat 2D panorama and moves this into a 3D image with interactive components. Some nice examples can be found on the internet. There is the panorama of World War II European Landmarks website (http://ww2panorama.org) (accessed 10/07/2005) which has full screen panoramas of World War II related sites around Europe. Another website with full screen QTVR panoramas can be found on http://vrm.vrway.com/projects/italian riviera/fullscreen/cervo.html (accessed 10/07/2005).

Works Quoted

Andrews, Lew, *Story and Space in Renaissance Art: the Rebirth of Continuous Narrative*, Cambridge: Cambridge University Press, 1995.

Bianchi Bandinelli, Ranuccio, *Hellenistic-byzantine Miniatures of the Iliad (Ilias Ambrosiana)*, Olten: Urs Graf, 1955.

Bonnemaison, Joachim, Tolstoï, Tatiana & Durand, Régis, *Panoramas. Photographies 1850-1950. Collection Bonnemaison*, Arles: Actes Sud, 1989.

Celant, Germano & Fondazione Prada Milano, *Sam Taylor-Wood*, Milano: Nava Web Industria Grafica, 1998.

Davidhazy, Andrew, (http://www.rit.edu/~andpph/articles.html) 3/04/2000. A few of the article titles are: *Basics of strip photography*; *Basics of strip enlargers*; *Bracket for strip photography*; *Introduction to panoramic, peripheral and scanning photography*; *Camera for conical peripheral and panoramic photography*, *Instant strip photography, Peripheral Portrait Photography with Improvised Digital Strip Camera*.

Davidhazy, Andrew, 'Peripheral Photography', in: *Industrial Photography*, vol. 36, no. 1, 1987: 28-31.

Dubois, Philippe, *L'acte photographique*, Paris-Bruxelles: Fernand Nathan-Editions Labor, 1983.

Francastel, Pierre, *Peinture et société: naissance et destruction d'un espace plastique de la Renaissance au cubisme*, Paris: Denoël-Gonthier, 1977 [originally published in Paris-Lyon: Audin, 1951].

Gombrich, Ernst H., 'Moment and Movement in Art', in: *Journal of the Warburg and Courtauld Institutes*, no. 27, 1964: 293-306.

Howard, John A., *Aerial Photo-ecology*, London: Faber and Faber, 1970.

Joray, Marcel (ed.), Richter, Hans & Read, Herbert, *Hans Richter* (Plastic Art in the Twentieth Century), Neuchâtel: Editions du Griffon, 1965.

Lamblin, Bernard, *Peinture et temps*, Paris: Publication de la Sorbonne-Klincksieck, 1981.

Lawson, Stephen, *Change by Degrees*, Wheeling (West Virginia): Stifel Fine Art Center, 1993.

Lawson, Stephen, *Forms in Light: Photography and Sculpture,* London: Talbod Rice Gallery, University of Edinburgh, 1988: n.p.

Lippincott, Kristen *et al.*, *The Story of Time*, London: Merrell Holberton, in asssociation with National Maritime Museum, 1999.

Maekawa, Osamu, 'The Panorama and its Subject' in: *Aestethics*, no. 9, 1999, (http://homepage1.nifty.com/osamumaekawa/panoramasubject.htm) (accessed 08/08/2005).

McBride, Bill, 'Panoramic Cameras 1843-1994', in: *Photographist*, no. 104, 1994/5, Whittier, California: 19-22.

Méaux, Danièle, *La Photographie et le temps. Le déroulement temporel dans l'image photographique*, Aix-en-Provence: Publications de l'Université de Provence, 1997.

Millar, Jeremy & Schwarz, Michiel (eds), *Speed, Vision of an accelerated age*, London: The Photographers Gallery, Trustees of the Whitechapel Art Gallery, 1998.

Molino, Jean, 'Fait musical et sémiologie de la musique', in: *Musique en jeu*, vol. 17, 1978 : 37-62.

Oettermann, Stephan, *The Panorama*, New York: Zone Books, 1997.

Read, Simon, *Seamarks*, Ipswich: Southampton City Art Gallery, the European Visual Art Center, 1990.

Read, Simon, *Time and Tide*, Ipswich: Ipswich Borough Council, 2000.

Richter, Hans & Gray, Cleve. *Hans Richter by Hans Richter. Pioneer of Dada and the Experimental Film*, London: Thames and Hudson, 1971.

Schivelbusch, Wolfgang, *The Railway Journey. The Industrialization of Time and Space in the 19th Century*, Leamington Spa-Hamburg-New York: Berg Publishers, 1986 [originally published in Munich: Carl Hanser Verlag, 1977].

Small, Jocelyn Penny, 'Time in Space: Narrative in Classic Art', in: *The Art Bulletin*, vol. 81, no. 3, 1999: 562-575.

Snelson, Kenneth, *Full Circle, Panoramas of Paris, Venice, Rome, Siena and Kyoto*, New York: Aperture, 1990.

Souriau, Etienne, 'Time in the Plastic Arts', in: *The Journal of Aesthetics and Art Criticism*, vol. 7, no. 4, 1949: 294-307.

Sturgis, Alexander, *Telling Time*, London-New Haven (Conn.): National Gallery Company-Yale University Press, 2000.

The Art Council of Great Britain, *Chinese Painting and Calligraphy from the collection of John M. Crawford Jr.*, New York: The Pierpont Morgan Library, 1965.

Van Gelder, Hilde, *Temporality and the Experience of Time in Art of the 1960s*, PhD Diss., Leuven, 2000.

Van Gelder, Hilde, 'The Fall from Grace, Late Minimalism's Conception of the Intrinsic Time of the Artwork-as-matter', in: *Interval(le)s*, no. 1, 2004: 83-103.

3 _ CRITICAL REALISM
INSTITUTIONS

1 _ AGAINST AFFIRMATIVE CULTURE
RENÉ BLOCK'S APPROPRIATION OF 'CAPITALIST REALISM'

Catharina Manchanda

Questions concerning the social relevance of artistic practice have been a central aspect of Critical Theory since Herbert Marcuse's publication of his essay *The Affirmative Character of Culture* (1937). They surfaced with renewed vigor in Germany during the 1960s, as an increasingly active student body questioned authoritarian systems of power that manifested themselves in social, economic, educational, and political institutions. In the radicalized political context of the 1960s, the work of art became a target for critique, because it epitomized the capitalist consumer model. Rather than creating decorative objects that entered the consumer chain, there were growing demands that art should serve a critical function. While these were popular ideas amongst theorists and a number of artists, René Block's embrace of such views, as an art dealer, was exceptional. This essay looks at the idealism that informed Block's gallery practice in the early years and investigates his appropriation of the term "Capitalist Realism" that was coined by a group of Düsseldorf artists in 1963.

René Block opened his Berlin art gallery in 1964. Within half a decade it grew into one of the leading venues for contemporary art in Germany. His roster of artists included Joseph Beuys, Klaus Peter Brehmer, Karl Horst Hödicke, Konrad Lueg, Blinky Palermo, Sigmar Polke, Gerhard Richter, Dieter Roth, and Wolf Vostell, as well as international artists such as Gilbert and George, Dan Graham, Richard Hamilton, Allan Kaprow, Nam June Paik, and many others. He had a special interest in Fluxus and Performance art, but as of the late 1960s he also showed American Minimal Art and the conceptual work of Marcel Broodthaers. Looking back at seven years of gallery practice in 1971, Block characterized his gallery as a "moral institution" (Block, 1971: 15). This unusual statement indicates that he understood the art gallery to serve a social as well as an economic function. Block's chosen venue in Berlin was far away from the newly emerging center of contemporary art in the Rhineland and the following discussion will reveal that this location was significant and corresponded with the art dealer's conceptual ambitions.

Block's inaugural show was a group exhibition titled *Neodada, Pop, Décollage, Capitalist Realism*. The term "Capitalist Realism" first surfaced in April 1963 in a letter to a newsreel company, written by the artist Gerhard Richter. It was an advertisement for a painting exhibition by himself and his friends Konrad Lueg (better known as Konrad Fischer), Manfred Kuttner, and Sigmar Polke, which they organized in a building scheduled for demolition in downtown Düsseldorf. Richter provocatively wrote:

> "For the first time in Germany, we are showing paintings for which such terms as Pop Art, Junk Culture, Imperialist or Capitalist Realism, New Objectivity, Naturalism, German Pop Art and the like are appropriate. Pop Art recognizes the modern mass media as a genuine cultural phenomenon and turns their attributes, formulations and content, through artifice, into art." (Richter, 1995: 16)

The term "Capitalist Realism" became known, however, through a happening which Richter and Lueg organized in a Düsseldorf furniture store several months later. Although this collaborative project has been well-documented, I will briefly summarize the key aspects of the event, because they are crucial to understand the inherent provocation and the artists' use of the term before considering its resonance for the gallery keeper René Block.

The full title of the Düsseldorf event was *Life with Pop: A Demonstration for Capitalist Realism*. Inside the store, Richter and Lueg had created a middle-class living room interior where they displayed themselves, dressed in suits and ties, as living sculptures on a set of contemporary furniture that was placed on makeshift pedestals. The middle-class furnishings were complemented by refreshments, a television with a live broadcast of the evening news, and a documentary about the Adenauer era. A Beuys felt suit and a box containing slabs of margarine contrasted with the otherwise conservative decorum. The re-contextualizing of the artists within the commercial setting of a furniture store underlined the role of the artist as producer and product ready for consumption. Richter and Lueg led several 'guided tours' through the store's furniture displays where a few of their photo-based paintings were on view (Block, 1971: 31-35; Küper, 1997: 233-36). The critique of the artwork as commodity, which increasingly occupied leftist intellectuals in the 1960s, found ironic expression at this 'happening'. The event's evocative title *Life with Pop: A Demonstration for Capitalist Realism* raised many questions: Was it intended as a celebration or a satire of Pop art? Was it meant to demonstrate that the new 'realism' of Pop art was as much ideologically tinged as Soviet-style 'Socialist Realism'? Did it ridicule the complacency of middle-class culture and demonstrate that artists and viewers alike were trapped by the mechanics of consumer culture? Or, was it directed against the modernist notion of the artist as autonomous genius who was thought to produce art outside the framework of everyday life? The event pushed sensitive buttons. Definitely, the new reality of a divided country was one part of the equation, but the playful packaging of such ambiguous and explosive ideas made the artists' stab at the artistic, economic, political, and social contradictions all the more subversive.

One should emphasize that realism in art was a loaded term in West Germany in the 1960s. It was at once associated with the Nazi past as well as with Eastern-style Socialist Realism. As such, it symbolized the political other. It stood for a tainted past as well as the wrong post-war political choice East of the iron curtain. As an alternative to state-sanctioned representational art, abstraction, or more precisely, abstract painting, was elevated into a moral and political necessity in the 1950s in West Germany.[1]

At a time when abstraction was regarded as the gold standard in West Germany, Pop art reinvigorated the debate about reality and representation. Demands for a new engagement with everyday life and the social conditions in a capitalist society were rooted in the writings of the Frankfurt School. With the rise of the German student movement in the mid 1960s, the texts of Herbert Marcuse, Theodor Adorno, and Walter Benjamin gained new importance, particularly Marcuse's 1937 essay *The Affirmative Character of Culture*. Marcuse criticized the separation of spiritual, idealist values from a social context, a split between the artistic realm of beauty and everyday needs. In his words:

> "What counts as utopia, phantasy [sic], and rebellion in the world of facts is allowed in art. There affirmative culture has displayed the forgotten truths over which 'realism' triumphs in daily life. The medium of beauty decontaminates truth and sets it apart from the present. What occurs in art, occurs with no obligation." (Marcuse, 1968: 114)

Pop art could be read as a new realism that seemed to reconnect high art with the everyday. Stefan Germer characterized the appeal of 'Pop' within leftist circles as follows:

> "In the light of Marcuse's theories, Pop art could be interpreted as a move to make art more democratic by abolishing its elitist alienation from practical living; following Benjamin, Pop could be seen as the elimination of the artwork's fetish status and authorial sanction." (Germer, 1996: 12)

If Marcuse and Benjamin allowed a positive interpretation of 'Pop', Adorno's critique of consumer culture and his call for the avant-garde to function as an instrument of critical negation provided material for a critique. Viewed from an Adornoesque perspective, the early reception of Pop art as a critical realism appeared far more problematic. One of the leading forums for left art criticism in the 1960s was the Munich magazine *Tendenzen*. In a 1966 essay, the Marxist art historian and magazine co-founder, Richard Hiepe, reflected on the emerging 'New Realism' in the arts. From the vantage point of the left, the re-engagement with the real (inaugurated by Pop art) was viewed as a welcome opposition to modernist forces, promoting an age of abstraction in the 50s and early 60s. Yet, Hiepe objected that Pop art succumbed to the very consumer culture it depicted or attempted to criticize. His view was shared by others. In 1968, when the Kassel *Documenta* celebrated Pop art in grand style, both the art and the institution were criticized by a radical wing of the German student movement as patently bourgeois and affirmative (*Tendenzen* 1968: 148; Berliner SDS-Gruppe Kultur und Revolution 1968).

René Block's inaugural gallery exhibition situated itself at the center of the ongoing debate about realism and representation that was triggered by Pop art. Block showed ten German artists, among them Manfred Kuttner, Konrad Lueg, Sigmar Polke, Gerhard Richter, as well as Klaus Peter Brehmer and Karl Horst Hödicke. It also included Wolf Vostell, who created décollage works in the early 60s, but was beginning to make a name for himself as a 'Fluxus' and 'Happening' artist. In the context of this show, the playful provocation and ambiguity, which marked Lueg's and Richter's use of the term 'Capitalist Realism', disappeared. In later interviews, Richter kept stressing the fact that the term was intended to have event character and was not meant to function as a new 'ism'. "Lueg and I used 'Capitalist Realism' as a slogan for a Happening", he said in 1970. "And that's how it caught on. It was not so much about our work as about that particular Happening" (Richter, 1995: 62). This was not entirely accurate, since Richter had previously used the term to promote his and his friends' work in the context of other catchy labels. However, in both instances the reference had been tongue-in-cheek. Once René Block decided to choose 'Capitalist Realism' as a label behind which any number of artists could be lined up, the term lost its playful and disrespectful punch and became didactic. For Block, who hoped to create an alternative gallery practice, 'Capitalist Realism' embodied the idea of an art form that confronted social, political, and economic reality and dovetailed with leftist demands for a critical new role for art. And for a brief moment in the second half of the 1960s artists such as Brehmer, Hödicke, and Vostell created some explicitly political and thought-provoking work that seemed to corroborate his thesis.

René Block's most explicitly political exhibition in Berlin was *Hommage à Lidice* (1967). The show was held in memory of a Czech mining village that had been destroyed and its inhabitants massacred by the German SS on 10 June, 1942, as a reprisal for the assassination of SS leader and Deputy Reich Protector of Bohemia, Reinhard Heydrich. Block asked more than twenty artists to create works that would be donated to the museum in Lidice.[2] Significantly, this provocative show took place in the now divided city of Berlin, which was the former seat of the National Socialist government. Moreover, it took place a few months after a German student was fatally shot and killed during a political demonstration in Berlin, at a time when student protests were starting to escalate.[3] In 1968, at the height of violent street demonstrations, Block published an edition of prints titled *The Graphic Art of Capitalist Realism*. The portfolio contained prints by Klaus Peter Brehmer, Karl Horst Hödicke, Konrad Lueg, Sigmar Polke, Gerhard Richter, and Wolf Vostell; in short, a group of artists who had also been shown in Block's inaugural exhibition. Most of the work in the portfolio was deceptively subtle. Polke's *Weekend Home* (1967) hinted at the growing affluence of the middle class and Konrad Lueg's *Babies* (1967) was taken from an advertisement of baby articles. Here again, the plump baby features spoke of middle-class prosperity. The only reference to violent conflict came from Wolf Vostell's *Starfighter*. This fighter plane was developed by Lockheed Aircraft Corporation in the early 1950s and was subsequently selected for use by NATO allies. After World War II, German rearmament was tightly controlled and remained controversial, particularly within Germany, where a sizeable anti-war and anti-nuclear movement had developed. Vostell's *Starfighter* pointed to the controversy surrounding the plane's continued use despite its poor performance, which was highlighted by several serious accidents in 1965. The image also served as a chilling reminder of the country's recent past and the devastating role the German air force had played during the Third Reich. Since this past remained largely repressed in everyday life, Vostell's *Starfighter* was a stark contrast to the images of growing affluence in the portfolio.

In 1971, René Block published a *catalogue raisonné* of prints by the six artists who had also been selected for the 1968 portfolio. At this time, the dreams of radical political and social transformation had lost momentum and there was considerable disillusionment amongst leftist intellectuals and activists. Block's catalogue was again titled *The Graphic Art of Capitalist Realism* and contained a polemical introduction by the art dealer, programmatically titled *My Last Word*. In this brief text, Block acknowledged that the social order in West Germany as well as in Socialist countries was still under negotiation and stated that he never viewed "Socialist Realism" and "Capitalist Realism" as polar opposites. Instead he declared: "I realize today that Capitalist Realism would have had to become a Socialist Realism if it had taken its agency for the masses seriously" (Block, 1971: 30). Block illustrated his argument with juxtapositions of Socialist Realist art and what he thought of as Capitalist Realist works, and supplemented them with quotes about art, reality, and alienation from the represented artists, as well as historical and contemporary literary and political leaders such as Bertholt Brecht, Walter Ulbricht, Kaiser Wilhelm II, Heinrich Mann, and Che Guevara. Among others, he reproduced a painting by the East German artist Harry Blume, *Riders for Peace* (1963), next to Konrad Lueg's *Boxer* (1964), which depicts Muhammad Ali and an opponent; the painting *Us* (1964) by the Soviet artist Janis Osis, next to Sigmar Polke's *Crowd II* (1969); *The Conquerors of Winter* (1963) by the GDR artist

Paul Pedak, next to Gerhard Richter's *Sailors* (1966); and *The Survivors* (1963) by the East German Willi Sitte, next to a conceptual piece by Klaus Peter Brehmer, which is titled *Coping with the Past, an Example* (1967).

Crucial differences were brushed aside in these provocative juxtapositions. The most obvious discrepancy was the state-funded nature of Socialist Realism compared to the individualistic projects of the West German artists. Ideologically tinged by government policy, Socialist Realism was necessarily didactic and propagandistic. By comparison, these West German artists' works were the products of an ironic and distancing view. Methodological differences, such as the critical engagement of the matrix of reproductive media, were crucial to Polke's and Richter's work, but their subtle interventions remained without comment. Many of Brehmer's works operated with the partial cancellation and reinterpretation of images. Brehmer's piece hinges on the image of a government-issued, Third Reich postage stamp bearing a portrait of Adolf Hitler. Brehmer partially cancels the portrait through abstract forms and phrases. Thus, the artist investigates the country's distancing from its past and the fluctuating historical interpretation, through the ephemeral nature of the postage stamp. Inadvertently, Block's juxtapositions illustrated that the work of the West German artists raised questions about the representation of history, memory, and media stereotypes, while the Socialist Realist work attempted to write history by creating images that anchored the political party line.

Clearly, Block's image-text collage was designed to spur further discussion. If the images were selected according to similarities in subject, but differed considerably in method and style, the chosen quotes from politicians, artists, and literary figures that accompanied them were equally contradictory. Among others, he cited Kaiser Wilhelm II on art as the repository of ideals and quoted East German party leader Walter Ulbricht to the effect that contemporary art should express the needs and concerns of working people. Freed from their political and historical contexts, these provocative quotes marked opposite ends of the intellectual spectrum and invited debate. Block's perplexing *catalogue raisonné* and introduction come into focus if one considers the publication date. In 1971, as the activist phase of the student movement came to a close, the question of the role of art in contemporary society remained of pressing concern to leftist intellectuals. In this context, Block's publication was far more than a simple inventory of artist prints. It had the character of a manifesto, except that his polemical introduction referenced "Capitalist Realism" as a historical relic, rather than an art for the future. The concluding paragraph of the introduction summed up Block's profound disillusionment with the West German artists' recent choices:

"Since 1968, Konrad Lueg has not made any more art [...] Polke and Hödicke are mostly concerned with aesthetic processes [...], Richter escapes into the 'fine arts', Vostell involves the audience far less often in his art and published ideas, and Brehmer dreams about the good life [*Funktionärsdasein*]. For me, Capitalist Realism remains an epoch of the mid 1960s, to which I feel very close." (*Ibid.*)

Block's disappointment was the disappointment of an era. As early as 1969, Richard Hiepe's search for an art that enabled a critique of the social and political status quo, led him back to the photomontage techniques of the 1920s and early 1930s. He celebrated the photomontage, in particular for its pointed commentary about social, economic, and political aspects of reality (Hiepe, 1969: n.p.). This re-evaluation of the artistic methods and processes of the early 20th-Century avant-gardes and disenchantment with contemporary artistic production also characterized other leftist writings in subsequent years as the activist phase of the student movement came to a close. Revisionist essays of the mid 1970s by influential writers such as Andreas Huyssen and Peter Bürger, invoked the artistic methods of the early 20th Century, notably collage, montage, and agit-prop theater, while despairing over the insufficiencies of contemporary artistic production (Huyssen, 1975: 77-97; Bürger, 1984). If Block shared this sense of disappointment vis-à-vis the political status quo it was, however, with a clear appreciation of many contemporary artists' acute choice of subjects and methods. Block's criticism implied that he expected these artists, which he had represented since 1964, to embrace his interpretation of 'Capitalist Realism' and view themselves as political and social advocates who put their art in the service of a political cause. What he interpreted as a lack of commitment to further develop a socially and politically engaged 'Capitalist Realism', was in fact the incompatibility of his utopian vision with the artists' ironic approaches. Block's dream of an art gallery that functioned as a "moral institution" had been fueled by the idealistic enthusiasm of the student movement and its theorists, but was no longer tenable when that movement collapsed. The text also revealed the intrinsically problematic nature of Block's approach. He bestowed a unifying term upon a diverse group of artists and viewed their exploration of ideas outside the confines of that definition as equivalent to betrayal. While it is perfectly legitimate for an artist to dedicate his or her work to a special cause, it is highly dubious if a dealer (even the most supportive and enthusiastic dealer) makes that choice for the artist. In the end, the irony of Block's terminological appropriation remains the willingness to sacrifice the artist's self-determination in a political struggle for greater freedom for the individual.

[1] Key purveyor of such ideas was the influential art historian Werner Haftmann who linked abstraction with political freedom. With his 1954 publication *Malerei in 20. Jahrhundert*, he rewrote the history of the pre-war avant-garde to the

detriment of realist movements such as New Objectivity and others with an overtly political agenda, notably Berlin Dada and Russian Constructivism. In addition to his 1954 publication, which went through numerous reprints, Haftmann was able to solidify his argument in three consecutive Documenta exhibitions in 1955, 1959, and 1964.

[2] Among those was Richter's painting *Uncle Rudi*, a portrait of his uncle in military uniform. It spoke of the troubled history not from the vantage point of historical judgment, but operated from an emotionally charged personal image that was ambiguous because it was self-implicating.

[3] Benno Ohnesorg was killed in June 1967 at a protest demonstration on the occasion of the Shah's visit to Berlin. Massive student protests followed this event. In the spring of 1968, the assassination attempt on the student leader Rudi Dutschke led to massive and often violent street demonstrations. The students' anger was largely directed at the Springer publishing house, because one of its conservative boulevard dailies (*Bildzeitung*) had portrayed Dutschke as a dangerous subversive. The attacker had carried an incendiary newspaper clipping from that paper. For several weeks, students around the country staged mass demonstrations and blocked delivery of Springer publications.

Works Quoted

Berliner SDS-Gruppe Kultur und Revolution, 'Kunst als Ware der Bewustseinsindustrie', in: *Die Zeit*, no. 48, November 29, 1968. [SDS stands for 'Sozialistischer Deutscher Studentenbund.]

Block, René, 'Bericht über 'Eine Demonstration für den Kapitalistischen Realismus' von Konrad Lueg und Richter, am Freitag, den 11. Oktober 1963, in Düsseldorf, Flingerstrasse 11 (Berghaus)', reprinted in: Id., *Die Grafik des Kapitalistischen Realismus: K. P. Brehmer, Hödicke, Lueg, Polke, Richter, Vostell, Werkverzeichnisse bis 1971*, with assistance by Prof. Dr. Carl Vogel, Berlin: René Block, 1971: 31-35.

Block, René, 'Mein letztes Wort (ich will hier nicht klären warum)', in: Id., *Die Grafik des Kapitalistischen Realismus: K. P. Brehmer, Hödicke, Lueg, Polke, Richter, Vostell, Werkverzeichnisse bis 1971*, with assistance by Prof. Dr. Carl Vogel, Berlin: René Block, 1971: 15, 30.

Bürger, Peter, *Theorie der Avantgarde* (1974), trans. Shaw, M., foreword by Schulte-Sasse, J., Minneapolis: University of Minnesota Press, 1984.

'Dokumente und Stimmen. Anti-Kulturzentrum Westberlin', in: *Tendenzen*, vol. 9, no. 52, 1968: 148

Germer, Stefan, 'Intersecting Visions, Shifting Perspectives: An Overview of German-American Artistic Relations', in: Beudert, M. (ed.), *The Froehlich Foundation: German and American Art from Beuys to Warhol*, London: Tate Gallery, 1996: 12.

Haftmann, Werner, *Malerei im 20. Jahrhundert*, München: Prestel, 1954.

Hiepe, Richard, 'Zur Theorie der Fotomontage', in: Id. & Fischer, K. M, *Die Fotomontage: Geschichte und Wesen einer Kunstform*, Ingolstadt: Kunstverein und Stadttheater Ingolstadt, 1969: n.p.

Huyssen, Andreas, 'The Cultural Politics of Pop: Reception and Critique of US Pop Art in the Federal Republic of Germany', in: *New German Critique*, vol. 1-2, no. 5-6, 1975: 77-97.

Küper, Susanne, 'Gerhard Richter: Capitalist Realism and His Painting from Photographs, 1962-1968', in: Gillen, E. (ed.), *German Art From Beckmann to Richter: Images of a Divided Country*, Cologne-Berlin: Du Mont-Berliner Festspiele and Museumspädagogischer Dienst Berlin, 1997: 233-36.

Marcuse, Herbert, 'The Affirmative Character of Culture (1937)', quoted from: *Negations: Essays in Critical Theory*, trans. Shapiro, J. J., Boston: Beacon Press, 1968: 114.

Richter, Gerhard, 'Interview with Rolf Gunther Dienst, 1970', in: Id. & Obrist, H.-U. (ed.), *The Daily Practice of Painting: Writings 1962-1993*, trans. Britt, D., Cambridge (MA)-London: MIT Press & Anthony d'Offay Gallery, 1995: 62.

Richter, Gerhard, 'Letter to a newsreel company, 29 April 1963', in: Id. & Obrist, H.-U. (ed.), *The Daily Practice of Painting: Writings 1962-1993*, trans. Britt, D., Cambridge (MA)-London: MIT Press & Anthony d'Offay Gallery, 1995: 16.

2_ BEYOND COMPASSION

HOW TO ESCAPE THE VICTIM FRAME
IN SOCIAL DOCUMENTARY PHOTOGRAPHY TODAY

Inge Henneman

Wrong Time, Wrong Place: a Case-Study

Wrong Time, Wrong Place, a multidisciplinary project on the actual situation of refugees in Belgium, opened on March 10th in the Antwerp PhotoMuseum. It presented the results of four creations: a double photographic mission on the one hand, a film- and a writing-commission on the other hand, and it was aimed at generating and staging a variegated series of meetings with refugees in Belgium today. As a curator of the PhotoMuseum I initiated and coached the double photographic mission and was privileged to collaborate with Nick Hannes (1974) and Dieter Telemans (1971), two young Belgian photographers whose work had been focusing until then on social and political documentary of worldwide conflicts. The aim of this compilation of portraits in pictures and text was to bring up for discussion the dominating one-sided and often negative media image of the refugee (and in particular the non-admitted refugee) through new, more complex forms of representation.

Nick Hannes's documentary photo-essay displays the official politics of the Belgian asylum rules. In four sequences of nine color photos each, he demonstrates the various steps in a request for asylum. Dieter Telemans portrayed non-admitted refugees and people waiting for years and years for a decision about their application. In another photographic series Telemans shows zones of illegal residence: empty places where the *sans papiers* hide. Bart Demyttenaere (1963) –a writer of children's literature who recently also published books on poverty, suicide, and the prison system in Belgium– reconstructed from intensive conversations with political as well as economic refugees five survival stories. In addition to this, he talked with a social worker at the Antwerp Public Welfare confronted with refugees each day –within a professional context and bound by rules and regulations. In exploring his subject, he also came across the unsuspected story of both his grandmothers taking refuge during World War I and being received abroad. Finally, Yasmina De Backer and Wim van den Eynde –known for their reports on Flemish local television– produced a montage of filmed interviews with Belgian refugees of World War I as well as testimonies of minor war refugees from Chechnya, Rwanda and Kosovo, applying for asylum in Belgium.

The exhibition presentation's aim was to detach the refugee's figure from the symbolic files monopolized by politicians and from the stereotypes employed by the press, by letting the viewer deal with unique faces, specific stories, and real social conditions. The aesthetic presentation of Nick Hannes' monumental series of color photos, the installation of Bart Demytennaere's book on a reading table, surrounded by Dieter Telemans' black and white portraits and sites, and the projection of the documentary with past and present stories from refugees, all invited to empathize with and reflect on the refugee's condition in Belgium. The educational part entailed a graphic presentation of the complex asylum procedures, a school exhibition guide, and a stylish collage of (self-)portraits by young Belgians and refugees, made at workshops with Nick Hannes in the asylum center in Kapellen (near Antwerp).

Until the end of 2006 the exhibition toured asylum centers, libraries, and cultural centers. Since this project aims at presenting different viewpoints and new positions within the complex social issues of the refugee problem, we could not do without the expert's assessment of real-life partners, intervening in the present or keeping the memory of past refugees' stories alive. In this case, the PhotoMuseum cooperated with the 'In Flanders Fields' Museum of Ypres, the Public Welfare Services of Antwerp, and Fedasil, the Federal Agency for the reception of refugees. Next to the bureaucratic problems, inevitably inherent to a collaboration of that many partners, the making of this project has been a long and winding road. For each partner brought not only his or her own expertise, but also a private agenda, a particular way of dealing with images, not to mention the inevitable control mechanisms that accompany each step of a publicly funded exhibition of this type.

Wrong Time, Wrong Place provides everything one needs to make a good case-study of the central issue of this volume: Do visual arts still have the potential to critically question the socio-political reality of today? My discussion of this case will express it in concrete terms, bringing it back to a story about 'Good Intentions' and 'Unintended Consequences'.

In Pursuit of the 'Right Time, Right Place'?
The question presenting itself to me as a photography curator since the realization of this project is not so much whether contemporary visual arts still have the potential to critically question today's socio-political reality –I think (good) art and social documentary photography

are always defying the status quo, but rather which contemporary context has the potential to make a difference in the social debate. The critical potential of some or other photographic series is obviously much dependent on the context within which it is shown. Hence, the basic question should become: Which context will facilitate the political impact of today's visual arts?

Critical social documentary and the better press photography are more and more shown in galleries and (photography) museums instead of in newspapers and magazines. What does this shift in the photographic image's context mean? The cultural world can never influence public opinion the way the journalistic world can. It simply doesn't have a similar social reach. Initially, museums are places in which a certain form of 'contemplation' is made possible and rarely if ever is the museum public 'mobilized' into political action. However, in the aesthetic framework of the museum the public's response to social-critical photography can go beyond the fleeting and subjective reaction of 'pity' and may at best lead to empathy. Expecting more would be an illusion. With this account of the project on refugees, I hope to indicate how important the role of the exhibition space has become. A photo gallery (as in the PhotoMuseum), a war museum (as in Ypres), a community center (once the exhibition started touring), a library in a problem area (as in the case I will study in detail), they all make up as many audiences, modes of reception, and reactions by the press and political administrations as you like…, but please notice the appalling predictability of these responses!

In this sense the disenchanting reception of the *Wrong Time, Wrong Place* project constitutes an actual echo of the fundamental principle of Allan Sekula's influential article comparing Stieglitz's *The Steerage* with work by Lewis Hine (Sekula, 1975). Not only do Stieglitz's and Hine's photographs represent immigrants applying for asylum –in the broad sense of protection and shelter, but Sekula also demonstrates clearly that the context in which photographs function, determines in a decisive manner the status and the interpretation of these pictures. *The Steerage,* seen from the point of view of its support *Camera Work*, devoted to photography's emancipation as an art, is valued because of its aesthetic potential, while Hine's work is introduced as an argument in a totally different social struggle for liberal reform. Nevertheless, questions of place and space never completely exhaust the meaning of a photograph's 'text', as is argued also by recent scholarship on the social underpinnings of Stieglitz's style in *The Steerage* (Bochner, 2005: 157-58). For this reason, I would like to make a continuing plea for critical realist photography as text and for its ability to ask the right questions straight to our face –apart from the representation's place, support, and politics. I will argue briefly that Dieter Telemans and especially Nick Hannes are able to go beyond the victim frame, leading the tone in many social documentary photography projects, and indicate their search for a way out, 'beyond compassion'.

The Last Free Space?

Interviewed by *Camera Austria*, Alfredo Jaar claims:

> "I still believe images are more necessary than ever. But I also believe that the political and corporate landscape of our times is full of control mechanisms that will not allow certain images to exist in their proper context. As artists are producers of meaning, we need to contextualize images properly. We must create a framework for their political efficiency. And the space of culture is probably the last free space remaining where this can be done." (Jaar 2004: 47)

Contextualizing images as properly as possible is exactly what a curator needs to do as well. The space of culture seems more than ever to be the proper place and opportunity for sharing other points of view. Yet, it is highly questionable whether this free space also provides the optimal context for the political efficiency of the images we display. After the opening of *Wrong Time, Wrong Place*, the press remained very silent, except for a half-hearted description here and there in a newspaper or the publication of photos without any mention of the global concept. Nobody examined the subject matter –though it is highly relevant and extremely delicate in Antwerp politics, where the ultra-right-wing is monopolizing the asylum debate. For many –captivated and moved– viewers the PhotoMuseum seemed indeed the right place for a close observation of the images and stories. However, the press and the political scene considered it just another cultural event, 'a nice photo exhibition'. There was no reaction from the contemporary art and photography sector either. The critics qualified the exhibition as a merely journalistic and educational project. The aesthetic bias of Nick Hannes' imagery in particular passed unnoticed. So, the exhibition fell between two stools, a fate it possibly shares with many so called 'social-artistic' projects. And though the attendance wasn't disappointing, I was somewhat disillusioned and started doubting the enforced multidisciplinary 'human interest' framing of the photographs. Had the sting been taken out by the humanizing discourse? Did the didactic staging put aside the viewers' imagination? Did the compelling way in which the attention was drawn towards the subject matter constitute a major obstacle to looking at the images? Had I been relating too much to the audience and not enough to the photographs? Was the political comment on the relation of photographer, writer, curator, and the 'other' shouted down by the humanistic argument (concerning the other's trauma and sorrow)? Questions also raised by Dirk Lauwaert in his review of Susan Sontag's *Looking at the Pain of Others*, where he calls this ability to empathize with others sheer fiction: "Imagination is the unique ability to reverse roles. [...] You can never literally take the other's view [...] it is the result of distance and aesthetics" (Lauwaert, 2003: 2). Analogous questions were largely discussed in the steering committee of the project.

The different agendas were weighed against each other over and over again and we got stuck in oppositions: moralist stances versus aestheticism, edutainment and white cube paradigms, democratic versus elitist reflexes.

Next stop for the exhibit was the 'In Flanders Fields' museum. There the emphasis was rather put on the connection with the refugee and war history of the Belgian people, since the exhibit was taken up as a contemporary section of the multimedia interactive presentation of World War I. Piet Chielens, the museum's coordinator and co-initiator of the exhibit, supervised the montage of interviews with young refugees and the last 1914-1918 witnesses. In his view these testimonies differ little. The panic of flight, the confrontation with the untold evils of war, and the laborious search for a new place to live are experienced and passed on by both groups in much the same way. As Chielens puts it: "During World War I almost a quarter of the Belgian population took flight, today we wonder whether we as a society should receive refugees" (Chielens, 2004: 135). This moral message and educational viewpoint informed several workshops that took place in Ypres, especially with young people, at which refugees were invited to witness. The opening on April 15th 2005 was covered on prime-time by the Flemish public broadcasting company VRT, one minute long… In retrospect I regretted that, partly due to the compelling 'historicizing' argument that 'refugees' stories are of all seasons and universal', Nick Hannes' and Dieter Telemans' photo series were far too much read as a social-political illustration, merely confirming what was assumed. The photographs' specificity as well as the openings towards other forms of representation of the refugee's social figure had been obliterated, held hostage so to speak by the 'common interest' and the appeal to the viewer to identify.

Since June 2005 the exhibit goes bilingual and the publication has been translated into French as well –by Fedasil, which organizes a tour along public libraries, refugee centers, town halls, cultural and community centers, etc. An official administration's participation in this social critical project may seem paradoxical and definitely not innocent, but at least it preserved us from a simplistic rendering of the facts. For especially in the refugees' distressing stories, Fedasil is represented as an 'enemy', whereas Nick Hannes' photographs visualize some of the less gentle aspects of the Belgian asylum system for the first time, such as the surveillance policy in the closed refugee centers, the emergency centers, and the transit centers from which refugees are repatriated [fig. 12]. That, nevertheless, a one-sided partiality and hence a full identification with the victim is out of the question is, I think, the strong point of the project and this is certainly due to the collaboration between very different partners. In the exhibit there are clearly two parties and they represent both sides of the same system. The process of dehumanization revealed in Hannes'

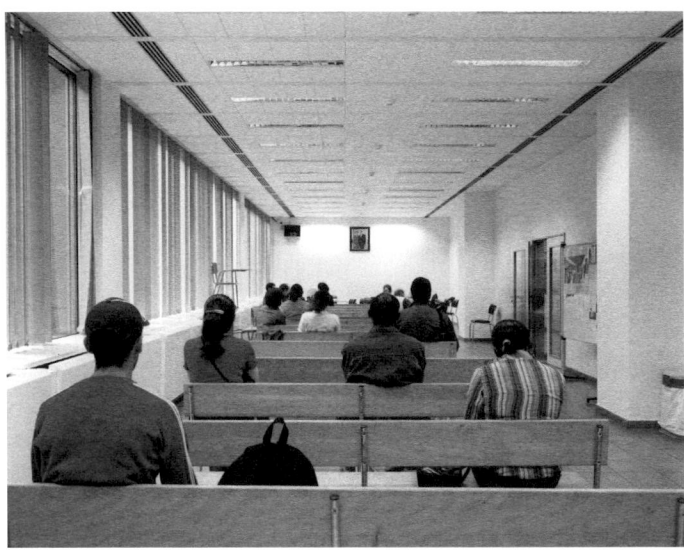

Fig.12 Nick Hannes, *"CGVS Wachtzaal 2"* (original in color).

pictures may be familiar to the whole (and to any?) official (reception) system, no matter how social its rules of conduct or guiding principles **[fig. 13]**. The discomfort with this system is not only a basic sentiment of the refugees, but also of the officials dealing with asylum policy and of those responsible for its implementation, such as Bob Pleysier, director of Fedasil, and Mieke Candaele, communication manager of Fedasil, who joined the project.

Fedasil officially justified its participation claiming that their services not only guarantee a qualitative relief of refugees in their open centers, but that they are also working towards a more realistic perception of the refugee and a larger integration of the centers in society. Next to Fedasil's expertise in the area of preliminary research and contacting refugees –and *sans papiers*– prepared to testify in front of the camera and the author, they acted as a mediator in order to require the official permits to photograph for example inside the Foreign Affairs building, where refugees are screened, searched, and interviewed. In exchange for this help, Fedasil and Foreign Affairs claimed a balanced spread of the photographs showing the repressive aspects of the system as well as 'linguistically and stylistically correct' captions and public comments. At the very last moment Foreign Affairs for instance instructed the removal of the word "illegal" from the entire exhibition's lettering. "Illegals" don't officially exist and what doesn't exist has no numbers nor statistics. The alternative term was "asylum seekers beyond legal proceedings". Fedasil as well as the Antwerp Public Welfare were the most ardent advocates within the steering committee to

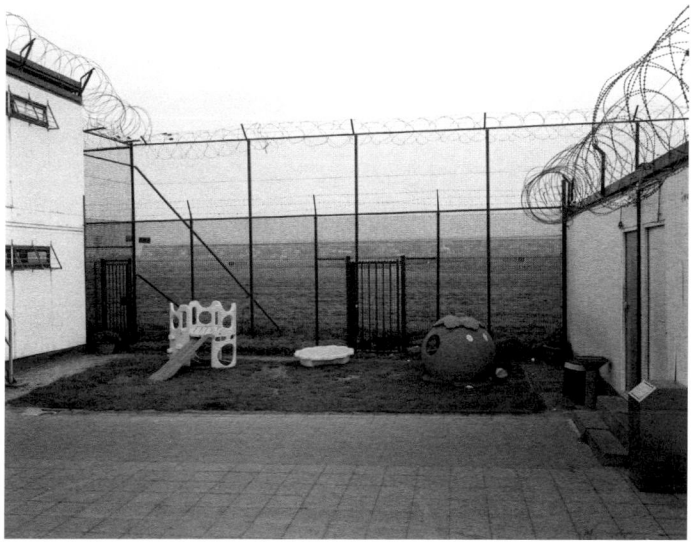

Fig.13 Nick Hannes, *"Melsbroek speeltuin"* (original in color).

promote a maximal spread of the results of the fourfold creative mission: their financial input was linked to as wide and democratic a dissemination of texts and images as possible and to a large accessibility to a young audience. This ambition was reflected in the educational brochure and the exhibition's itinerant character, as well as in the avoidance of specialist language and the involvement of a mainstream publisher (Roularta Books) in the publication. More than once I have been questioning my role as a photography curator within this steering committee. As a matter of course the Museum has to deal with actual social themes and needs to accommodate all kinds of pictures about the world. And why not use the best commissioned photography as an instrument to intervene in the public debate, since the demand for counter-images and the revelation of hidden abuses can stimulate new forms of representation? But didn't I leave the cultural world too far behind in this construction? To top it all, there were the "sincere congratulations" artists and steering committee received at the opening of *Wrong Time, Wrong Place* in Brussels on June 20th 2005 –World Refugees Day– from Christian Dupont, federal Minister of Social Integration, responsible for the Belgian asylum policy. As a result there were some impassioned discussions and mixed emotions afterwards. Wasn't the whole project intended to expose the failing asylum policy, to critically question a poignant social reality and to break the taboo of the 'illegal' stranger? The photographers as well as the writer felt themselves outsiders; they even wanted to be outsiders in order to witness all this human suffering in the margin. Was the system willingly supporting the criticism, but recuperating it at the same time?

In its press notes on the exhibition, Fedasil actually stresses the a-political character, introducing the exhibition as a presentation of four personal, artistic visions displaying a warmly human and balanced view on refugees. Who is ultimately responsible for what? Would Minister Dupont share this discomfort he himself provokes?

Next exhibition stop was the new Permeke library in northern Antwerp, situated in a neighborhood (the *Seefhoek*) where many potential refugees and illegals live. This very prestigious and expensive project had successfully opened its doors some months before. Since it was announced as a meeting place for a large audience, Fedasil considered it an attractive exhibition space. Yet, two weeks before the opening –the leaflets are printed, the transport arranged– Antwerp city council pronounces its veto. A local newspaper proposes the following analysis:

> "According to the Mayor photographs interpreting the issues of asylum seekers and refugees don't belong in the new temple of culture in the *Seefhoek*. In the PhotoMuseum in the classy South of Antwerp, where this well balanced exhibition resided with success a few months ago, there wasn't any problem… but not in the Permeke library! Mayor Janssens claims the exhibition would give a 'wrong' signal in the *Seefhoek* and would only reinforce the bad image of the district." (Heirman, July 1st 2005: 18)

A national media hype thus starts. Interested journalists all of a sudden start calling. According to me, this is because of the news value of a political blunder and because in a couple of days the exhibition grows into a symbol. Socialist Mayor Patrick Janssens argues that "an exhibition about refugees only reinforces the bad image of the neighborhood, whereas the library wants to change this image" (Van Hove, June 30th 2005: 3). The extreme-right-wing party Vlaams Belang congratulates Janssens. City alderman for culture Philip Heylen retracts his decision, but isn't able to convince the rest of the board. The council then plans to transfer the exhibition to the Antwerp Fashion Museum. In *De Standaard*, a national newspaper, Nick Hannes declares:

> "Can you imagine a bigger contrast between the glamor of fashion and the world of non-admitted refugees? It is precisely in a neighborhood like the *Seefhoek* that the exhibition could wipe out lots of prejudices, this is the very audience we want to reach! Everybody is walking past this library!" (Verhoeven, July 2nd 2005: 33)

I was quoted in the same article, adding: "In the museum the pictures are beautiful, in the *Seefhoek* they suddenly become dangerous". I don't remember having used the word "dangerous", though. Ultimately, Fedasil decides to cancel the exhibition in Antwerp and the Permeke library remained empty that summer. Better no exhibit at all than one about refugees? In a press message the steering committee states that:

> "With its verdict that our exhibition would stigmatize a part of the town, Antwerp city council has broken the positive élan this exhibition was welcomed with in other places. It has stigmatized the refugees. What we want with this exhibition is exactly to invite the audience to look at refugees in another way." (Press release of the steering committee, July 4th 2005)

Above all, this unsavory media hype demonstrates the importance of the place where images are shown. As Dirk Lauwaert writes: "Photographs do possess a proper explosive power, but this energy is never controlled and directed by the photographs themselves, it is always stirred up by the context. This context is the barrel in which the photo-bullet is put" (Lauwaert, 2003: 1).

Framing / Blaming Time and Place and not the Victim

To photograph is to frame. Unfortunately, very often the same frames are used in social documentary photography, frames deeply rooted into the medium's tradition, especially in press photography, frames which photographers seem rarely able to evade. Journalists also employ frames to construct the news. As communications scientist Baldwin Van Gorp puts it, the frame is the concept which unites a limited selection from a large number of possible elements into a coherent and comprehensible entity. In a recent research project on the representation of newcomers in the Belgian media he demonstrated how two frames were frequently applied: the "victim frame" and the "intruder frame" (Van Gorp, 2006). The victim frame is constructed around the archetype of the vulnerable person in need of help and protection. This kind of victim evokes sympathy, but is also passive, weak, useless and not in a position to help himself. So, taking care of him involves some costs. In the intruder frame, on the contrary, the archetype of the villain turns up as well as the image of the stranger as a barbarian. In the newspaper photographs investigated by Van Gorp, the refugee's image as an innocent victim predominates. In the text coverage the intruder frame was overriding.

Without falling back into victimization, Dieter Telemans as well as Nick Hannes offer, each in their own way, an image of the asylum problem in Belgium. Whereas Dieter Telemans wants to provide a face and an understanding of the social environment of the non-regulated refugee –the largest group– in a series of 'portraits' and 'places' **[fig. 14]**, Nick Hannes is focusing on the official route a refugee has to pass through in Belgium. In the portrait series of *sans papiers*, not capable of a recognizable presentation for fear of an arrest or repatriation, Telemans chooses

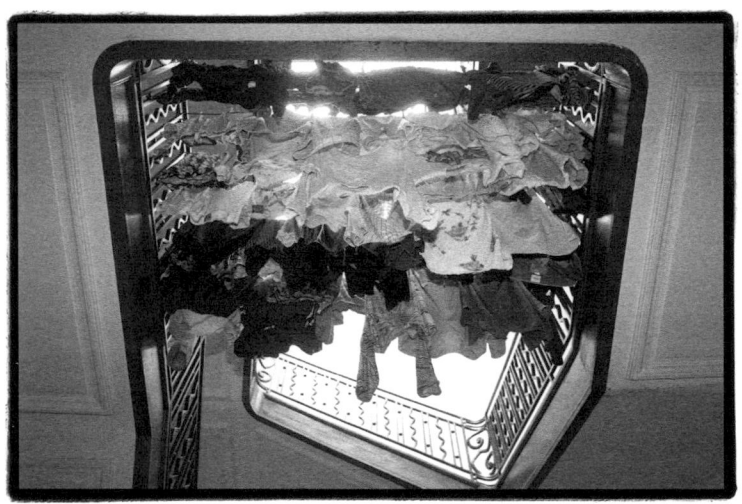

Fig.14 Dieter Telemans, *"Ambas 1"*.

to reveal the human being behind the stereotype. His aestheticizing black and white approach translates the respect for the human dignity of these *sans papiers*. Nick Hannes on the other hand exposes the mechanism of 'dehumanization', so familiar to the bureaucratic battle of procedures during the request for asylum. Telemans is wondering 'who' the refugee might be, whereas Hannes is questioning the 'where' and 'how' of the asylum's condition as a temporary situation in which people reside.

Telemans' portraits are conceived to be looked at in combination with the story of the person portrayed. The alternation of vivid glances of the people looking at us in the present and quotations from the story of their lives, by writer Bart Demyttenaere, was a way to avoid the one-sided exposure of the refugee as a victim. Mostly the dramatic moments occur outside the photographer's frame, but the combination of text and image helped correct this flaw. Another strategy consisted in the use of an unusual frame, not representing the refugee as a burden, but as a person who has quite a lot to offer to his host country, be it professionally or culturally. So, the pretty Klaudia appears to be a top model, although an illegal one… Finally, Telemans used detours and symbolism to secure the anonymity of some of his sitters, while honoring their testimony by focusing on a certain detail or prop, suggesting what is significant for this person, as well as on the shadow, symbolizing the disappearance into an insecure existence. So Dhurba, who spent his entire young life as a domestic slave, is looking at the camera as through a keyhole. Telemans photographs four fingers reading in *braille* the word 'peace', four fingers belonging to the hand of a political prisoner who went blind after his tortures in Sri Lanka [**fig. 15**]. These portraits clearly resulted from 'encounters' with a whole range of unique people, on the run for various reasons. Next to the quotation of the sitter, a brief indication has been added on the 'status' of the person with regard to the asylum procedure: asylum application considered or rejected. The rather rough grain, the printing of the black negative frame along with the rest of the image, the aestheticizing *clair-obscur* and compositional direction, and the meticulous leaving out of any specific context place these photographs within the tradition of engaged photography and into the rhetoric of the 'committed photographer'. These stylistic effects draw the attention too much to the medium itself, though. In the photographs of the zones of illegal residence then, there seems to be all too little distinction from more general settings of places, significant of poverty or exclusion, such as reports on decay, slum landlords, and the outsider's hiding places in the margin. These places do appeal to the stereotypes of the stranger as a barbarian (traces of wilderness, primitive behavior and a threatening *dehors*) as well as to the victim figure in need of help who can barely survive unprotected. From this point of view aestheticism becomes irrelevant, but weakens the shock of a genuine confrontation with an unbearably harsh 'state of affairs'.

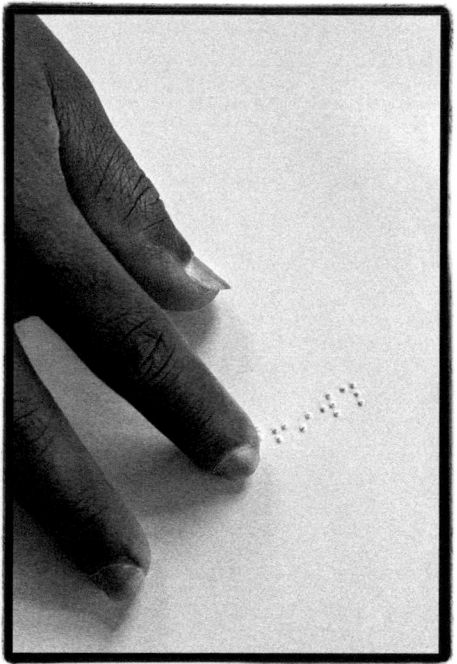

Fig.15 Dieter Telemans, *"Ruben"*.

Nick Hannes gave priority to the refugee's context —the 'where' and 'when'— at the expense of the 'what' and the romanticizing question of identity. How does the registration, the investigation, and the interrogation proceed at Foreign Affairs? In what way do the refugees inhabit the 'open centers' (Jodoigne, Kapellen, and Sint-Pieters-Woluwe)? And what is taking place in the 'centers for illegals' (Merksplas, Transitcentrum 127 at Melsbroek and the building of the Maritime police in Zeebrugge)? The photographs demonstrate the fact that 'the' refugee does not exist. What does exist, is a certain condition in which refugees without any distinction find themselves, a condition without reservations out of sheer necessity a passive situation of uncertainty and an awaiting of the 'yea' or the 'nay' by the Ladies and Gentlemen of the jury. Hannes too does not get round the typical victim-framing; often he focuses on children and families with children. He shows the playground in Melsbroek from behind the fence, men wrapped up in blankets appearing inconsolable, passive figures waiting, bored stiff, helpless, and resigned. Even the macho, chunky, and tattooed Eastern European who has to take a T.B.-scan is defenceless, being left at the mercy of Belgian asylum procedures and regulations. But Hannes manages to enlarge the alienating distance between refugee and refugee center and throws it right back into our faces as a question: how do human beings move, behave, live, exist in the space we mark out for them? This spatial infrastructure is extremely impersonal and fluctuates between a check-in counter, a police station, medical practice or courthouse where the 'trial' must proceed. The refugee centers' architecture seems to hesitate between a camping site, a mental hospital and a prison. Hannes demonstrates how the other's body is reduced to a 'requesting party' and a mere (file) number. He draws our attention to the political meaning of these non-sites: the determined chill, the inevitable neon light, the fake materials, and the uniform furniture. The asylum place is arranged as a provisional waiting room, a transit zone that at the same time seems to be located within and beyond the frontiers, where newcomers are tolerated but also guarded. Hannes manages to employ enough distance to enlarge the anachronism and the maladjustment of the refugee to his circumstances, without losing the involvement with the portrayed. He does not expose the other as a victim, but represents in his photo essay the individual's vulnerability and malaise, being confronted with a (relief) system.

Works Quoted

Bochner, Jay, *An American Lens*, Cambridge (Mass.): MIT, 2005.

Chielens, Piet, 'Epiloog. Een actuele kunstenaarsvisie. Hans Op De Beeck: 'Border'', in: Id. *et al.*, *Vluchten voor de oorlog. Belgische vluchtelingen 1914-1918*, Leuven: Davidsfonds, 2004.

Heirman, Frank, 'Expositie Uitgewezen', in: *Gazet Van Antwerpen*, July 1st 2005: 18.

Jaar, Alfredo, 'The Mise-en-scène is fundamental', in: *Camera Austria*, no. 86, 2004: 41-7.

Lauwaert, Dirk, 'Waar het allemaal goed voor is. Over Sontag', in: *De Witte Raaf*, no. 106, 2003: 1-3.

Press release of the steering committee, *'Verkeerde Tijd, Verkeerde Plaats' en 'Le Salon des refugiés' gaan [sic] niet naar Antwerpen*, e-mail, July 4th 2005.

Sekula, Allan, 'On the Invention of Photographic Meaning', in: *Artforum*, no. 13-5, 1975: 36-45.

Van Gorp, Baldwin, *Framing Asiel. Indringers en slachtoffers in de pers*, Leuven: ACCO, 2006.

Van Hove, Jan, 'Antwerps college schrapt tentoonstelling vluchtelingen', in: *De Standaard*, June 30th 2005: 3.

Verhoeven, Frank, 'Vluchtelingen naar Modemuseum', in: *De Standaard*, July 2nd 2005: 33.

3_ THE LOTTERY OF THE SEA

Frits Gierstberg

As I'm writing this short essay, newspapers are reporting on the recent conclusions of analysts announcing that the global shortage of oil will already reach us by the year 2010. The latest news also tells us that oil and gas companies are opening up a new frontier: the seas around the North Pole. The old fishermen's village and small harbor city of Hammerfest (Norway), close to the Barentsz Sea, is experiencing an era of unprecedented prosperity as a result of investments in new underwater drilling technologies that make formerly inaccessible reserves available for the world energy market –a market momentarily driven by India and China's immense and fast-growing need for oil. The USA, Canada, Iceland, Norway and Russia are fighting over the rights to exploit oil and gas reserves in other locations in the icy northern seas –the most 'invisible' of all seas on the globe. The lucky citizens of Hammerfest now seem to have won the jackpot in the 'lottery of the sea'. Global capital has moved its focus to the shores of the most nordic city in the world, indeed thereby expressing its 'spirit of adventure'. Could it be that 'risk' for the economy is exactly what 'the sublime' is for aethetics? This is the question that Sekula asks himself at the beginning of his new film, *The Lottery of the Sea*.

The story of Hammerfest is not part of Allan Sekula's new documentary film. However it does exemplify quite well the topicality of the issues that Sekula addresses in his three-hour filmic journey back and forth across the globe, from Athens to Barcelona, Amsterdam, Lisbon, New York, Genoa and Yokosuka, with long stop-overs in Panama and on the coast of Galicia, Spain. In the proposal for such a film he writes, together with film-maker Noël Burch: "Our premise is that the sea remains the crucial space of globalization. Nowhere else is the disorientation, violence, and alienation of contemporary capitalism more manifest, but this truth is not self evident, and must be approached as a puzzle, or mystery, a problem to be solved" (Sekula, 2002). This is precisely how *The Lottery of the Sea* is structured: it explores different smaller and larger bits of a giant puzzle. So it is an ambitious project, but nowhere does the film fall into generalizations and abstractions. Rather, it proceeds at a steady pace from one particular situation to another, unravelling bits and pieces. We follow Sekula on his route and we stay close to his own experiences, almost to the point where one gets the feeling that we are his traveling companions, guided by his low key voice. In the voice-over, Sekula reflects and comments on the connections between the various pieces of the puzzle. American foreign policy seems to be one of the major driving forces in the global maritime world, and not the most beneficent one if we are to believe Sekula's cynical comments when he refers to the invention of ship registrations in poor countries (often established by the USA), the ongoing 'war on terror' or the collision between an American submarine on a demonstration tour and a Japanese fishing boat. More like a demonstration of 'The Military Industrial Entertainment Complex' someone had said –had it not been for the nine Japanese maritime students who died in the crash.

But Allan Sekula does not tell us, the viewers, too much. Rather, he records and *shows* us the ongoing events and daily situations in the (mostly) harbor places he visits. (Spoken) text and image often run parallel, just like in the book *Fish Story* (1995) of which *The Lottery of the Sea* can be seen as a filmic counterpart. The film therefore is not a documentary in the common sense of the genre. It does not make a clear and final statement but leaves the viewer with large parts of the complex puzzle still unsolved. *The Lottery of the Sea* as a clearly subjective filmic montage reflects on various aspects and effects of the globalizing economy with the sea playing a leading role. It is a critical report and investigation at the same time. Many, if not all parts of *The Lottery of the Sea* are filmed with the camera hand-held. Here, the artist is a reporter, registering everything that happens before the camera lens. This becomes the most obvious when he is recording one of the many public demonstrations that can be seen in the film. In other scenes this is less obvious, the camera is at distance and seems more stable and controlled. It lets events go by without changing its frame or focus, staying fixed on the object or detail. In these cases one can easily imagine the different shots to be photographs as one recognizes a certain distanced, pensive style which is characteristic for the photographs in, for instance, *Fish Story*. Sekula reads us the eloquent lines of his own writings, often with wit and irony, creating double layers of mental and 'real' images and thoughts while we are watching the film. At several points in the film, he makes clear that he is the one who is filming, thereby both underlining the subjectivity of the film and questioning the role of the artist and his medium. Is he a reporter? A visual artist? A critical realist? A political activist? This is underlined by the numerous moments when the artist himself enters the frame, or when his voice is heard not in the voice-over but in the film itself. At one point in the film he suddenly pops up out of the water and jumps towards the film camera with his photo camera in his hands. At the American Naval Base in Yokosuka he shares his amazement with us when he discovers a mural painting that visualizes, amongst others, Ansel Adams with his view camera. In Barcelona he answers a demonstrator who asks him where he is from. There, he makes a boat trip through the harbor during what seems to be a workshop with students. In the Panama Canal Zone we see him holding the camera in the side mirror of a moving car from which he is filming. At another time in the film a policeman, controlling a demonstration, unconsciously poses the more philosophical question of whether we are dealing here with a participating observer, whom he is threatening to beat in the meantime ("no press", we hear someone saying in the background). Later on in the film, again during a demonstration, Sekula films his own reflection in a shop window on which somebody (the artist?) has written "Activist?" –a question that addresses the position of the artist at that very moment: is he participating in the demonstration? Should he? Can his work be considered a from of protest, even if it is not making any overt political statements about, say, the policy of the World Bank? Evidently the artist is no 'fly on the wall', a neutral 'scientific' observer of reality.

Sekula obviously sympathizes with the protesters he films. The film contains a number of long shots of just one person, often a young woman, who is participating in a demonstration or –in one particular case– helping with clearing oil from the beaches in Galicia. Generally speaking he films protesters in a rather respectful way, as individuals, and in groups almost as if they form a community, sharing one single cause for the moment. A community that is dancing, marching and making music (or a lot of noise!) together. Some scenes in the film where demonstrations are shown, are in fact big noisy concerts, a kind of politically inspired *Musica Povera* as they are almost entirely constructed with found objects, non-musical instruments. Sekula seems to be recording the cacophony with great pleasure, for minutes we listen to and watch the rattling, drumming, banging, whistling, clapping. Does he see any connection with the 1960s in the sense that a global movement for peace and a better world is coming up, in the form of anti-globalists? We have already seen their protests against the World Bank in Seattle which have artistically taken a visual form in Sekula's slide sequence *Waiting for Tear Gas* (1999). In this film we can actually hear the protesters. Sekula may have had plans for it already at that time. In any case *The Lottery of the Sea* seems to offer some hope, both for the (critical) arts *and* for the world. In Barcelona he films the protests of local citizens near the end of the Diagonal Mar –the extension of one of Barcelona's modernist boulevards towards the sea. At this point a huge re-urbanization process is taking place. Shopping malls, exhibition spaces, leisure ground, spectacular architecture and luxurious apartments will reshape this part of the city's connection with the sea into an area that is only partly accessible for locals. It is one of the many places in the world where globalized capital is invading local communities only to push these aside in favor of 'football heroes, Saudi princes, international gangsters'. Almost unbelievable and shocking is the scene filmed in Galicia in December 2003, where hundreds of voluntary workers try to clean the rocky beaches from La Coruña to Cape Finisterre after the oil tanker Prestige broke in two in the dangerous currents off the Spanish coast. An immense 'workforce' of old and young people together, dressed in rubber boots and white plastic suits, smeared with oil, embark upon the impossible task of removing the oil by hand from the stones, rocks and animals washed upon the shore. Here, the lottery of the sea took a much nastier turn... which it tends to do every nine years in Galicia according to the statistics.

We also learn that dockers are uniting in a democratic global-scale collective in order to protect themselves against the global powers of the ship and cargo companies they work for. A spokesman who tells us all this in front of the camera also makes the stunning remark that every time there is a conflict in the harbor of Barcelona, Elia Kazan's 1954 Hollywood classic *On the Waterfront* is broadcast on television, presenting the workers' unions in the dubious light of organized mafia. Dockers, sailors, marine biologists, crane drivers in their 'gigantic playstation' moving containers, Sekula films them all while they are at work rendering them 'visible'. Sekula clearly resists the notion that we are living in the age of the volatile and immaterial world of the internet. The fact that hard physical labor and workers have disappeared from sight in the West, doesn't mean that they belong to history. We would all die if it weren't for the hardship of farmers and sailors. We do live in a time of the global sweatshop –but it has to stay out of sight.

The film begins presenting the image of a huge ship sailing past, piled high with shipping containers, in sharp contrast to the amorphous flow of crude oil spilled by the broken Prestige oil tanker near the coast of Galicia: images of gains and losses, investment and risk, modernism and the abject. In between a shot of a microtome cutting slices of a small fish to be put under the microscope –slices of reality prepared to be analysed. Then it quickly moves on to Athens, the birthplace of the Agora and democracy. Sekula films the meat market –'where everything is fresh, but dead'. He links such seemingly unrelated scenes as the mysterious killings of stray dogs in the streets of Athens before the start of the Olympics, a Galician driver of a bulldozer who hilariously loses his cap in the oily dirt, a Millionnaire's Fair in Amsterdam (even more hilarious), and a Barcelonan sailor demonstrating how to make the perfect *paëlla*. It is typical of his working method to weave together small, everyday experiences that may or may not have a symbolic meaning, with the bigger events that are much more obviously connected with the theme of the film. It makes the film rich in references not only to global politics and maritime history, but also to art and film history (*The Lottery* contains bits of the history of film as well). And last but not least it makes the film fun to watch –the three hours pass quickly. In the meantime we are given many opportunities to relate our own experiences to what we see. The film ends sadly with a shot of slowly and tragically dying squids on the quays of Piraeus. Singer Phil Ochs continues to sing the dramatic song about sailors that started the film. Then the last shot shows a bright and shining full moon. I wonder what that could mean. Time to act?

Afterword

Sekula's documentary method and approach were discussed in the context of an academic program with a symposium, debates and exhibitions around critical realism and the work of the Belgian sculptor Constantin Meunier (1831-1905) (Van Gelder, 2005). A first version of *The Lottery of the Sea* was premiered at this event (September 2-4, 2005). Under the title *Shipwreck and Workers. Version 2 for Leuven*, Sekula for the first time in his artistic career had installed various large format photo works in open-air spaces at different locations outside the building of the STUK Arts Centre in Leuven, an indeed shiplike architecture designed by the Dutch architectural firm Neutelings Riedijk. The film premiere was embedded in a film program with screenings of amongst others *Misère au Borinage* (Henri Storck and Joris Ivens, 1933), *Les enfants du Borinage, lettre à Henri Storck* (Patric Jean, 1999), *Moeder Dao de Schildpadgelijkende* (Vincent van Monnikendam, 1995) and *Drifters* (John Grierson, 1929). Also Sekula's first film, *Tsukiji* (2001), was shown. This program placed Sekula's film in the tradition of 'critical realist documentary' film and was partly a tribute to Storck and Ivens as well. Sekula's decision to work in the medium of film, outside of the confined gallery space and within a local/historical context causes a triple deepening of his already rich oeuvre and adds challenging new perspectives to the actuality and possibilities of critical realism today. We hope to see more. As the world oil reserves are running empty or becoming harder to access, the global capital will no doubt act more aggressively and 'adventurously'. Stakes will be higher, risks bigger. Sekula is offering us the tools to discuss and understand the dynamics of this process and perhaps, if democracy has its way, we will be able to control better who wins, and who loses, in the lottery of the sea.

Works Quoted

Sekula, Allan and Burch, Noël, 'Notes for a Film', in: *October*, no.100, 2002, 83-87.

Sekula, Allan, *Fish Story*, Düsseldorf: Richter Verlag/Witte de With Center for Contemporary Art, 1995.

Van Gelder, Hilde, "Social Realism' Then and Now. Constantin Meunier and Allan Sekula', in: Id. (ed.), *Constantin Meunier. A Dialogue with Allan Sekula* (Lieven Gevaert Series, vol.2), Leuven: Leuven University Press, 2005, 71-91.

EPILOGUE

1 _ A DEBATE ON CRITICAL REALISM TODAY

Hilde Van Gelder & Jan Baetens

(The following pages offer a slightly shortened version of the public debate that closed the Conference on 'Critical Realism in Contemporary Art. Around Allan Sekula's Photography' on Sunday September 4th 2005 at STUK Arts Centre.)

Jan Baetens: The notion of 'critical realism' brings to mind a wide range of ideas, convictions, and practices. But a canonical and universal definition on what it is or should be, seems to be lacking. What is 'critical realism', how is it related to the work of Allan Sekula and to the lectures of this conference? Yet, the first thing to do may be to clarify our position toward 'realism' in general and the whole set of accompanying notions such as the 'indexicality' of the sign, the 'authenticity' of the producers, and so on…

Hilde Van Gelder: A good way to start, might be to go back to Tom Mitchell's paper, where he made a strong claim against any ontological definition of realism. I would like to add to this that it is not possible either to define realism in terms of style, of a set of neatly listed stylistic features. For me, realism should be defined in terms of research methods. When a work is realistic it is the result of a method that testifies to a certain artistic and social engagement.

WJT Mitchell: Realism doesn't come by nature. Realist photography, as I argued in my lecture yesterday, is a project; it's basically a search for some reality. We should avoid the idea that photography is or has ever been realistic in itself. Realism has to be earned; it has to be struggled for. It is a historical, contextual and critical account of a state of affairs. The real is of course the target of this process, but every reality remains a construction, it is the tapestry we weave out of the information we gather during this research. Realism is a project in relation to that process and critical realism would be some critical relation to some constructed reality.

Catharina Manchanda: I agree with this vision, but I suggest we include in our approach to critical realism also issues related to the specificity of the media involved in the project. What an author is, or a medium, or a project, cannot be defined in universal terms.

Allan Sekula: So far we have proposed that realism is a matter of convention, and that conventions are fought over and change over time. At the same time, these conventions are not reducible to stylistic fundamentals, and have to pass different sorts of extra-aesthetic tests to qualify as both realist and critical. Hilde Van Gelder has proposed the test of research rigor and the test of socio-political oppositionality, of focused dissent from the existing political order. Oddly enough, those two tests put us fairly close both to the model of the 'experimental novel' followed by Emile Zola, and to his personal political bravery in the face of reaction and anti-Semitism in the Dreyfus affair. However –and here our chosen terms get very confused– Zola was, for Georg Lukács, neither a realist nor a critical realist, but a naturalist. (Remember, by the way, that Zola was a strong influence for Constantin Meunier.) Indeed Zola called himself a naturalist, but for Lukács the term was deeply pejorative. And remember that Lukács invented the term "critical realism" as a counter to the socialist realism or Zhdanovism that became the official aesthetic of the Soviet Union with the 1934 Writers' Congress. Critical realism maintained contact with the deep currents of history and resisted the sentimental clichés of an official Stalinist aesthetic that Lukács, late in his life, described as "establishment naturalism". For Lukács, the high road of critical realism was taken by Thomas Mann, by Maxim Gorky, and within the later Soviet period, by Alexander Solzhenitsyn. According to Lukács, these later realists achieve a grasp of the social totality similar to that achieved in the 19th Century by Balzac, before realism degenerated into the descriptive naturalism of Zola. I'm sorry to rehearse all of this, which some of you know already, but the opposition between realism and naturalism has been less sharply defined in art history, and Lukács himself even lamented that art historians used the two terms interchangeably. Furthermore, the ultimate failing of literary naturalism was, for Lukács, precisely its photographic character! Lukács even spoke of the photographically illustrated works of social reportage of the 1920s as especially heinous examples of degraded naturalism. Photomontage he dismissed as "one-dimensional". So where does that leave us? Are we barking up the wrong tree? Or does this force us to take the dialectical bull by the horns? If photography is the bad object of Lukács' critical realism, can it be reworked into the fundamental element of yet 'another' critical realism, one much more modernist in character, that still seeks contact with and understanding of social totality? This is precisely why I wanted to bring Meunier forward from monumental figurative sculpture into a context bracketed by photomontage and surrealism, but also linked to the portrait and the documentary photograph.

Piet Van Robaeys: Would it be useful to define realism as anti-idealism and critical realism as a democratic art?

Marjan Sterckx: I think this can be interesting indeed, for instance when one wants to understand better the position of Meunier, whom one might consider the Belgian Courbet. For him, realism was really a style, but during his life this realism was considered too raw, too democratic. This style didn't work; it didn't reach the public he wanted to reach, so he wanted to come back to more traditional forms of painting and sculpture.

Inge Henneman: The historical complexity of realism is often overlooked or simply forgotten. Critical realism is of course a search for reality, but there is a third in the game and that third is the aesthetic, and the success or failure of critical realism has also to do with the aesthetic choices that are made at a certain moment for a certain audience. The work by Nick Hannes I discussed this morning is a good example of that complexity and these choices. In his pictures, he didn't address the reality of what he saw, at least not directly, but he constructed a kind of theatre piece, a kind of *commedia dell'arte* in which the social figure of the immigrant becomes an actor, and he shows us the absurd relationships between subject and environment. So, when it comes to move people, which is the aim of critical realism for me, then you also need poetry, metaphors, fiction, imagination, and all kinds of frames.

WJT Mitchell: I would like to make a comment on what has been said about what is considered the opposite of (critical) realism, namely idealism. Idealism has been described as falsified, falsifying, and so on. But I think that realism is a kind of idealism too, in the sense that it aims at truth and not just truth as an object that is ready-made or given, but truth as something that has to be uncovered, truth as the result of a certain labor. There is always a work to be done, a project to be corrected and this comes close to the romantic idea of the artist as a solitary worker. The truth may turn out to be awful and it usually is, but the meaning of it is never clear. After our discussion yesterday I kept asking myself: is Andreas Gursky a realist or is he idealizing late capitalist architecture and making a beautiful spectacle of it? We can put it in a realist frame, but also admire the beauty of his work. In discussions on critical realism, reception issues matter a lot. But I have one other question. We talk about critical realism and documentary, and we often think that we have lost something, but my impression is that in cinema we are living in a golden age of documentary and critical realism. Michael Moore and many other filmmakers are creating a popular thirst for films which tell the truth, e.g. films on the war in Iraq and popular films that are not confined to the gallery space. Documentary cinema is so popular now that it is keeping up the industry of Hollywood.

Allan Sekula: I wouldn't go that far, but certainly, the tolerance for documentary is much more limited within the culture of still photography. Cinema remains a realist, or at least naturalist art, especially in its popular forms. But photography became an art by renouncing referentiality and embracing the doctrine of *l'art pour l'art*, so the lineages of documentary have an uneasy status. I argued a long time ago that Alfred Stieglitz's *Camera Work* was heavily committed to a symbolist agenda, and this left the practice of someone like Lewis Hine out in the cold. This exclusion is not recuperable by being reduced to a mere difference in 'stylistic motivation', as John Szarkowski of the Museum of Modern Art tried to have it. As for Gursky, it would seem that 'documentary' in this vein consists in a kind of monotonous perfection by way of PhotoShop of the funereal shabbiness of certain exemplary capitalist spaces, such as the Hong Kong stock exchange. He makes them seem more grand and monumental than they actually are, and thus is actually even less of a critical realist than Zola, who came up in *l'Argent* with a wonderful set of more or less scatological metaphors for the flow of humanity around the Place de la Bourse. Gursky's overall project is a variation on Albert Renger Patzsch's *Die Welt ist schön*, tempered, perhaps, with a kind of fatalistic cynicism. No doubt there are those for whom Gursky's globetrotting is an attempt to grasp Lukács' 'totality', but I'm not convinced. There is always something weirder around the corner that tells us more about everyday capitalist reality, especially in an entrepôt city such as Hong Kong, so thoroughly given over to shipping and shopping. The average Hong Kong crime film gets closer to this reality, simply through what one sees in the background of the action.

Hilde Van Gelder: May I make a comment on that? I think that the problem with Gursky's 'totalities', as you present them, is that they are unclear or at least that they also conceal what he is really doing. I am thinking also of the argument that Rosalind Krauss makes about Jeff Wall in her essay on James Coleman (Krauss, 1997: 29). There she accuses him of pastiche because he somehow hides what he is really doing.

David Green: I think one of the problems of this type of work is that it is simply too open to fetch any meaning. It may be disrespectful, but Gursky's work makes me think sometimes of a kind of circus act, a kind of spectacle. It impresses people. So I wouldn't discuss Gursky in the context of critical realism.

Wouter Davidts: To continue Tom Mitchell's thought on the new documentary, I would like to say that one of the interesting aspects of Michael Moore's work is that it demonstrates how you can deal with the truth while constructing the reality behind it, while using elements that are not real as such. I think that one can be very critical without being literally realistic. Realism, in the narrow sense of the word, is not an absolute imperative for a critical stance towards reality.

WJT Mitchell: I see the point, but I disagree on Moore. You should show me the point where he is lying about, where he is false about. There are no lies in his movies; he doesn't play with reality in that sense. Certainly he's taking a point of view and one of the things that makes me talk of him as a realist, particularly in his film on the Columbine High School shooting, is his effort to find out something. His documentaries are always constructed as inquiries. You might disagree with the answers, but the method is that of critical realism. And in the case of Columbine, one of the most astonishing things is that he doesn't find the answer. It's a process of investigation and that leads him into new territories, which were unexpected for him too. In the first scenes of the 9/11 film, where he portrays the relationships between the Bush family and the Saudis as a kind of back-story to September 11th, well, you could debate that and I thought it was a flaw of the film myself, but, aside from that, you should tell me where he is lying.

David Green: To come back on Gursky, one should ask questions about intentionality. Can one be a critical realist without having the intention to be one? For example, it has been argued by T.J. Clark that Jackson Pollock's work stands in a 'critical' relationship to the norms of a dominant social and economic class in the immediate post-war period in the USA. In this sense, Clark argues that Pollock is a realist, much like Courbet was a realist, though Pollock may not have been conscious of this. He may not have intended his work to be taken in this way. So, maybe Gursky too is a realist…

Hilde Van Gelder: But not a critical realist…

David Green: Well, that's the question. You're quite right to ask the question. I agree also with Tom Mitchell when he was saying that in the late 70s and the 80s the term realism was becoming a substitute for the social and this shift is meaningful. 'Critical realism' also became an alternative to social realism, which was no longer acceptable, not even, or perhaps especially, amongst artists on the left.

Allan Sekula: Yes, and that was the same period in which Margaret Thatcher, speaking to a women's magazine, famously said: "There is no such thing as society. There are individual men and women, and there are families". So there was pressure from the right as well. On the left, it was more a question of renouncing old-fashioned 'reflectionist' theories of culture, which had regarded political or cultural superstructures as mirror images of the economic base. This renunciation was of course part of the linguistic turn in the human sciences. The implications of this for the practices of film and still photography were more thoroughly worked through in Britain, in the journal *Screen* and in publications such as *Photography/Politics*. The parallel questions were asked in a more isolated and altogether more eclectic and less programmatic way in the United States. I remember a show of British and North American work that Victor Burgin and I co-curated at the San Francisco Art Institute in 1977. We called it *Social Criticism and Art Practice*. We would never have considered using the term 'realism'. But earlier, when John Baldessari invited Fred Lonidier and me to show together at CalArts in 1973, we cooked up the title

'Socialist Realism', meaning it as a joke, and as a provocation to the rich kids we imagined to be so plentiful at CalArts. After all, we were both socialists and realists. To give you an idea of the context, and of the absurdity of our gesture, this was the time when David Salle and Eric Fischl were both studying painting there. The odd thing for 'official' photographic culture is that in the decade of the 60s, otherwise fraught with political conflict, the sanctioned turn was toward disengagement and ironic distance. This shift was polemically charted in John Szarkowski's *New Documents* exhibition at MoMA in 1967, which presented the work of Diane Arbus, Gary Winogrand, and Lee Friedlander. It was an enormously influential exhibition. One could say that the dominant attitude surrounding Pop Art was imported into the sphere of photography, but what resulted was also tinged with the spirit of the 'new journalism'. For example, Arbus had published photo stories frequently in *Esquire* magazine, which was considered the home of the new, subjectivized journalistic prose-writing, typified by Gay Talese and Tom Wolfe. Taking MoMA as the arbiter of photographic meaning in the fine arts, it is significant that the museum was able to mount a show of British photography called *The Thatcher Years* in 1991, when a similar show called '*The Reagan Years*' would have been impossible, since it would have had to explicitly contend with a decade of counter-revolution at home and abroad. For example, could Susan Meiselas's photos of the El Mozote massacre in El Salvador have been omitted from such an exhibition, and would these have sat well with pictures of the rich by Tina Barney or Larry Fink? Or what about a small section devoted to work done about the AIDS epidemic that Reagan ignored, ranging say from Nicholas Nixon to David Wojnarowicz? It's not that certain of these artists weren't exhibited at MoMA, or that at least some of these themes surfaced from time to time. It is that 'politics' can only be imagined to exist somewhere else, and that the name Reagan cannot be conjured with at an institution that draws its trustees from the ranks of the ruling class. The Atlantic, on the other hand, is wide enough to establish ironic distance.

Catharina Manchanda: I wonder if I can go back to a general question and ask whether critical realism may be defined as a method rather than a style. Fritz Heubach, who was the editor of the important German art magazine *Interfunktionen* in the early 70s, responded with a scathing critique of the simplistic approaches to realism, prompted in part by *Documenta 5*. He felt that one of the biggest problems was the preconceived notion of reality as something absolute or given, equally perceived by all and readily definable. Given the complexities of portraying the real, he suggested both a structuralist and psychological approach instead. He emphasized the need for highlighting structural relationships and promoted a circular and descriptive approach, rather than the mere representation of objects.

Allan Sekula: As early as 1921, Roman Jakobson argued that realism is always a response to earlier realisms, a renunciation of stale stylistic formulae. So the method of realism is one of substituting a new style for an older conventionalized style. One could say that for Jakobson there is no naive realism, there is only naive conventionalism. So he absorbs realism into the *telos* of the avant-garde. A photographic portrait by August Sander is not operating in the same way as a portrait by Nadar, and maybe the conditions of Sander's project –faced as it was with mass society and totalitarianism– made the category of the individual more problematic. *The Panthéon Nadar* is a manifestation of bourgeois-republican-bohemian optimism. Sander's *Antlitz der Zeit* is a manifestation of republicanism in crisis. The implicit heroism and genius of Nadar's figures no longer works: intellectuals and artists and composers take their places alongside the bourgeoisie and the proletariat and those between, distinguished only by the individualistic shadow of their initials.

Catharina Manchanda: As Inge Henneman's presentation made very clear, you really need additional information. A portrait in itself cannot communicate the social, political, and economic complexities.

Inge Henneman: As a curator, you have to edit the images, you have to construct the representation as a whole.

Allan Sekula: Or the artist does so him or herself, as Nadar and Sander in fact did.

Hilde Van Gelder: I think it is time to contradict ourselves. After all that we have said on critical realism as a method, can't we say that critical realism is also a style? Let's suppose for a moment that we are art historians of 2060 and that we would say that Allan Sekula was the initiator of the critical realist style and that many young artists were following him. How would you feel about that?

Allan Sekula: Well, I wouldn't feel anything, because I would be dead. But assuming I could feel something, it would be sadness that art history was still primarily the history of style, and that young artists were still seduced by style. A more interesting story would be how cinema and photography and literature and the graphic arts collided and resulted in new forms, sometimes even with old and seemingly obsolete materials.

David Green: The very notion of realism, more specifically the idea of critical realism, could only at one time be perceived and received within the framework of what realism was in the fields of painting and sculpture. It is because painting and sculpture were no longer seen as viable vehicles for realism in the 1970s, that it became possible to think of critical realism in new ways, primarily through the media of photography and video. Those media seemed to be more democratic; they seemed to be able to reach a larger audience. If addressing the 'real' is now once again becoming a possibility in painting and sculpture, it is thanks to this broader evolution, which was in the first place an anti-painting and anti-sculpture movement.

Hilde Van Gelder: I think the work of Gerhard Richter (or Luc Tuymans and Dirk Braeckman, as presented in the lecture by Liesbeth Decan) might fit well into such a picture. You have to start with an analysis of the strategies of the photographers, compared to those of the painters, and to go back to a close reading of the works, as you did in your own reading of Richter (Green, 2000).

David Green: I would like to insist on the fact that the very means of representation need to be addressed as closely as possible. General questions on indexicality, referentiality, etc, are important, but they cannot be separated from their concrete manifestation in particular forms.

Wouter Davidts: The notion of medium is crucial indeed. As an architect, I would like to mention here the 1979 book *Modern Architecture* by Manfredo Tafuri and Franceso Dal Co. They state in their introduction that architecture is a cultural project which has to relate to the enormous processes of socio-economic transformation unleashed in our modern, industrialized society. For them, architecture must be realistic, i.e. try to deal and to cope with these new conditions, or as they say "to gaze squarely and without any deforming optic at the reality of the new human condition". Architecture, they remark, is a form of "intellectual work" or "concrete work" in every sense, to use the Marxist definition. This implies that architecture must not merely relate to the existing conditions, but rework them through the specificity of its own medium. For Tafuri however, the critical first and foremost resides in the definition and the choice of a 'project', the decision to set up an autonomous space of reflection that serves as a theoretical frame of reference and signification for all the work that stems from it. The critical is thus not only something that comes afterwards —something that the resulting work 'reveals', but also something that precedes —that resides in the personal decision to pursue certain questions or matters, to first and foremost pursue a reflective enterprise that defines one's position towards reality. And therefore, I think that criticality has more to do with attitude than with method. The former is as essential as the latter. The selection of a specific medium comes afterwards and is relative. So therefore, I believe that these ideas can be applied to photography too. The problem with much of so-called critical photography is that there is no underlying and guiding project or that it's simply ill-defined. It only 'reveals' something about things that end up in front of the camera, but there's no particular reason why these things did so in the first place.

Inge Henneman: The specificity of the medium is dramatically important in photography. When contemporary photographers like Dieter Tielemans reproduce the frame or the negative of their pictures, as I've tried to show in my lecture, when they exhibit their compositional techniques, etc, that can be, for some of them, a way to show that they are committed and that they are working within the field of critical realism. The use of a certain style and of a certain rhetoric is a way of showing engagement. The example of the Bechers should be mentioned here too and the fact that their style has been widely copied is important. For me, Allan Sekula is also one of the examples or models of critical realism and this has also to do with his recognizable style. I think one should take into account that critical realism is not just intellectual, but also technical and stylistic. Many critical stances become styles.

David Green: I agree with you completely, but one of the things that continue to amaze me most is the fact that all styles, even the 'critical' ones, are today so easily appropriated by fashion and the fashion industry, which of course destroys their critical impact. Yet this phenomenon enables us also to better see what the work by Allan Sekula is about and how style in his work is constantly intertwined with process and method.

Allan Sekula: It might be useful here to distinguish critical realism from institutional critique, which is largely concerned with the immanent criticism of the art institution. One mode spirals outward, the other inward. But at best each engages both internally and externally. A Michael Asher project cataloguing the deaccessioning of works by MoMA is as much about property relations in advanced capitalist society as it is about the museum institution as such. The fantasy of a gift 'given in perpetuity' is one of final escape from the hard realities of the market. It turns out that this is another bitter lesson in the neoliberal principle of total marketization and 'flexibility'. The donor's gift is as fungible as an auto worker's pension.

Catharina Manchanda: I would like to link the critique of the institution with the critique of the framework. And I would like to argue too that critical realism remains strongly determined by its subject, which I feel should be defined as the subject of the social.

WJT Mitchell: And 'social' itself is used as a substitution for 'socialism'. Of course, this brings us to a completely different issue. If we are to distinguish between naturalist realism and critical realism, it is imperative too to separate critical realism and socialist realism. Socialist realism was anything but critical and anything but realist, in the sense we have been discussing. It was propaganda, an idealization of a hoped for reality to come, not an existing reality to be represented truthfully.

Wouter Davidts: I want to come back to my last remark. I often get the idea that photography –especially in the age of digital photography and the total availability of the apparatus– has become a rather easy medium for so-called critical art practices. Photography can set up a rather effortless relationship with the world. I am thinking here, amongst others, of the total inflation of site-specific art and their use of images, whether photographic or filmic. Much of this work is marked by a highly romantic idiom of exploration and revelation. The world that one encounters, is merely revealed, but not concretely engaged with. It seems rather easy to use photography in order to reveal things that never had been noticed or that had remained hidden, but the larger picture or the underlying narrative stays out of focus. The camera often functions as a rather romantic device, as it represents the tool that allows capturing things that are believed to go unnoticed by the regular gaze.

Allan Sekula: That is why the invitation to go back to Meunier here in Leuven was so compelling. The underlying narrative involves repression and forgetting and a discredited history of radical thought. Meunier imagined workers as citizens at a time when socialism was still a dream. The only way we can reconnect to the promise of radical democracy is to propel ourselves back to those figures who predate 1917 and the subsequent embalming of revolutionary movements. Otherwise we accept by default the other Thatcher *dictum*, that "there is no alternative" to neoliberalism. So this is more than an academic or antiquarian question.

WJT Mitchell: In the academy political and social issues are debated along the same lines and within similar perspectives. They often behave as claustrophobic institutions within a public sphere that is insufficiently tackled. Yet, there is space for debate and there are people that are pointing towards what is outside. My heroes at this moment are Edward Said and Noam Chomsky.

Allan Sekula: Both of whom have practiced a kind of 'critical journalism' peripheral to their academic fields. Does the art world, which is culturally libertarian but economically tied to the most anti-democratic forces in society, and which has very powerful codes of professional behavior, capable of sustaining a similar sort of 'aberrant' job description?

Catharina Manchanda: The traditional notion of artistic 'community' has become very problematic indeed.

Inge Henneman: The need to discuss critical realism is also the need to address certain social and political issues. Yet, what has not been sufficiently stressed is that this debate should be conducted in other public forums than the art scene, like the magazine world and the journalistic world. There is a huge problem if the art world is the last remaining refuge and the last free space for critical thinking and critical realism. There is a problem if a place like *Documenta* is the place where you have to go if you want to see uncensored images of the world. A very restricted public is addressed in this way, whereas the topics should involve all types of audiences. It is a pity that the interesting documentary photographers of today have to come to the museum because they are no longer welcome in the press. And if they manage to publish books, like Geert Van Kesteren on Iraq, why should it be coffee table books?

Frits Gierstberg: This is a very dangerous evolution indeed. As a representative of a public cultural institution, the Dutch Photo Museum in Rotterdam, I have always tried to avoid staying aside from the social and political debate. The Museum should be a platform for this debate. In the case of critical realist photography, the curator himself should also behave as a critical realist, i.e. behave in a way that is both critical and realistic. Since one works with and thanks to public money, one has always to find a balance between what one can do and what is impossible, to see how far you can go. Certainly in our job, where it comes down to show or not show what can be seen or what cannot be seen, the very work of a curator is critical in itself.

Inge Henneman: And don't forget museum people don't have the same political expertise as other agents in the public field. We are not Said or Chomsky. In a way, we are much more naive. Moreover, we are not always perfectly placed to judge the value of the pictures that are being submitted to us. Who are we to judge whether this or that documentary work on the war in Iraq is 'better' than what is being shown elsewhere? I can use my art standards, but here we are confronted with other questions.

WJT Mitchell: That's the reason why for me critical realism is always collaborative work. Some elements can only be evaluated by other people –and I know we always collaborate with ourselves, and this might be one aspect too to be added to the discussion on critical realism and medium-specificity. This may be just a conjecture, but I think medium-specificity may be (just) a stumbling walk in the path of thinking of what critical realism should be now. It makes us nostalgic for a classical stage of a medium that we want to hold on to. I think we have to be very careful about turning medium-specificity into a fetish object. What always impressed me about Allan's work is that he is a researcher. He looks things up, he has read a lot and that's why I think of him as a kind of collaborative artist. Also the fact that he is drawn by invitations such as Meunier: it drew you into something that might not have been.

Allan Sekula: Without Meunier, there would have been no way to do what I have done here. Hilde Van Gelder showed me Meunier, an artist about whom I knew something, but not a lot, and over time a conversation developed, between Hilde and me and Meunier and Crystal Eastman. We could also start thinking of 'dialogical realism', which might be another term for critical realism. Broadly speaking, people are seeking new ways to speak of the relationships between economics, politics and culture. People in the anti-globalization movement, meeting last year in Porto Alegre, tried to place cultural questions solidly on the agenda for the first time, perhaps as an antidote to a certain 'economism', and also because the spheres of ideology and the media are so important.

WJT Mitchell: Last year, I visited an exhibition at the Los Angeles MOCA, curated by Nato Thompson (*The Interventionists*). It was a survey of some collaborative projects by the homeless, made in the USA during the 90s, like emergency habitations, multi-purpose shopping carts for advanced scavenging, all kinds of crazy stuff. This mix of performance, mass culture, and political interventions, I find most interesting. There's something schizophrenic about the idea that you are walking into an art gallery, you are looking at pictures, and this somehow is an act of critical realism or an act of participation. And the interesting curatorial worker is the one who will be able to reach also outside the walls. This is something else than to be fetishistic about medium-specificity. The medium will be a means to work through a project. The studio, the art gallery, and the space of exhibition are also means to an end.

David Green: One of the things that have happened is the transformation of the gallery space during the last ten years. An art space is no longer necessarily the space we go to in order to look at objects. The proliferation of installation art has introduced us to a new way of interacting with the gallery. It used to be a presentation of 'bits and pieces', but I think this is changing. Now it's a different kind of spectator that is needed, a spectator that has to think and put things together, a kind of lacing and piecing of information. Think, for example, of Ann-Sofi Sidén's video installation *Warte Mal* (1999) that was quite remarkable in this regard. The subject of the work was the sex industry that had developed on the Czech-German border, following the Velvet Revolution of 1989. It utilized a labyrinthine lay-out of video monitors, which carried hours of interviews with prostitutes and pimps, and the local inhabitants of the town. You could walk from screen to screen, but you had to make something of this for yourself. It became a much richer work than being just a single screen documentary. This is an example of what has been happening to the art gallery in general, it has become a different place. I won't take sides in this debate on medium-specificity, certainly since we start too often from a too simple idea of what a medium is. In the case of cinema, for example, when we reduce it to narrative cinema, this is very clear. We need a more open kind of 'text'. But what we haven't discussed is the question which type of spectatorship you want.

WJT Mitchell: When you move in into a video installation, and the last *Documenta* or the last Venice Biennale were good examples of that, you feel like you're going to a film festival that doesn't know how to be a real film festival. In a festival you walk in and you watch a film and then another film, and that's a kind of medium-specificity which I also respect, but the merger between cinema art and video and the gallery space is really unpleasant now. You receive much more information than you can possibly manage and this should become the project of an institutional critique, but it has of course to be done by artists. We are now in a very awkward stage. We all get paralyzed by endless black boxes with films running. What do they tell? There hasn't necessarily to be a narrative, it can be something else, like a sales pitch, but you need to organize the material. One of the works I most admire in this regard is *Biotaylorism 2000*, by Natalie Bookchin of CalArts. A 30 minute automated PowerPoint presentation, which presents itself as a corporate 'infomercial'. It's a hilariously funny half hour of mainly found images about the biotechnological industries, filled with statistics, quotations, documents of all kinds, but it is really that deadpan, ironic presentation that is urging you to invest in a product that would be high-risk and high-return, harvesting rare genes from third-world bodies for instance. Actually, you don't need to see the whole thing to get the point, although seeing the whole thing is also quite satisfactory. The video makers should be very cautious about what they want the spectators to actually see and understand if they are just passing by in a gallery. Conversely the gallery people should try to figure out how we deal with the special demands of this medium in relation to the framing medium of the art gallery.

Jan Baetens: I would like to come back to the initial remark by Hilde Van Gelder, that critical realism is not a style but a method. It is a stance which she later invited us to criticize and we can link it, in a certain sense, to the issues of medium-specificity we are now debating. Personally, I think that critical realism is a style indeed, not one style, but a style that is modulated in function of the medium that is being used. There exists now, I think, a kind of consensus of what might be considered critical realism and one of its most salient markers is the very fact that a work is reached through a certain method. Method is part of the notion of style. Style can be rather easily historicized. There are certain periods in which it becomes possible to think of critical realism and in those periods it's rather easy, retrospectively of course, to list a number of rather fixed features of what is critical realist. I strongly believe in that idea of style, and method is part of that idea for me. It is not something that is opposed to it. If I had to define what critical realism today is, I would add also that some types of subject matter are automatically decoded as critical realist, whereas others are not. If you make a report on immigrant workers, you will be a critical realist. If you make a series on academic life, the risk that your work will be taken as an example of critical realism is very low. It may be seen as an example of social critique, but not of critical realism. The same goes for purely formal markers, such as the accumulation of data. It's not a coincidence that you needed a year, so to speak, to know what was being shown in the last *Documenta*. And there are also markers at the level of the exhibition context: the fact that you show something in a museum, rather than in another place, automatically reduces the degree of the critical realist part of your project.

Hilde Van Gelder: I agree with you, since you enlarge the notion of style to include elements such as method and presentation context, which are elements of style for me too.

David Green: I think it is necessary to give a tighter definition of style than you both did.

Jan Baetens: I would define it rather as a kind of social practice, in the meaning that cultural studies has been defending, i.e. as a network of formal, contextual, historical, and institutional relationships that construct a work and that this work in its turn is constructing too, of course. But that's pretty general too, I admit.

Hilde Van Gelder: It should be stressed that Allan Sekula's work does not function that way at all and this is also due to the fact that the presentation contexts always fit the work so well.

Jan Baetens: Let me put it in a more polemical way. Without a serious reflection on medium-specificity, critical realism cannot work, since you have to have a perfect knowledge of your material, and that material includes of course (also) things like method and exhibition context, if you want to achieve a certain goal. Moreover, how can you be a critical realist without having precise goals, which are both critical and realist? What's most hampering our reflection on medium-specificity is of course the fossilized and essentialist meanings of the concept we inherited from the past, but one can only hope that this is changing. I go on thinking that it would be a great mistake to exclude from the discussion on critical realism notions such as subject matter and formal characteristics. The project or the intention never suffices in itself, it has to be materialized and contextualized, and then one enters the field of style and medium-specificity.

WJT Mitchell: Medium-specificity matters a lot indeed, but if one accepts to define media as social practices, we are turning away from fixed essences, from specifications of technical and material circumstances. Medium-specificity is also something that people produce with their skills, their habits, their conventions, their styles. With medium-specificity the danger of reification is never far away. Yet, medium-specificity can also be a project for critical realism. One has to find out what a medium can do, because you never know it before you start. It's an investigation. So, I don't want to make a choice between intentions and projects on the one hand and medium-specificity on the other hand. You have to tie all these things together; otherwise you have unreflected practice on the one hand and good or bad intentions on the other hand.

Frits Gierstberg: I would like to come back to the issue of quantity and multiplication of data. You have to consider also from a purely instrumental viewpoint and ask yourself what is the most efficient way to work. Hans Haacke for instance has proven that it is possible to obtain strong effects with one composition. What matters in the context of critical realism is what the image is going to reveal about reality.

Jan Baetens: I totally agree, but in the case of Haacke, I wonder if the same effect would have been achieved if he had used painting instead of photography. The medium issue is absolutely crucial here. The same composition made with painterly means wouldn't have functioned, at least not in those years. You could not have been considered a serious critical realist in those years if you didn't use photography.

Frits Gierstberg: Yes and no. I think that the basic issue in the case of Haacke's work is to see that an image works as a narrative and that the artist chooses the material that fits best that narrative purpose.

Allan Sekula: Haacke's real estate photographs, from a work which led to the cancellation of his scheduled show at the Guggenheim Museum, were rather casual. He tilted his camera up at the buildings, with none of the perspective-correction niceties of architectural photography. In fact, they could have been photographs made by real estate agents. They were marked by the conceptual spirit of photography at that time, more 'images' than 'photographs'. The impact of these pictures had entirely to do with his parallel research into the convoluted network of slumlords that owned the pictured buildings. Here photography is primarily a recording technique; questions of medium-specificity are less important. If one were to complain that the photographs are 'pedestrian', that's beside the point.

Catharina Manchanda: Well, this question of real estate might bring us back to that of the presentation context. How do you bring projects like those on real estate together and what are the institutional pressures?

Jan Baetens: I would like to add a remark on the supposed incompatibility between critical realism on the one hand and aesthetic effects on the other hand. Allan Sekula's work clearly demonstrates that this is a false opposition.

WJT Mitchell: In Allan Sekula's work, the aesthetic effects are very strong, like in *Fish Story* in which there is that wonderful image of the contour left by a wrench that had been taken away from a table full of dust two years after the closing of a factory, and whose very 'implicit presence' is a kind of metonymy for the whole project and the whole subject (and of course for the medium of photography itself too…). This comes very close to the idea of the single photograph telling it all and that is somewhat counter to Allan's methods of creating a photographic archive, but nevertheless, every once in a while, for some spectator a photograph will be remembered as such a type of picture. For me, it's the end of a thread one can pull out as a way of leading one into the labyrinth of the archive.

Catharina Manchanda: The idea I would like to add is that it gets almost impossible to get away from the question of the aesthetic, because conceptual photography appropriated the banal descriptiveness that is associated with a documentary style (for instance in the work of Ed Ruscha or Robert Barry). In fact, these artists mimicked the deadpan, anonymous documentary style in order to invert it. It is conceptual art, of course, but the photographs they created or used productively exploited the documentary aesthetic and the associations of objectivity that come with it. If you say that you can't make a worthwhile aesthetic style when making critical realism, that is fiction of course. Even an anti-style has an aesthetic and ultimately it becomes recognizable as yet another style.

Allan Sekula: I don't mind re-introducing the notion of the aesthetic, as long as we try to think in terms of multiplicity. Aesthetic potentials might well be realized within the image itself, or perhaps in relations between images, or between image, text, page, site or whatever other elements the work activates. Then we would have to see pictorial style not as a definitive end, as the aesthetic surplus that confirms the art status of the image, but as an interrogative tool or means, alongside others. When one works in this way, the photograph poses the question, "what does it mean to picture in this way in this context?"

Works quoted

Green, David, 'From History Painting to the History of Painting and back again: Reflections on the Work of Gerhard Richter', in: Green, D. & Seddon, P. (eds), *History Painting Reassessed. The Representation of History in Contemporary Art*, Manchester: Manchester University Press, 2000, 31-49.

Krauss, Rosalind, "'… And Then Turn Away?" An Essay on James Coleman', in: *October*, no. 81, Summer, 1997.

2_ INTERVIEW WITH ALLAN SEKULA

Katarzyna Ruchel-Stockmans

Allan Sekula's interest for the world of labor brought him to an intriguing vicinity of the 19th-Century Social Realist art. Since the city of Leuven celebrated the centenary of Constantin Meunier's death in 2005, it seemed a matter of course to invite Sekula to make an intervention that could relate to Meunier's legacy. He was asked by Hilde Van Gelder and the Museumsite Leuven to make a double exhibition in Leuven. Early in spring his *Dear Bill Gates* posters were hung at various locations in town, where they entered into a dialogue with the monumental work of Constantin Meunier. In September the images from Sekula's *Shipwreck and workers. Version II for Leuven* were installed at STUK Arts Centre. Breaking away from his earlier practice, Sekula showed the entire series as an outdoor installation, imitating the billboard advertisement. At the same time an international congress was organized in Leuven by the Lieven Gevaert Research Centre for Photography and Visual Studies ('Critical Realism in Contemporary Art. Around Allan Sekula's Photography'), which aimed at developing a discourse on what has been termed 'critical realism' in contemporary art. This attitude, which was recognized by Benjamin Buchloh, entails the engagement of an artist in broad social, political, and cultural issues.[1] For Sekula, art is always already implied in some kind of politics. However, the exhibition *Shipwreck and workers* raises not only social-political issues, but manages to implicate them in artistic and historical questions of the image culture in a broader sense.

The following interview with Allan Sekula took place on September 1st 2005.

Katarzyna Ruchel-Stockmans: The exhibition *Shipwreck and workers. Version II for Leuven* is an outdoor installation of billboard-size panels with photographs, which are hung at the two entrances and in the courtyard of STUK Arts Centre in Leuven. They all show working people of various professions, except for the panoramic view of a shipwreck. I'm wondering how the idea for this exhibition has come into existence? When you showed *Shipwreck and workers* for the first time in Vienna earlier this year,[2] you referred to Walter Benjamin's Angel of History.[3] In a passage from the *Theses on the Philosophy of History* the angel is the one who sees the past as a sequence of disasters and piling debris. It is actually quite a catastrophic vision, whereas this collection of photographs is, except for the *Shipwreck* triptych, almost optimistic and cheerful. Isn't there a contrast in it?

Allan Sekula: I very much wanted and intended that contrast. Although there are some photos of Americans and Asians, the series is primarily an imaginary sampling of Europe, with more photos from France than anywhere else. Front and center, or if you want, first and last, both in Vienna and Leuven, were the two triptychs from Istanbul: the shipwreck on the Sea of Marmara, and the goldsmiths at work. And the pregnant question of the moment is: will Turkey join Europe or not? (Both the Turkish right-wing Islamists and the new Roman Catholic pope share the desire to abort this union.) In Vienna the battle line against the Ottoman Turks was drawn more than once: in 1529 and 1683. And the Chamber of Labor, headquarters of the Austrian syndicalist movement, was an apt place to evoke the specter of the very Turkish workers who already contribute –very often in the unorganized sectors of the economy– to the prosperity of Europe. (I come from California, where the labor movement originated in the 19th Century with a militant anti-Chinese platform, so the contradictions between working-class nativism and more radical and internationalist aspirations is not unfamiliar to me.) Similarly, the Catholic university town of Leuven, with –among others– student contingents of right-wing Vlaams Belang and Opus Dei, was a place to ask again the obvious question: whither Europe? Shipwreck of the super-state, apocalyptic rematch of the Battle of Lepanto, or massive hive of the golden bees? Or none of the above?

While working on the Vienna exhibition in the late spring of 2005, I was thinking as well of the ongoing project in Leuven. After I finally saw Meunier's *Monument to Labor* alongside the port of Brussels, it hit me that the Vienna project was already a big step toward the project for Leuven.

Up to that point I had been thinking of the Borinage, and the line that led from Meunier to Joris Ivens and the Dardenne brothers, and the rather surrealist technological and economic history that leads from the coal mine to the barge elevator. But this is something I would like to come back to later, with more time to actually work and make photographs in Belgium.

I wanted to make this exhibition outside the walls of the museum or art space. From the beginning I was uncomfortable with the space upstairs (inside the STUK Arts Centre) because the show was scheduled for the late summer when the university is closed. I remember how active it was however here in the bar at STUK, even during my first visit during the Christmas break. So it seemed best to think of a work that would take advantage of the good weather, STUK being a destination for a beer or a movie, if not for a specialized indoor art presentation. This was consistent with the outdoor placement of my poster project *Dear Bill Gates* in close proximity to Meunier's sculptures and to his former studio in the old medical amphitheatre. So the explicit dialogue between outdoor photography and public sculpture was joined in a more precise way.

The Vienna project opened the door to a new way –new for me– of presenting pictures, and this led, through the encounter with Meunier, to the idea of a portable and temporary 'monument for labor'. Of course a portable and temporary monument is all we can count on in a epoch of factory-closings and aggressive de-localization of production. You might even say that –in keeping with the prevailing neo-liberal ethos– I'm being 'flexible'.

In Leuven I added two panels, one with a text and a small diagram and one with montaged photographic reproductions of Meunier and Giacometti sculptures of the human body, in full and in part. Both sculptures are both implacably static and gestural in a dramatic way and to me they capture something of the elemental embodiments of Greek theater. The real test for an image may well be not its ability to hold the wall of a museum, but rather its ability to function as a theatrical backdrop in the absence of any dramatic action. It is as if the spectator, by reading the text and contemplating the images, produces a little play for him or herself. A philosophical play: like a *Lehrstück* by Brecht or maybe even a piece by Beckett. But of course there is a cast of characters, but they are offstage, elsewhere in (or, rather, 'on') the building and its immediate environs. So it is an exploded or disassembled play, just as *Aerospace Folktales* (1973), one of my early projects, was a 'disassembled movie'.

Katarzyna Ruchel-Stockmans: By appropriating the sculpture of the *Puddler*, but also by placing your *Dear Bill Gates* posters throughout the town, you engage in a sort of imaginary dialogue with Constantin Meunier. How do you perceive his work? Today you can read his Social Realism in two contradictory ways. On the one hand, his effort to monumentalize the worker can be seen as a confirmation of the existing social order, a heroicization of the lower class that serves only the aesthetic appetite of the upper class. On the other hand, it might be interpreted as a sign of social engagement of the sculptor who, as one of the first European artists, gave the ordinary worker a place in the iconography of monumental art.

Allan Sekula: I think Meunier is neither. Hilde Van Gelder's essay makes an interesting case that he is neither a socialist nor an aesthete.[4] He defines a new object of representation by means of

141

which he alters the formal possibilities of sculpture. It seems to me that the *Puddler* is the answer to the *Thinker*. Rodin's *Thinker* is very romantic and individualistic, and, one might add, nakedly Cartesian. Rodin is a late romantic idealist. It is a commonplace to say of the *Bourgeois de Calais* –even though it is a group sculpture– that the figures are all psychologically individuated, each takes his own tragic-epic-lonely stand. Rodin is thus taking the ideal of the bourgeois individual and projecting it backward onto the early history of the urban bourgeoisie. One can assume that this was also a consuming issue for Meunier, whose interchange of mutual influence with Rodin appears to have been considerable. As a 'response' to Rodin's backward time-projection of bourgeois individualism, Meunier turned his attention to a group of people whose humanity was not even acknowledged in legal terms, who were, in effect, disenfranchised toiling beasts. The *Thinker* thinks in a void. *The Puddler* thinks in the face of his own exhaustion. Meunier finds the idiosyncrasy of the individual within the collective burden of industrialized toil. This is very different from the fake triumphalism of Socialist Realism: the hero-worker who vanquishes the quota. It is unfair and anachronistic to see Meunier as a proto-Stakhanovite of representation. I appreciate his kinship with his other contemporary, the American painter Winslow Homer, whose pictures of struggling fishermen on the edge of the abyss have recently attracted the likes of Bill Gates for reasons I have tried to explore elsewhere. The acuity of observation in Meunier is consistent with a range of other realists, from Courbet to Zola. There is an inner life that the artist can record. But the inner life of the worker is always burdened by his or her physical exertion and exhaustion. Meunier was particularly sensitive to this. His sense of observation made him a precursor of neo-realism in cinema.

Nowadays, when the inner body is colonized in terms Foucault has described, when the body is relentlessly disciplined and leisure itself is converted into work, when all of life is submitted to the cycle of production and consumption, one realizes that it all began in the 1880s, with the coming of the second industrial revolution. In this sense Belgium was ahead of France, and it is no surprise that the American radical Crystal Eastman would find in Meunier a powerful metaphoric embodiment of the collective trials of the workers of Pittsburgh. (In light of our other conversations about critical realism here, it is interesting to note that Crystal Eastman met and was very impressed by Georg Lukács when he was minister of education of the short-lived Hungarian Soviet Republic in 1919.)

Meunier marks the end of monumental sculpture. We can now –in retrospect– ask ourselves who appeared in monumental sculptures one hundred years ago. First, the nobility, then the bourgeoisie, and then, with Meunier, the workers. The bourgeoisie had to seize the pedestal, to win the monument from the aristocracy, which is what happens in the *Bourgeois de Calais*. At nearly the same moment, Meunier presents a new kind of actor who is not yet really an actor –'*en soi*' but not *'pour soi'*– an emergent and incompletely realized subject; a subject who is not yet revolutionary but no longer comical, charmingly rustic or pathetic; a subject who is not yet a citizen, but who aims to be a citizen.

In other words, there is no simple answer to your question because this is not a matter of either/or. Meunier's bold language game was to introduce a radically new subjective content to an exhausted and increasingly depraved genre. The statues of King Leopold overlooking the beach at Zeebrugge are evidence of that exhaustion. Of course 20th-Century dictatorships would revive the genre, but that is only more evidence of our backwardness.

Katarzyna Ruchel-Stockmans: In that case, how would you define the present situation of the monument? You called your Leuven project an anti-monument to labor…

Allan Sekula: When doing this project, I was thinking about the grand photographic exhibitions from the 1950s, like *The Family of Man*, with large-scale photographs. Until now I wasn't making large-scale pictures myself. Maybe now the position of the outdoor advertisement, of the large-scale photograph is akin to that of monumental sculpture at the end of the 19th Century. In other words, everyone nowadays is colonized by little things (mobile devices, just like your little recorder here…), everyone hypnotically engaged with their text messages, and big things are becoming almost irrelevant. Micro-devices define the new field of communicative interaction and media-colonization, so there is something archaic in these big unwieldy panels of plywood on which my photographs are hung. I live in Los Angeles, which is a city with trivial but amusing monuments –an equestrian statue of John Wayne in front of the headquarters of the porn-and-gambling impresario Larry Flynt, for example– a 'post-monument' city in which the primary mode of Foucaultian discipline is automotive. Brussels, by contrast, is chockablock with monuments and yet as contemporary as Los Angeles in every other human sense. That is perhaps one reason I was so moved by Sarah Vanagt's film *Little Figures*, in which immigrant children 'give voice' to Brussels' noble figures in stone.

The photographs themselves come from the same period as the *TITANIC's Wake* series (1998-2000). Some of them were made during my stay in France in 1998 and some of the same people appeared in the pictures from *Titanic's Wake*: for example, you see the machinist Michel Boireau, who as a young man worked with Alexander Calder, and who now, in his late forties, continues to work in the same factory, building containers for hydrofluoric acid. I wanted photographs of people either absorbed in work or posing at rest, even if only for a brief moment. I also wanted modes of work that were of great historical longevity: woodcutting, seafaring, the *vendange*.

Katarzyna Ruchel-Stockmans: By the way, where did you find the goldsmiths? It's a very ancient-like profession in my opinion…

Allan Sekula: In Istanbul, near the Grand Bazaar, I climbed up into a labyrinthine inner courtyard and found men casting and molding jewelry and other golden artifacts, using cyanide of course, and with very little ventilation to carry away the fumes. The mold is a vessel, like a little ship or boat, but you pour the liquid into it, rather than pouring it into the liquid.

Katarzyna Ruchel-Stockmans: So, there is an iconographical link between the two diptychs, since the goldsmiths vessel is the negative of the wrecked boat…

Allan Sekula: You could say that. The golden ship is the one that makes it home. The shipwreck removes the gold from circulation. That's the archaic or mythic opposition that came to be literally true during the epoch of primitive accumulation, with Spanish galleons returning from Peru. Also, the time sequence of the *Goldsmiths* is opposed to the spatial panorama of *Shipwreck*. These are the two poles of photography: the sampling of time and the sampling of space.

Katarzyna Ruchel-Stockmans: Indeed there is a palpable opposition between the two. The *Shipwreck* triptych made me think of photomontage and the fragmentariness it entails. But even if there is no full view of the shipwreck, the threefold image makes a claim to a panorama. *Goldsmiths,* on the other hand, offers a sequence of consecutive actions that seem to defy the *decisive moment* (as defined by Cartier-Bresson). You could choose one of the three frames, why do you show all of them?

Allan Sekula: Because it was important in this case not to reduce the work process to a pose. The window frame marks out a continuous frame, like a film strip being pulled through a primitive projector with visible sprocket holes. This is the most emphatic of the pictures showing people absorbed in work. One could also say that it is Muybridge –another contemporary of Meunier– who destroys the privileged status of the single pose stolen from the flow of the moving body, and who thus also undermines the logic of monumental figurative sculpture. Cartier-Bresson rescues the 'pose' for surrealism, precisely by unleashing his own catlike subjective time. But this uncanny facticity of suspended movement only works in two dimensions and on a small scale.

My two triptychs from Istanbul are different from the rest of the pictures in the exhibition. All the others are –in a way– portraits. Even the woodworker, who seems to be in the middle of an action, is looking at the camera. Also the people from *Ship inspector* are very aware of my presence, as much as they are of the awkwardness and difficulty of their own interaction, which is a micro-instance of class struggle. So that there is a kind of theatricality to the scene, bringing me in as a spectator. But the *Goldsmiths* are absorbed in their work. We used to call this candid photography.

Katarzyna Ruchel-Stockmans: Your earlier exhibition practice often consisted of a picture gallery and a photo-sequence projection combined with a reading room. You called it a sort of disassembled movie. Since a few years you are actually doing film next to photography. Would you have chosen film earlier if this was an option or does this disassembled form of cinema have a value in itself?

Allan Sekula: Absolutely. The question is still valid. In this strategy of disassembling the question is how diffuse, how disassembled can a disposition be and still remain readable? How do you construct a complex and coherent array of images in a space dedicated to picking and choosing 'this image' or 'that one'. Since the early 1970s, I wanted to experiment with that problem, since it ran against all the genre expectations typically brought to still photography. Genre constraints are more forgiving in cinema. I tell myself I am serving an apprenticeship: first a 'city symphony' or two; then an 'essay film'; after that, maybe a 'fiction feature film'. I think one can attack the problem of genre in film from the inside, but with still photography, one has to attack from the outside, by introducing all sorts of 'impure' operations.

Katarzyna Ruchel-Stockmans: When visiting the exhibition in Leuven, one has to look for the photographs hung all around the building, from both entrances and on different levels and heights. They are not given, one has to wander around and make an effort in finding them. Moreover, there is a text panel with not the easiest piece of your writing. It also needs quite an effort of assembling from the spectator. In the pictures themselves you seem to include a lot of references to your earlier photographs or essays. How important is it for you that people actually read your comments or essays and that they are acquainted with the more general discourse around contemporary photography? Does the spectator have to search for ideas you invest in the images? In other words, how literate must your ideal spectator be and how much of his activity in assembling the disassembled elements do you expect from him?

Allan Sekula: It is a mistake to imagine an ideal spectator. The ideal spectator is a noble fiction, like Rodin's *Thinker*. We all muddle through whatever it is we encounter, picking up some threads, dropping others, missing some entirely. If we stick at it, we get another chance. All I can do is invite the spectator to become a reader and the reader to look. Having made that invitation,

I would have to imagine that 'competence' is something that can change radically, for better or worse. For example, art criticism is less competent now than it was thirty years ago, but that is a problem of institutions, not of innate or acquired abilities to perceive and understand and communicate. Basically, I think that one has to respect the capacity of audiences to look seriously and figure out how to do the work necessary to understand. I don't think works of art should require external glosses or external theoretical armatures for their legibility.

You could argue that it is somewhat easier in the documentary or essay film, because of the work done by the voice-over. In the plastic arts it is harder, because of the exclusion of verbal language. But think of the tradition of illuminated manuscripts, of William Blake and all the ancient text-image modes. It is modernism that sunders text from image, and ironically it does so in the name of Mallarmé, for whom text floats imagistically on the field of the page.

Katarzyna Ruchel-Stockmans: In your research into the history of photography, you traced the shifting meanings of archival photographs, which can be re-contextualized and re-appropriated according to the free will of the new owner/interpreter. Do you ask yourself how your own images can be re-used and appropriated in different contexts, including those that counter your intentions? Are you concerned with the 'afterlife' of your photographs?

Allan Sekula: Ultimately it's a losing battle, but yes, I try to have control of the conditions of reception to the extent that I can. For example, I allow only some images from *Fish Story* to appear in separate editions. Gallery keepers will ask me: "if you could just say yes to that one, I have five clients…", and I usually say no. I decide which pictures work on their own, and try to fight for a definitive view that the work is not a series of equivalent utterances, but a modulated ensemble, with different inflections, variations of tone and pace. Insisting on this larger unit of meaning is not the best marketing strategy.

Katarzyna Ruchel-Stockmans: So, your audience should be intellectually active…

Allan Sekula: Yes, that's another reason why I was interested in working in a university town like Leuven, home to an ancient Catholic university. We are facing the fragility of the humanist tradition in Catholicism. Remember that Meunier worked at the time of the first papal encyclical on the dignity of labor, which was an attempt both to stave off the new socialist threat and to ameliorate the worst aspects of capitalist exploitation. Before becoming the new pope, Cardinal Ratzinger was the mastermind of the Vatican's war on liberation theology and its 'preferential option for the poor'. In that sense, his politics are quite consistent with neoliberalism, which loathes peasants and everything about the life-world and moral economy of peasants. Now, in alliance with very conservative forces, Ratzinger is committed to re-evangelizing Europe. The more I worked on this project the more I found myself thinking about the last pope, the new pope and the whole spectacle of youthful faith in Cologne.[5] When Ratzinger worries about the future of the Catholic Church he is not really thinking about attacks from the outside, even if he refers to a threatening Muslim world, to Christian women marrying Muslim men and converting to Islam. What really matters is the inside, the secularization and demographic decline of Europe; the progressive sexual politics of Zapatero in Spain, whose agenda is very supportive of women and gay people. The concern of Catholic conservatives, exemplified by Opus Dei, but much larger and widespread, is to make sure that Zapatero's Spain doesn't become the ethical, demographic and sex-political model for the whole of Europe.

Remember that the oldest metaphors of a shipwreck are politico-theological: the monotheistic test enacted in the Book of Jonah, for example. Ratzinger warned metaphorically of the saltiness of the sea in one of his first papal homilies. The church is terra firma in a sinful sea.

Katarzyna Ruchel-Stockmans: How do you see your role as an artist in making such a political statement? Is it essential for art to become involved in the political issues of the time?

Allan Sekula: I think art always is political, one way or another. That is, on purpose or by default. For example, it is strange that current American art discourse is rife with praise for the baroque, in a country that lacks a feudal tradition, and is more Protestant than Catholic. For example, Frank Gehry is praised as the new Bernini. But nobody asks what is actually implied by these enthusiastic references to the baroque. What was at stake in the counterreformation? It was the re-inscription of faith against the conscience-driven rationality of the Protestant revolt. This was carried out through a spectacular excess of the image. What is our contemporary counterreformation? The re-inscription of the absolute and unalloyed dominion of capital in the wake of the collapse of bureaucratic state socialism. So: how do we build the meaning-machine to counteract neo-baroque spectacle culture?

Katarzyna Ruchel-Stockmans: The counterreformation is the period when propaganda in the more or less contemporary sense came into being…

Allan Sekula: You are absolutely right. What is funny is that the contemporary art world's defenders of the neo-baroque would say that the baroque is the essence of a non-political aesthetics. The new baroque claims to overwhelm with pure sensation, offering sheer unalloyed pleasure. None of this really happens. As you say, it is unabashed propaganda for sophisticated consumerism. How do we swim in this soup without turning into parboiled crustaceans, red on the outside and tasty on the inside?

Katarzyna Ruchel-Stockmans: In this overwhelming flood of images, in the culture after the visual turn, what is your aesthetic program? There is a clear aesthetic dimension in your photography. How do you define it yourself? You do have a certain 'style' that makes you recognizable…?

Allan Sekula: I don't think of myself as having a kind of signature style.

Katarzyna Ruchel-Stockmans: However, if you consider it from a different perspective, the aesthetic has an essential role in critical realist photography. How would you comment on Herbert Marcuse's saying that the only political impact art can have is in its aesthetic dimension? How do you see the relationship between the aesthetic and the politic?

Allan Sekula: Marcuse simplified his aesthetic argument in his last writings. The best Marcuse text on aesthetics is the early 'Aesthetic Dimension' essay from the 1930s that appeared in *Eros and Civilization.* As is well known, Marcuse was trying to strike a balance between Marx and Freud. Marcuse's key point is that for Kant the mediating function of aesthetic judgment is crucial to any engagement with broader human intellectual and practical problems. Aesthetics –the realm of "purposive purposelessness"– reconciles and mediates between the realm of reason and that of ethics. Shortly after Marcuse died in 1979, I reread the essay and realized that the anti-formalist reaction associated for example with conceptual art was more about Clement Greenberg's misreading of Kant, than it was about Kant. Many of us were reacting to the hegemony of abstract painting. And Greenberg was someone to tangle with in a very serious way.

Katarzyna Ruchel-Stockmans: Do you consider your work, both visual as well as essayistic, inspired by Walter Benjamin? Referring again to Benjamin's philosophy of history, it appeared to me that you are actually doing a similar thing to what he postulated. You are re-writing history in a new way, by analyzing historical images or reframing them in your photographic work. Do you see yourself as Benjamin's rebel who, by looking back in the past –in your case at 19th-Century realism– tries to redefine the way we see the contemporary world?

Allan Sekula: What interests me the most about the 19th Century is that it is much more complex than modernist caricature allows. Modernism, or shall I say: various modernisms, invented 'straw-man realism' in order to dismiss naïve reflectionism. Roman Jacobson argued in the 1920s, however, that realism is actually engaged in a complex discursive play, pitting newer realisms against older and seemingly exhausted or over-conventionalized forms of depiction. Anybody seriously studying the realist novel or realist painting knows this to be true from the evidence at hand. But I know plenty of artists, most of whom I try to avoid for my sanity's sake, who 'have a problem with photographs'. In other words, they are only comfortable when a work 'uses photography' in order to demonstrate some order of photographic or general representational poverty or inadequacy of meaning. So the medium is categorically dismissed, but for these high-minded meta-commentaries. This is a version of the master-slave dialectic from the side of the master, even when the work pretends to be a version of the slave rising from abjection into postures of resistance.

I think Jakobson's point is better understood within serious documentary film culture (I am thinking here of a range of people over many years, from Joris Ivens and Jean Vigo to Hartmut Bitomsky and Rithy Panh) than it generally is in the visual arts. In the visual arts the working and reworking of plastic material is of such central concern that, by contrast, the ambition to carefully represent a pre-existing reality is always liable to be tainted by an apparent failure of the plastic imagination. In other words, the imagination is imagined, in its essence, to be plastic. This is true even in an art world reluctant to use the term imagination, and is one of our unacknowledged ideological debts to romanticism, despite our vociferous post-modernism, with its incumbent distrust of 'creativity'.

That is why I was interested in Giacometti. If the arm is the semantic lever of Meunier's *Puddler,* then there is a strange continuity with Giacometti, who makes the arm into a pure lever: Giacometti's hand, with its spread fingers, is a kind of sail, or paddle. Giacometti separated volume from mass. Not so long ago, I heard Leo Steinberg describe Giacometti's response to a question about the thinness of his figures. Giacometti responded that the mass of his figures had to correspond to the actual mass of the beings he depicted. Bronze, being heavier than flesh and bone, dictated a thinner figure. So one could say that a realist principle was buried in Giacometti's push toward the analytical and seemingly reductive abstraction of the body. And this submerged realist principle was also echoed in the outer world of living and half-dead human beings in the wake of World War II.

I take seriously the sociological model of Bakhtin and Volosinov, for whom it was ultimately impossible to separate form from content, the word from usage and meaning, and the sign from the universe of living human dialogue. Volosinov's criticism of de Saussure can be aptly extended to the whole regime of contemporary criticism and art promotion, even if de Saussure himself is hardly to blame. The art world, in its love affair with bigger and bigger mausoleums, and with its reliance on the new pseudo-agora of the art fair —that is, a luxury bazaar with walk-on guest philosophers— is most head-over-heels in love with one big idea: that living contemporary art should approach the frozen but venerated status of a dead language. The lights dim and the conversation becomes a séance. The auctioneers gavel is just another form of spirit-rapping in an age in which no one is surprised when a living artist is the subject of a catalogue raisonné.

What is forgotten in all this, is that the human referent for the seemingly exhausted sign 'worker' is still operating somewhere, pushing the crates into the delivery dock, hoping to get immigration papers. And the artist, who is better off dead in the eyes of his collectors, is still working in the studio —or at least his assistants are, preparing for the next catalogue raisonné, which is guaranteed to be posthumous. This is necrophilia of a very high order.

Katarzyna Ruchel-Stockmans: What is the meaning of the little diagram you placed in your text on one of the panels?

Allan Sekula: It is a diagram illustrating work as defined by physics. The inertia of a mass is overcome by applying a force. That's what work is, in the strictest mechanistic sense. Agency is not specified. The agent could be a human, a water buffalo, or an earthquake. Physics has no particular respect for humanity, and that is why Marcuse's reading of Kant is helpful in pointing the way to ethics.

Katarzyna Ruchel-Stockmans: The schematic form of mass on this diagram resembles a cargo container from your earlier work…

Allan Sekula: I'm pleased that you see that, because it allows us to connect the physicist's definition of work with what Marx wrote in the *Grundrisse*. Bringing the commodity to the market is part of the production process, and a necessary part of the process by which a commodity is realized as such. So the seeming neutral and indifferent all-purpose physicist's definition has a definite spatial and even geographical logic. The sea lanes beckon, the song of the open road, the very 'ideology of adventure': it's all a matter of the money factory on the march. But the additional lesson here is that the commodity is not an essence or an ontological identity, but rather a status that can be refused or revoked or thwarted. So in this sense, the market is neither absolute nor inevitable.

[1] Buchloh, Benjamin, Sekula, Allan and Gierstberg, Frits (eds), *Allan Sekula: Dead Letter Office*, Rotterdam: Nederlands Foto Instituut, 1997: 10-12. The term 'critical realism' was coined by Georg Lukács in his theory of literature in *The Meaning of Contemporary Realism,* trans. Mander, John, London: Merlin, 1963 and recently redefined by Buchloh to describe Sekula's artistic practice. It was then applied by other scholars (Beausse, Pascal in an interview with Sekula, 'The Critical Realism of Allan Sekula', in: Art Press, no. 240, November, 1998: 20-26; Lundström, Jan-Erik, 'Realism, Photography and Visual Culture', in: Bertelsen, Lars Kiel, Gade, Rune and Sandbye, Mette (eds), *Symbolic Imprints: Essays on Photography and Visual Culture,* Aarhus: Aarhus University Press, 1999: 62-64). The same term, however, resurfaces in other contexts as well, notably in Brandon Taylor's book *Modernism, Postmodernism, Realism. A Critical Perspective for Art*, Winchester, Hampshire: Winchester School of Art Press, 1987: 156; and, outside art theory, in the philosophy of science developed by Roy Bhaskar.

[2] *Shipwreck and Workers (Version I)* was shown in the Museum in Progress in Vienna, June-September 2005, as a part of the billboard exhibition series *Worlds of Work.*

[3] Quoted by Brigitte Huck in the text accompanying the exhibition *Shipwreck and workers* in Museum in Progress, Vienna: http://www.mip.at/en/werke/640.html.

[4] Sekula refers to: Van Gelder, Hilde, 'Social Realism' Then and Now. Constantin Meunier and Allan Sekula', in: Id. (ed.), *Constantin Meunier. A Dialogue with Allan Sekula* (Lieven Gevaert Series, vol.2), Leuven: University Press, 2005: 71-91.

[5] Sekula refers to the XX World Youth Day in Cologne, August 18-21 2005, which was the first significant Catholic event attended by the new pope, Benedict XVI.

3_ PHOTOGRAPHY AS DIAGNOSIS OF CONTEMPORANEITY

Maria Giulia Dondero

As far as the political sphere is concerned, photographic images have always played a decisive role within battles for representational hegemony, thereby leaving their trace on each historical moment of contemporary society. Evidently, we are not dealing with the staging of opposing 'truths' but of textualities whose ultimate stakes are the antithetic effects of truth itself. However, this does not entail a merging of reality into discursivity, as there will always remain an effective 'inherence' amongst practices, lived experiences and the world into which each subject is thrust. The problem is that this inherence is not deployed as a configuration of meaning but through a discursivity comprising various perspectives, engagements, and inflections. Keeping this in mind, photography will function as a resource for the diagnosis of contemporary tensions, and this in the hands of social actors endowed with differing roles. The photograph enables a "thorough examination" (i.e. "a diagnosis") and the formulation of a judgment. In short, we are rather far removed from the idea that a photograph "shows" reality. By contrast, the photograph takes on a "symptomatic" mode of being, assuming "known" correlations with various degrees of intensity. But the semantic potential of this diagnosis and the illocutive force of the inscribed judgments function as a kind of "argumentation through images" and depend on the entries in the body of work, the types of "afference", and the status ascribed to photography (Rastier, 2001: 228).

It is within this theoretical framework that one can gauge the effectiveness of the immense photographic series entitled *Fish Story* (Sekula, 2002), a textual composite staking out a position against prototypical notions of globalization. At this very moment, the concept of globalization is undoubtedly at the heart of representational battles while informing the crisis of contemporaneous identity. This series, created by photographer and theorist Allan Sekula, has an artistic status, implying that the spectator is invited to saturate his or her semantization with figurative and plastic traits. Following Nelson Goodman, it can be said that this status guarantees that Sekula's photographs –as far as their textuality is concerned– will be endowed with a heightened semantic and syntactic density (Goodman, 1969). However, in itself, this does not suffice. In addition to its obligation to produce an immeasurable vista for the tensive connections between the enunciated (*énoncé*) and the enunciation (*énonciation*), one cannot fail to note that semantic and syntactic saturation is fundamental to a veritable "reasoning through figures" (Fabbri, 1998). In other words, it forms the basis for a diagnosis of humanity's contemporary 'globalized' political and existential identity. This allows us to do away with an ambiguity: in no way does artistic status compromise the testimonial efficacy of the photograph, nor does it force us to relegate the photograph's emotional dimension to a secondary position in relation to its cognitive dimension.

Theoretical Preliminaries

First and foremost, we must point out that our analysis diverges from both the aprioristic and sociological 'ready-made' knowledge concerning the phenomenon of globalization. Rather, it attempts to describe semiotically –prompted by the figurative level of photographic texts– how the political and existential identity of the immigrant laborer is called into question by *Fish Story*. Exclusively taking actual symptoms as its starting point, this photographic series presents perspectives on contemporary labor, and offers itself as a diagnostic deposit probing into the emergence of phenomena of globalization. Accordingly, our corpus will not exemplify the preconceived notion of a globalization commonly understood in terms of the infiltration, insinuation and hegemonic imposition of one (Western, liberal, etc) culture on a planetary scale. However, despite the fact that our focus is indeed concentrated largely on symptomatic forms of contemporaneity as signaled within a pertinent diagnostic framework (i.e. the corpus we are examining), this does not mean that we will only deal with what the photographs 'show' us. We will speak about the photos' figurative character, but this is not at all reducible to what the photograph supposedly 'illustrates'. Indeed, first and foremost, the figurative plane must be understood as an "inter-actantial" horizon (Basso, 2003) dependent on the polysensoriality of the values at play. Secondly, as Jacques Fontanille (2004) emphasized, the figurative is endowed with memory and tensive vectoriality (prefiguration). Lastly, the figurative character can take on different shapes in order to present irreconcilable inner tensions that require a semantic resolution through a *figural* key (in other words, it may warrant a rhetoric of the photographic image).

We know how figurality arises as a necessary but still tentative discursive profile that prefigures any argumentation, as is the case with scientific metaphors (Fabbri, 2000). In addition, figurality may infringe upon the institutional rules of communication, as when enunciation must rely on tropes so as to bypass the suppression affecting direct speech. Moreover, the figural is also anticipated in function of the subjectivity of the enunciation, which concerns the enunciator as well as the addressee, while taking into account the competence required for producing a frame for narrative transformations. Furthermore, the figural should not be considered as merely one figurative "area" distinguishable by virtue of its high density of features that may well become pertinent as objects of the natural world. Instead, the figural must be seen as the "construction of perspectives for discursive material emphasizing internal relations, especially in terms of the tension between plastic and figurative elements" (Basso, 2003: 29).

With respect to Sekula's work, one can safely say that, on the one hand, the photographer faces opposite social and political forces traversing the lives of immigrants in addition to the strong tensions regarding identity. On the other hand, Sekula is faced with a stratification of enunciations –especially concerning the representation of scenes and landscapes of labor– which precede and stigmatize *Fish Story* with notions such as alienation, deterritorialization, exploitation, and so forth (cf. Sekula (2002), especially the chapters "Red Passenger" and "From the Panorama to the Detail"). *Fish Story*'s internal figurality presents and elaborates a diagnostic space for a moving 'social body' showing contradictory symptoms, while its figurality also departs from commonplaces informing the battle for representational hegemony.

The majority of the images taken by the American photographer are set in some of the most important seaports of the world. As such, the series presents itself in the form of a contemporary cartography of harbor life. As the Indian theorist Homi Bhabha affirms, in these images "the harbor and the stockmarket become the *paysage moralisé* of a containerized, computerized world of global trade" (Bhabha, 1994: 8). The title, *Fish Story*, is decidedly emblematic, precisely because depictions of fishing boats, fishermen, fish or the sea are so rare. The only photos of harbor landscapes without containers are of deserted places, vestiges of the past, remnants of a forgotten world where it was possible, unlike today, to devote one's life to fishing. By contrast, the series contains representations of harbors, complete with naval machinery, cranes, trucks, and port workers. It is precisely from the semantic tension between the title of the series and the textual corpus that our analysis starts. The title's fish as well as the sea are conspicuously absent from the images. Assuming that the disjunction between the title and the photos is significant, we must examine how this semantic tension can ultimately attain some kind of resolution.

The Epic of the Container

While not exclusively political in its contestation, *Fish Story* offers a problematization of a state of identity through its focus on various contemporary harbors. *Fish Story* is a photographic work (and an essay) composed of seven image 'chapters' and two texts by Sekula that retrace the histories and theorizations of the representation of industrial and post-industrial labor, as well as the iconographic tradition of marine landscapes. In a certain sense, the objective of the two essays is to show how *Fish Story*, in its own eccentric manner, inserts itself within the Western iconographic tradition of labor and the harbor. A number of the series' images are representational configurations that correspond to the great romantic landscapes so prominent in 18th-Century Germany. However, contrary to the sublime landscape where man perceives his own grandeur by appreciating the grandeur of natural elements, *Fish Story* posits an epic of the machine and the container.

The seven photographic chapters of the series collect images taken between 1989 and 1994. The first introductory sequence of photographs is entitled *Fish Story* (1989-1993), and is comprised of images of the Los Angeles dock. *Loaves and Fishes* on the other hand is mainly concerned with the port of Rotterdam, but also features Gdansk and Barcelona. *Middle Passage* again focuses on Rotterdam, but presents images of the open sea, in this case the Atlantic, as well. *Seventy in Seven* is set in South Korea, as it focuses on Seoul and Ulsan while exploring the lives of the workers employed at the large naval company Hyundai. The fifth chapter, *Message in a Bottle*, shows photographs of Portuguese and Spanish harbors such as Puerto Pesquero, while *True Cross* contains images of Mexican ports such as San Juan de Ulua in Vera Cruz, as well as the Cuban port of Malecon. The final chapter, *Dictatorship of the Seven Seas*, resumes with the Los Angeles seaport and that of Hong Kong. All seven chapters show images of containers, cargo liners preparing or ready for loading, as well as anonymous dockworkers whose faces we can almost never see, and who are only identified by captions representing them as employees of large enterprises or naval companies, such as Hyundai, Mitsui, Evergreen, American President, and so forth. These loci are so striking because, instead of using their potential to signal identifying traits that might have exposed their provenance, they become so similar and indistinguishable that the suspicion arises that these photographs address the cultural processes responsible for the leveling of labor landscapes and for the neutralization of differences amongst dockworkers coming from every part of the world. From Rotterdam to Seoul, laborers of all seaports share the same existential condition: they perform a "relocation of the home and the world –the unhomeliness– that is the condition of extra-territorial and cross-cultural initiations" (Bhabha, 1994: 9). Indeed, in the global ports as photographed by Allan Sekula, everything has changed compared to the time when it was still possible to discern nationality through a boat, cargo, or through a naval company. Or, as Sekula writes:

> "Things are more confused now. A scratchy recording of the Norwegian national anthem blares out from a loudspeaker at the Sailors' Church on the bluff above the channel. The container ship being greeted flies a Bahamian flag of convenience. It was built by Koreans laboring long hours in the giant shipyards of Ulsan. The crew, underpaid and overworked, could be Honduran or Filipino. Only the captain hears a familiar melody." (Sekula, 2002: 12)

The gap with an irremediably lost time is marked by those images that feature boats of a distant past: sailing ships. However, these sailboats are only offered to the viewer in the form of small-scale models in naval museum displays, or the shop window of a jeweler. Even rowing boats are exhibited in the Prins Hendrik naval museum of Rotterdam, and passenger ships also featured there have become collector's items. Instead of sailing ships and passenger boats it is really the container vessel that is the protagonist of *Fish Story* –it is no coincidence that some critics proposed "Container Story" as a more fitting title. Besides, even living spaces can be confused with containers, as suggested by titles such as "Waterfront vendors living in containers" or "Mike and Mary, an unemployed couple who survive by scavenging and who, from time to time, seek shelter in empty containers". The container is a space signaling work. However, it can often also become a habitation, while anonymous living spaces can come to resemble containers, such as those built for the dockworkers of Hyundai in Ulsan. In all of these cases the existential landscape of man merges entirely with that of labor, as can be seen in the exhaustive assimilation symbolized by the figure of the container box that simultaneously stands for both the receptacle carrying and circulating commodities across the oceans (a box just as itinerant as the commodities it holds), and for the cubicle man is forced to live in. Just like goods, the migrant worker is held, restrained, packaged, parceled and prepared inside a container.

Be that as it may, it is essential that we don't stop by noting that the images almost exclusively show containers rather than fish. Thus, one needs to go further than art criticism and those sociological theories of globalization that merely point out that the title of the series refers to what the images contain *in absentia*, namely the natural element that has been substituted in our post-industrial society by the artificial element par excellence, i.e. the commodity. One needs to uncover a more profound motivation for the tension between the title and the text, without limiting oneself to an analysis of figurative representation. Instead, one must emphasize the figural dimension of the image, as the latter, as Pierluigi Basso stresses, "will not be reduced by us to prototypes of the imaginary nor to symbolic meanings" (Basso, 2003: 30), nor to broad generalizations that may pose the risk of losing sight of the rhetoric of the photographs we are examining. It is not so much a question of connecting opposites such as container and fish, the artificial and the natural, as art critics have done, but of turning one's attention to the simple fact that, before anything else, the container is something that envelops and encloses, within which contemporary humankind is rigidly bound to. Indeed, a fish is also 'contained', but unlike the container box, the water of the sea is a reservoir organically connected to its 'content'. A fish in the sea is thus 'contained' in a completely different manner compared to commodities (and people) inside a container. A fish is 'contents' as it is closely and biologically attached to its container, thereby forming an inseparable part of it.

A Fish Out of Water

From the semantic fracture between the title and the corpus emerges the tension between two types of receptacles, namely the container and the aquatic environment. Because Sekula's series confronts us with houses and containers instead of the fishing space of the sea, this means that its theme is linked to the *subtraction of natural environment*. If on the one hand the rigid container is considered hostile to man, while on the other hand the aquatic reservoir is presented as soft and as the guarantor of life to fish, we may propose that it is precisely the subtraction of the natural that enables us to compare the condition of the immigrant worker to that of a 'fish out of water': both risk death by suffocation. In contrast to 'man contained in a container', the organic and healthy relation of fish in the sea calls to mind the concept of *sacred* as defined by Gregory Bateson in his *Steps to an Ecology of the Mind* (Bateson, 1973). In the words of Bateson, the *sacred* is a "healthy ecology". For the 'fish out of the water' and for the migrant worker, the subtraction of the natural world presents itself as a violation of an ecological, salutary and sacred system. In *Fish Story*, the negation of the sacred relation, or the "disease" as Bateson calls it, sets in precisely because the necessary unity of a container with its contents has been lost. Through the subtraction of the natural, the relation between the receptacle and its contents has been damaged and profaned. If we can agree with Bataille when he states that "what concrete totality is to objects considered in isolation, the *sacred* is perhaps to the *profane*" (Bataille, 1998) ,one may realize that the disease, the profane, is describable in terms of separation and missing relations. In this sense, *Fish Story* is to be understood as a diagnosis through images.

> "To solve the "rebus" posed by Sekula's photographic series, it is necessary to take an anamorphic view, which plastically deflagrates the figurative landscape so as to be recomposed as the expression of a new (indeed figural) content, which although unstable, will appear in the form of a text's privileged isotopic connectors, since these

result from the perception of a structure made of more profound semantic relations." (Basso, 2003: 30)

"The Relocation of the Home and the World"

Fish Story contains only one representation of a fish out of the water. It is a photograph of an elusive eel trying to reach the small stream of water on the floor of a fish market in Pusan, South Korea. The eel's futile escape attempt is really an emblem of the human condition 'presentified' in *Fish Story*. In this image, the eel is a fish out of the water just like all the laborers of Sekula's series. The fish out of the water, or the "unhomely" laborer Bhabha alludes to, is extracted from his habitat and prepared as a commodity: at the market he is put on display, cooked, processed into a dish or packaged. The isotopy of 'man for sale' is corroborated by other images, in the photograph entitled *Engine-room wiper's ear protection* (Sekula, 2002: 56) for example, where the text composed in the first person, i.e. "I can not be fired. Slaves are sold", reminds us that, for the laborer, death will not come from the barrel of a gun, but from the imposition of economic laws governing the world market. Therefore, the contemporary "unhomely" worker is the locus of an identity riddled with powerful tensions between dispersive forces and rigid regulations. Rather than just a pamphlet on contemporary labor conditions and spaces, *Fish Story* is a reflection on the political tensions between conflicting forces of identity, a reflection on the relation between the non-organic and the profane, between a receptacle and its contents, between open dispersion and rigid containment, between cosmopolitan scattering and existential contrition. In short, *Fish Story* explores the tension between global dispersion and passionate homing.

159

Works Quoted

Basso, Pierluigi, *Confini del cinema*, Torino: Lindau, 2003.

Bataille, George, *Inner Experience*, Albany: SUNY Press, 1988.

Bateson, Gregory, *Steps to an Ecology of Mind*, New York: Paladin Books, 1973.

Bhabha, Homi, *The Location of Culture*, London/New York: Routledge, 1994.

Fabbri, Paolo, *La svolta semiotica*, Roma/Bari: Laterza, 1998.

Fabbri, P. *Elogio di Babele*, Roma: Meltemi, 2000.

Fontanille, Jacques, *Soma et sema, figures du corps*, Paris: Maisonneuve et Larose, 2004.

Goodman, Nelson, *Languages of Art. An Approach to a Theory of Symbols*, London: Oxford University Press, 1969.

Rastier, François, *Arts et sciences du texte*, Paris: PUF, 2001.

Sekula, Allan, *Fish Story*, Düsseldorf: Richter Verlag, 2002.

PHOTOGRAPHS

Art museum guards, Seattle

Shipwreck, Istanbul (triptych)

Seafarers, Limassol (diptych)

Ship inspector, Seattle (diptych)

Maritime museum curator, Constanza

Woodcutter, Thilouze

Oil deliveryman, Saché

Grape harvesters, Saché

Machinist, Tours

Goldsmiths, Istanbul (triptych)

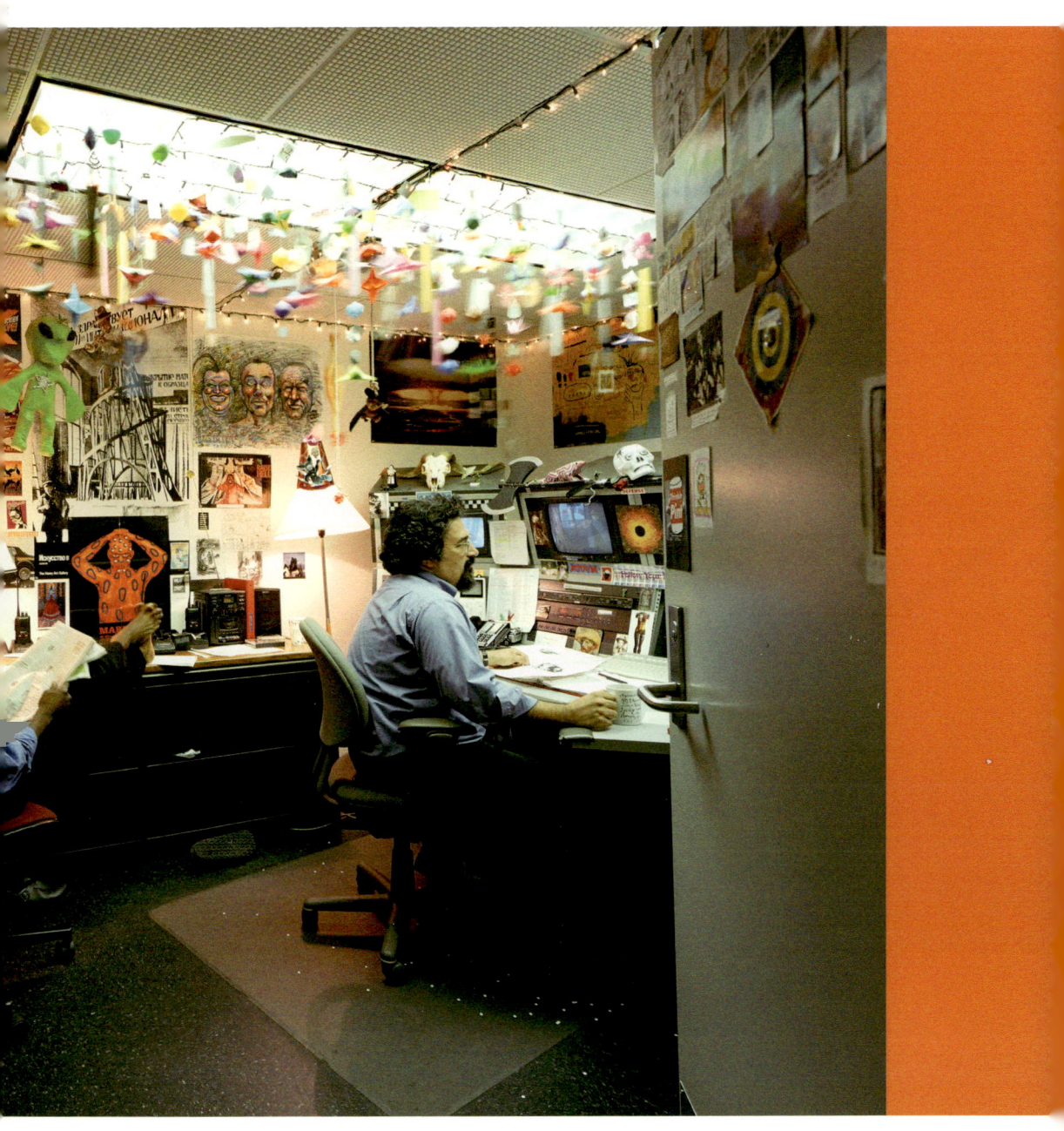

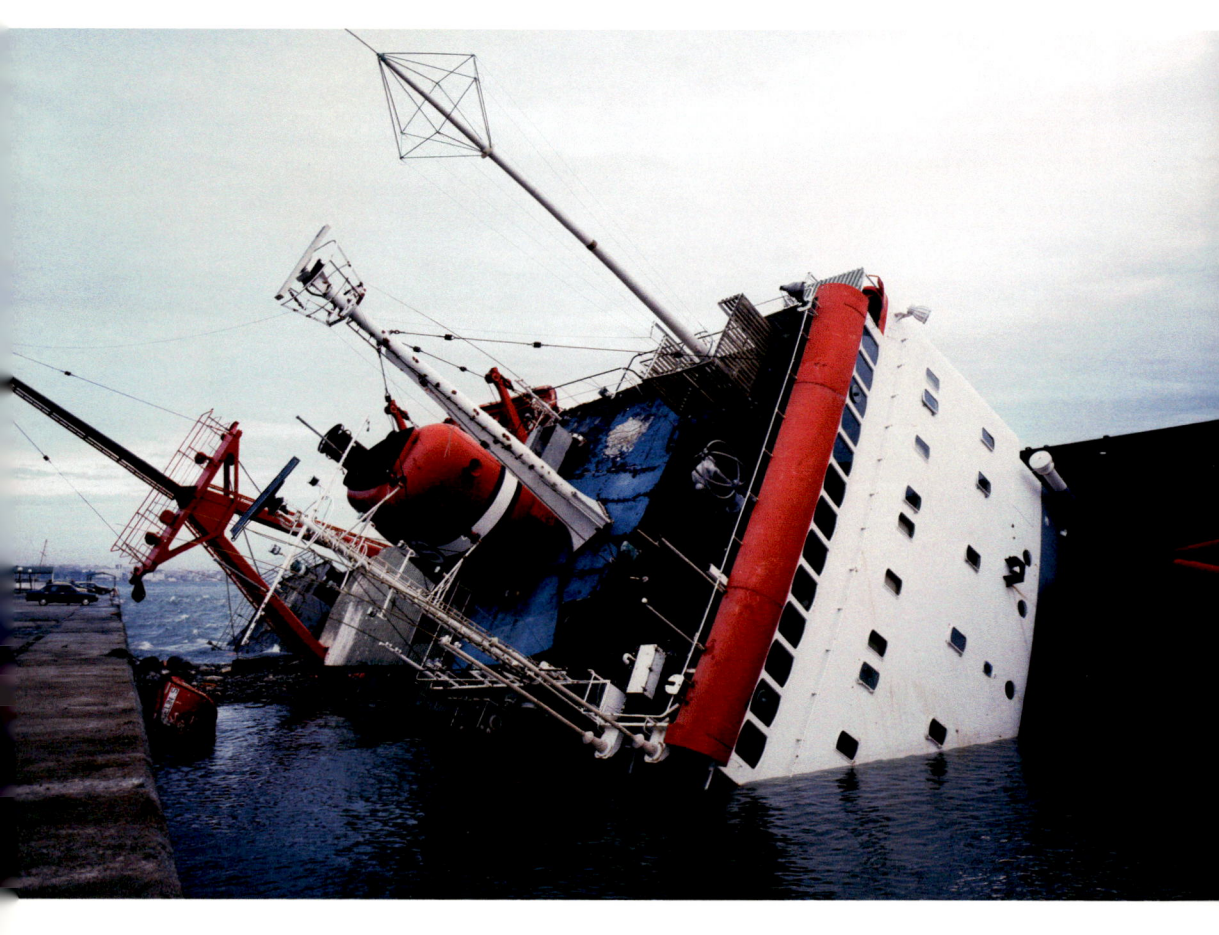

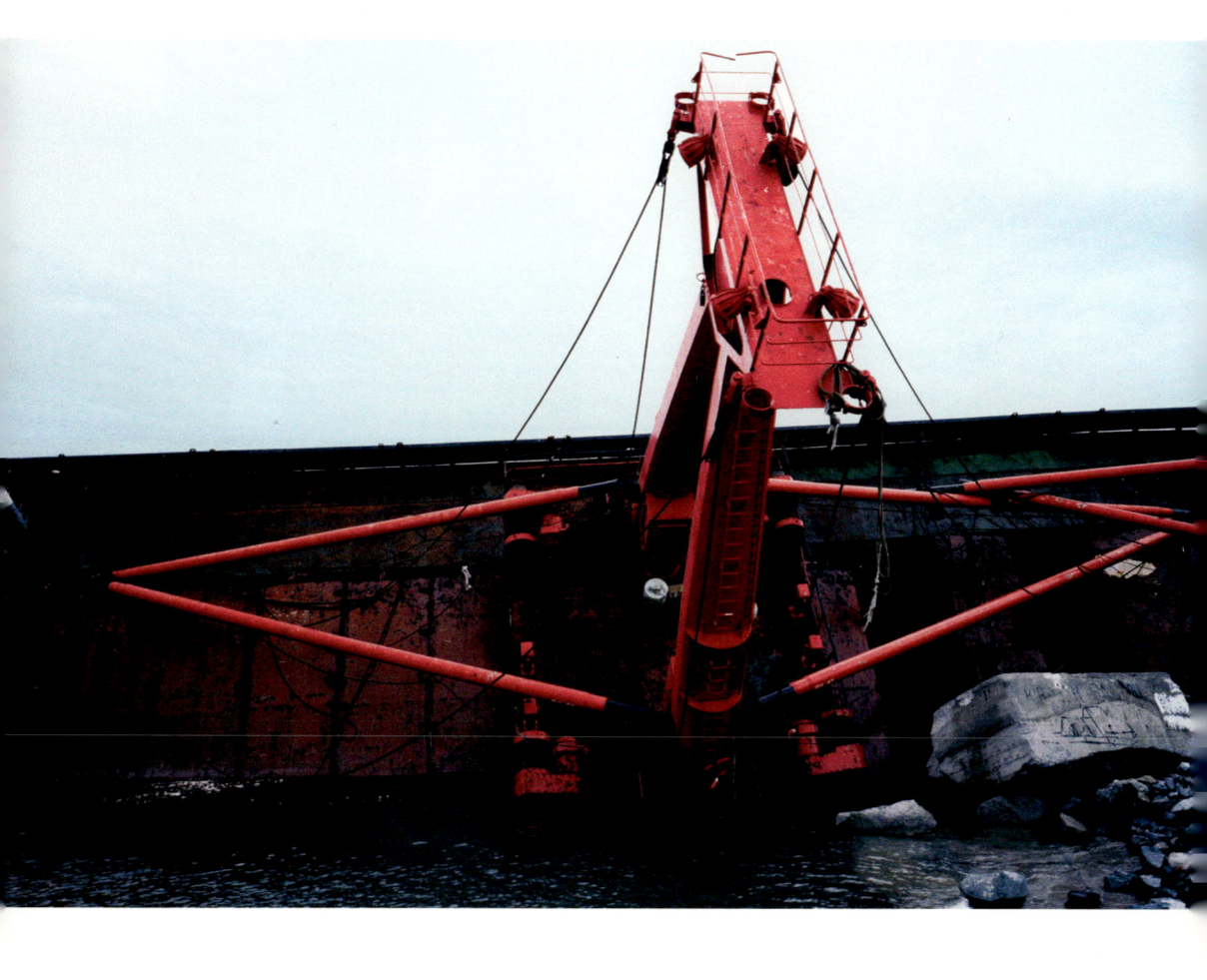

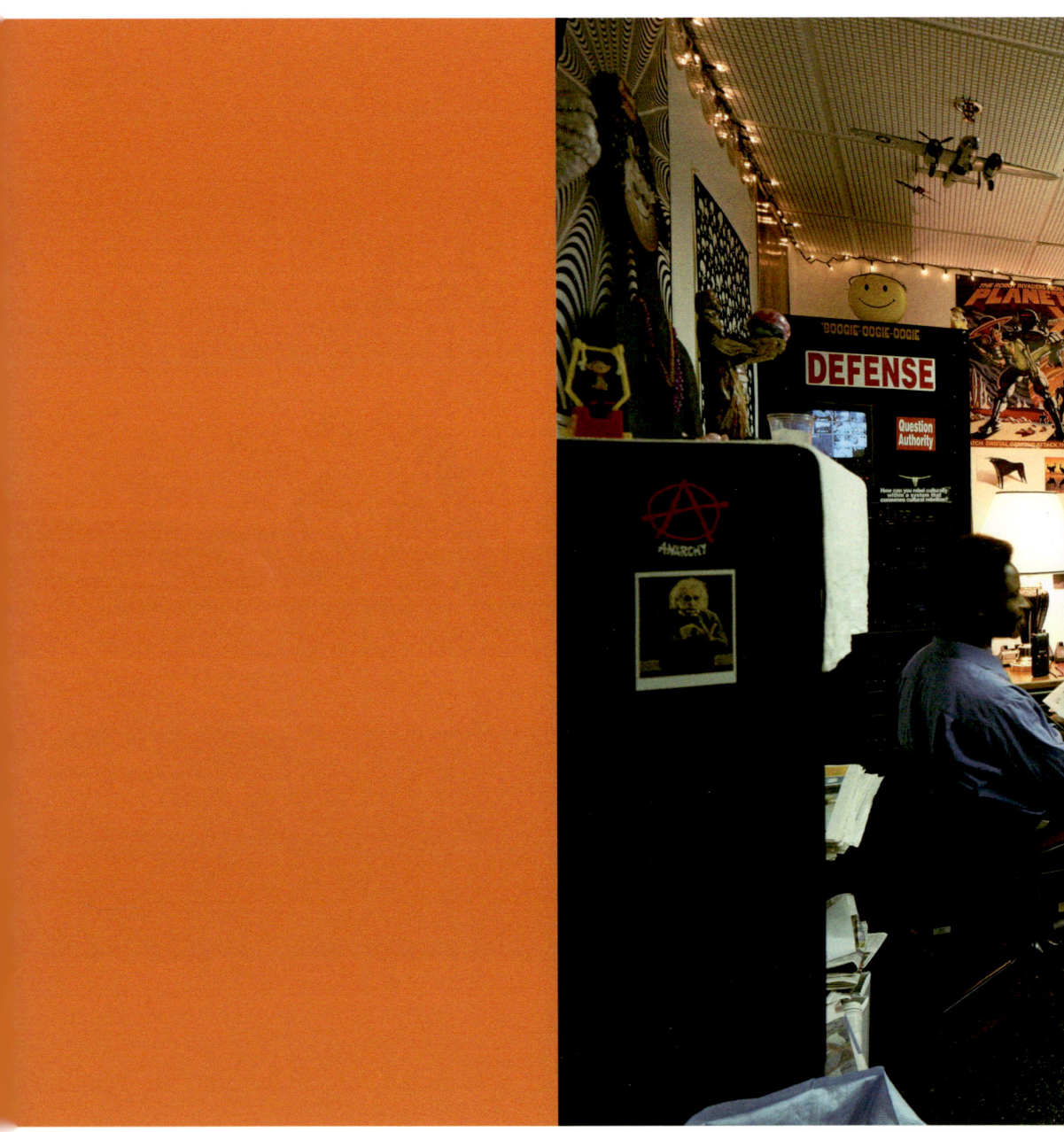

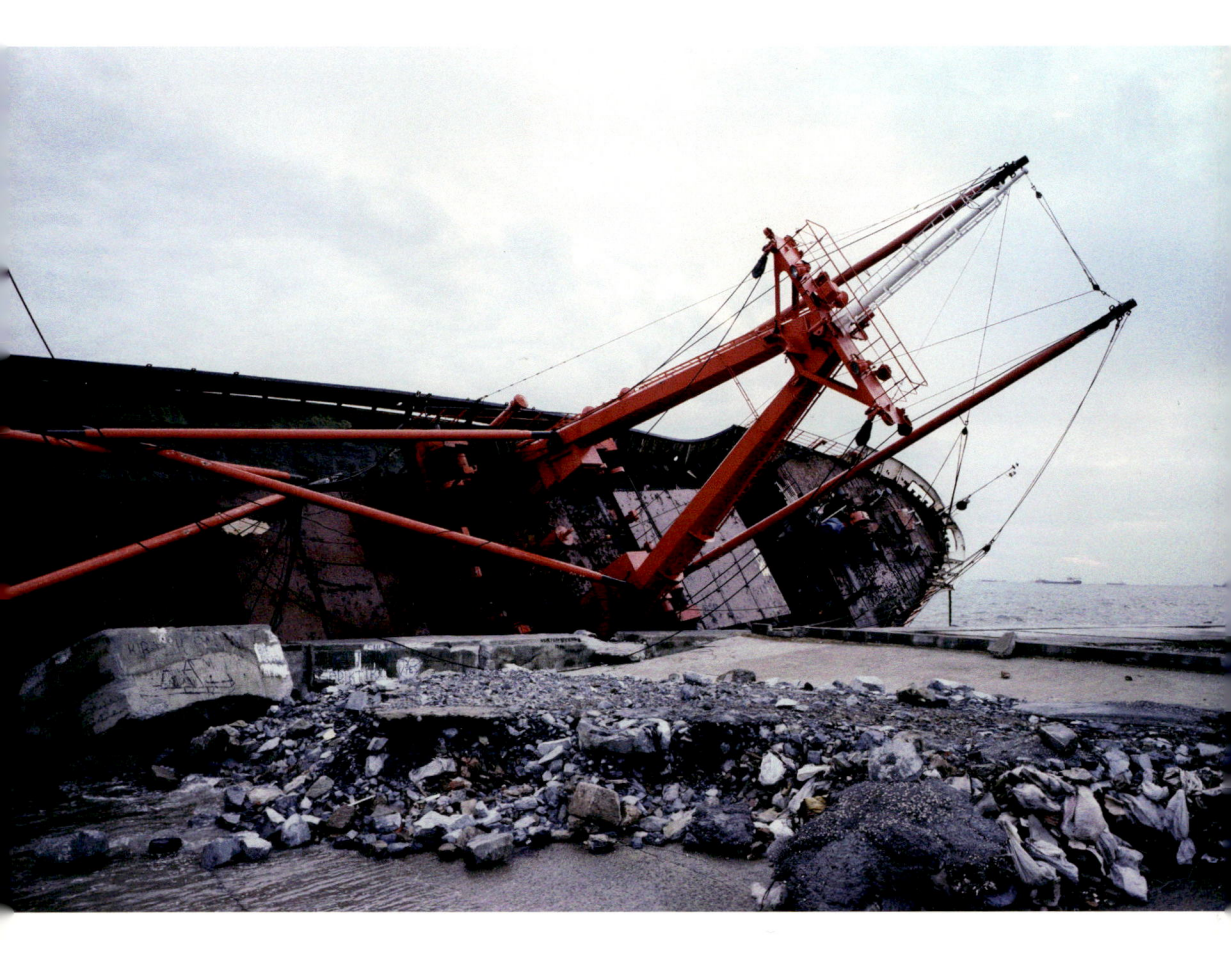

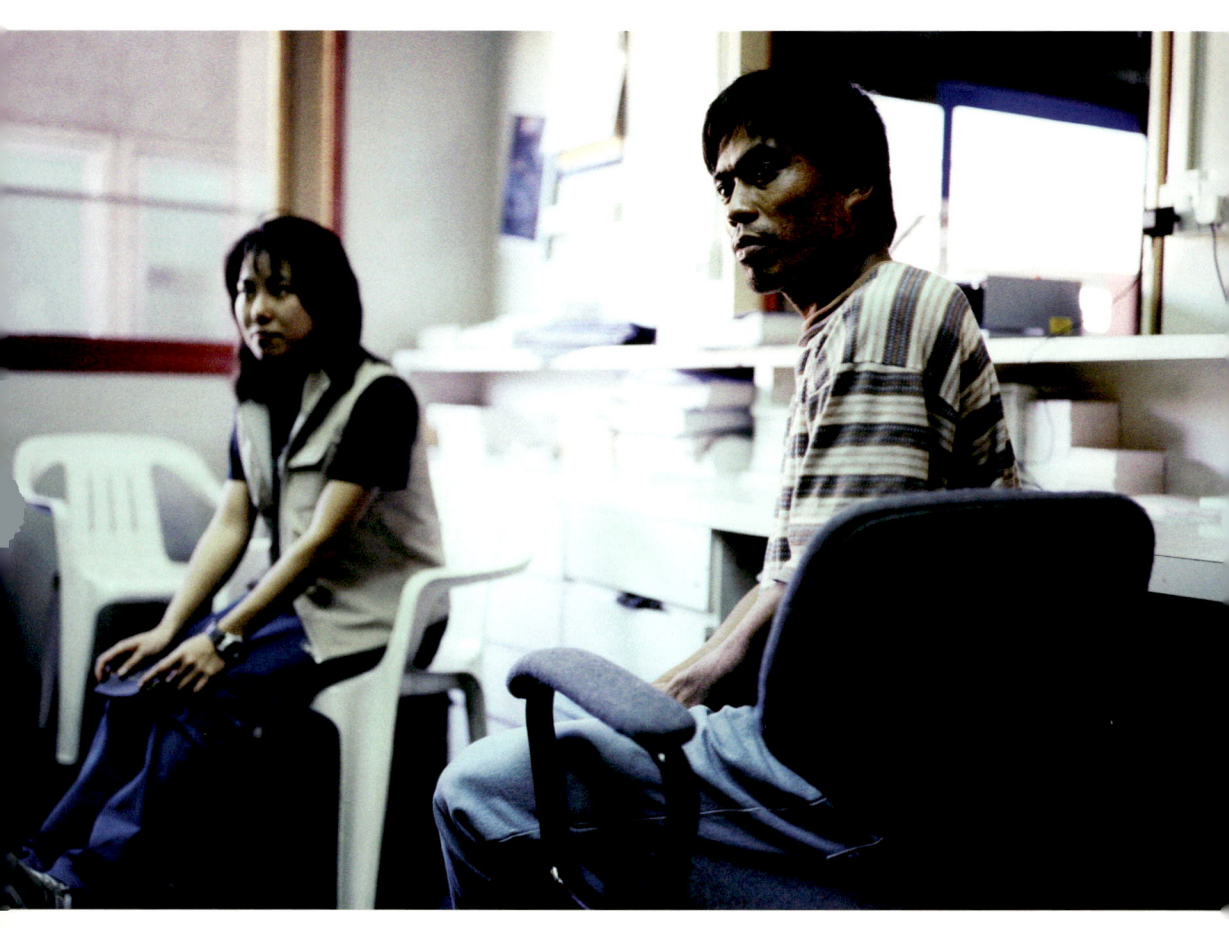

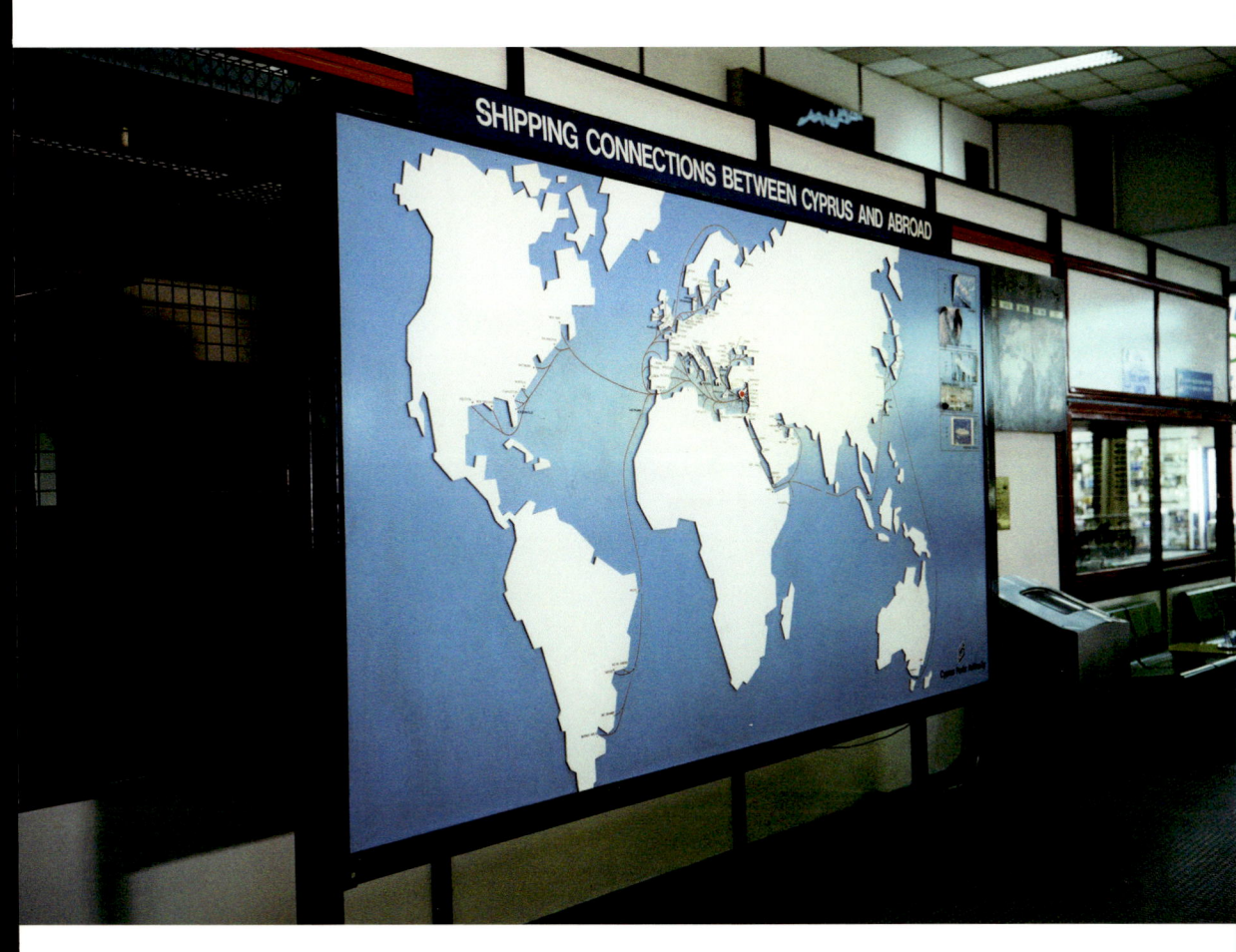

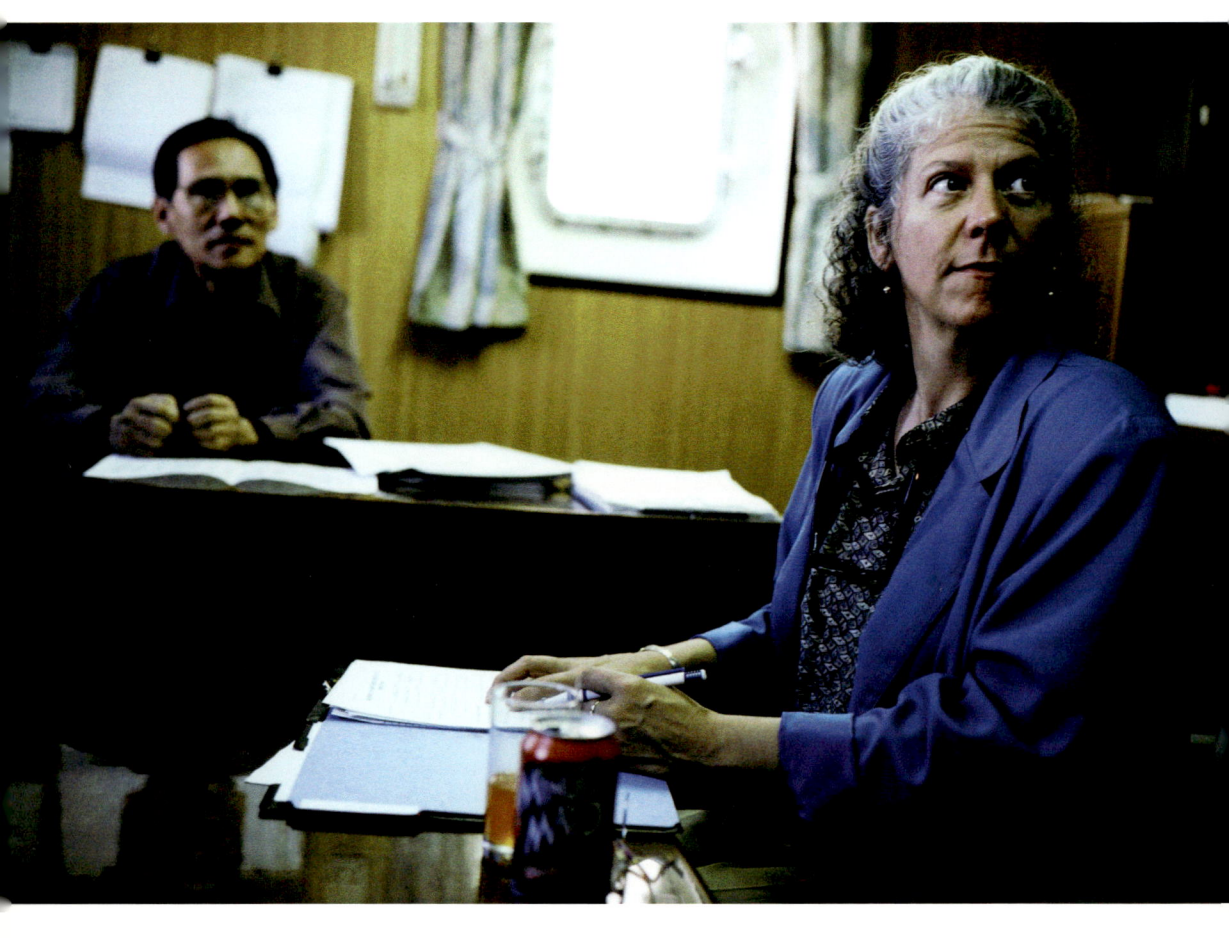

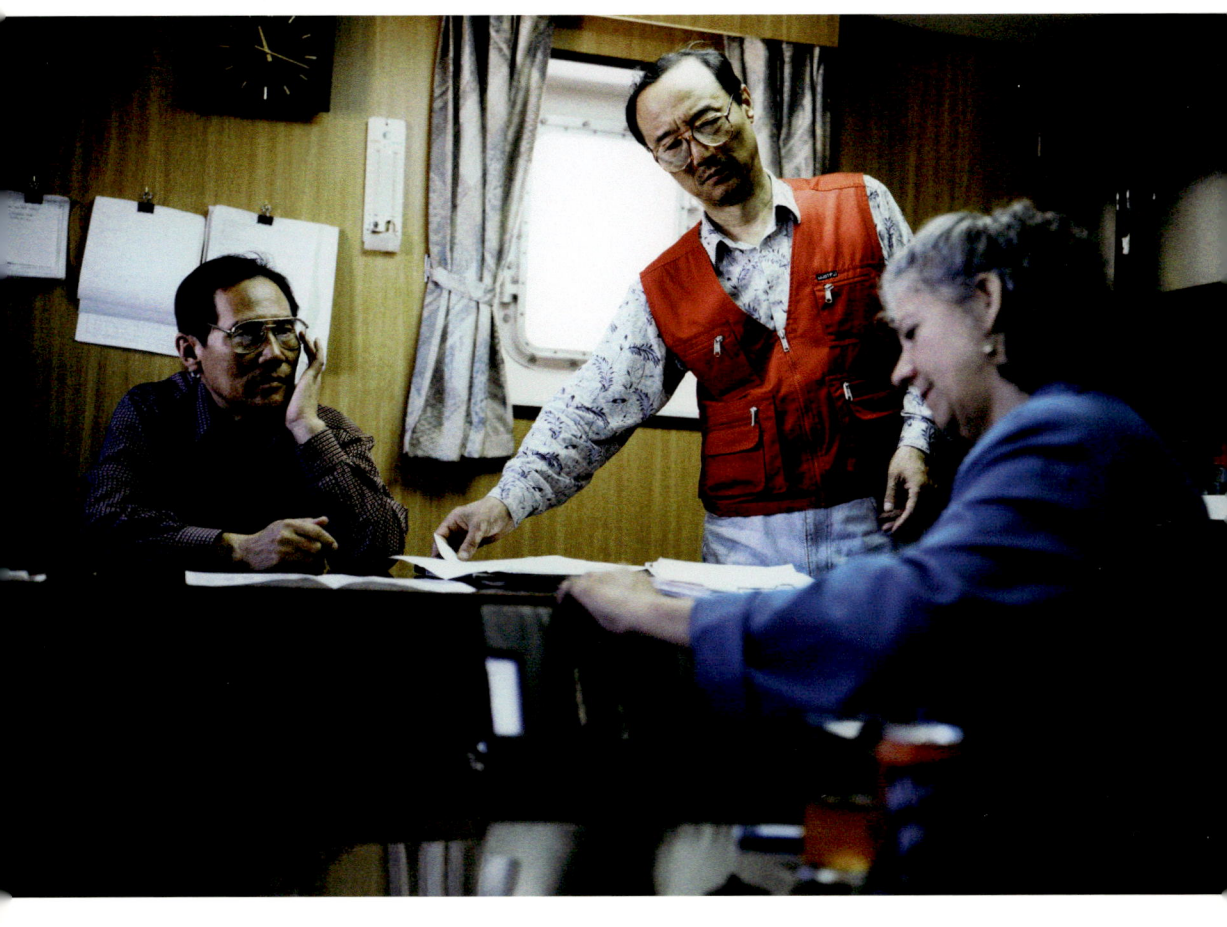

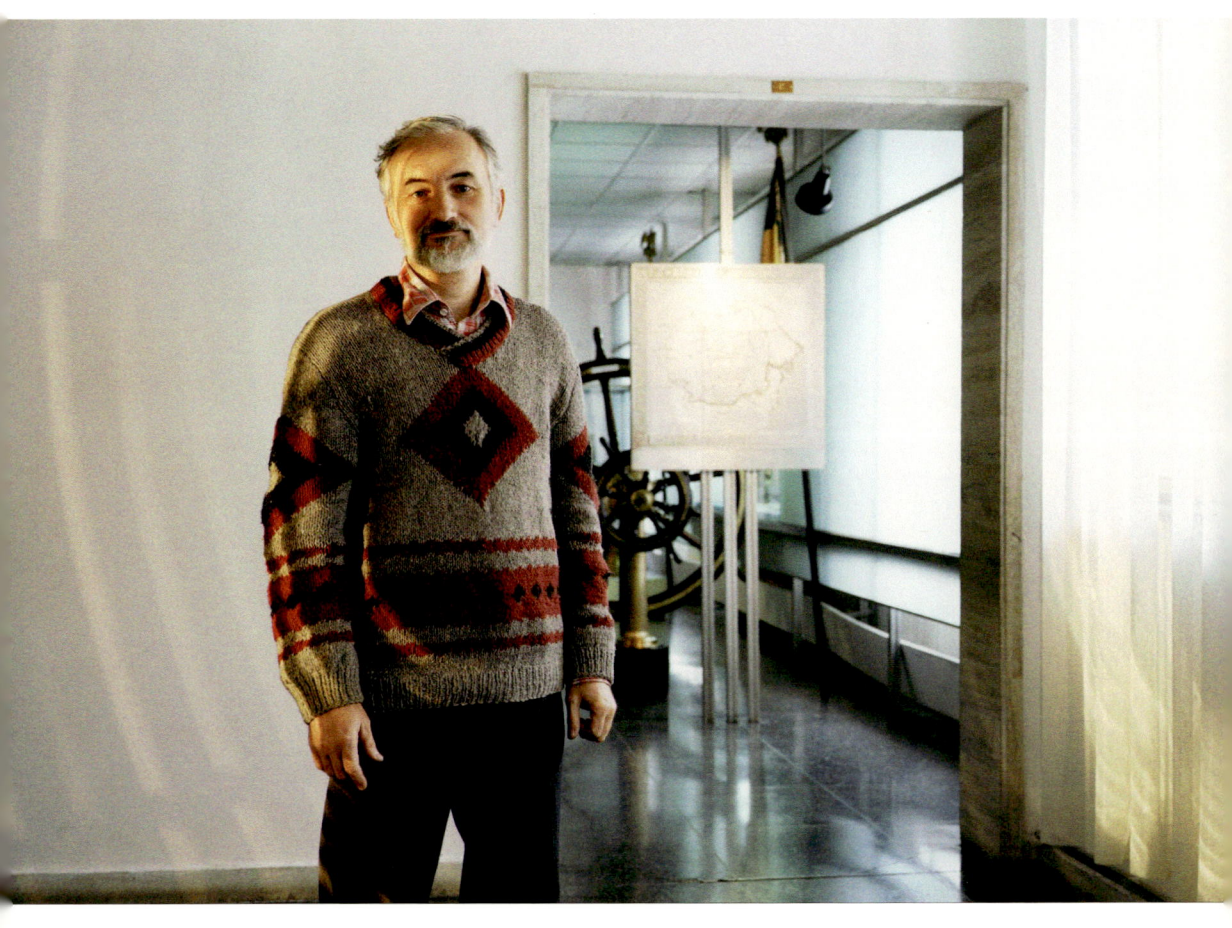

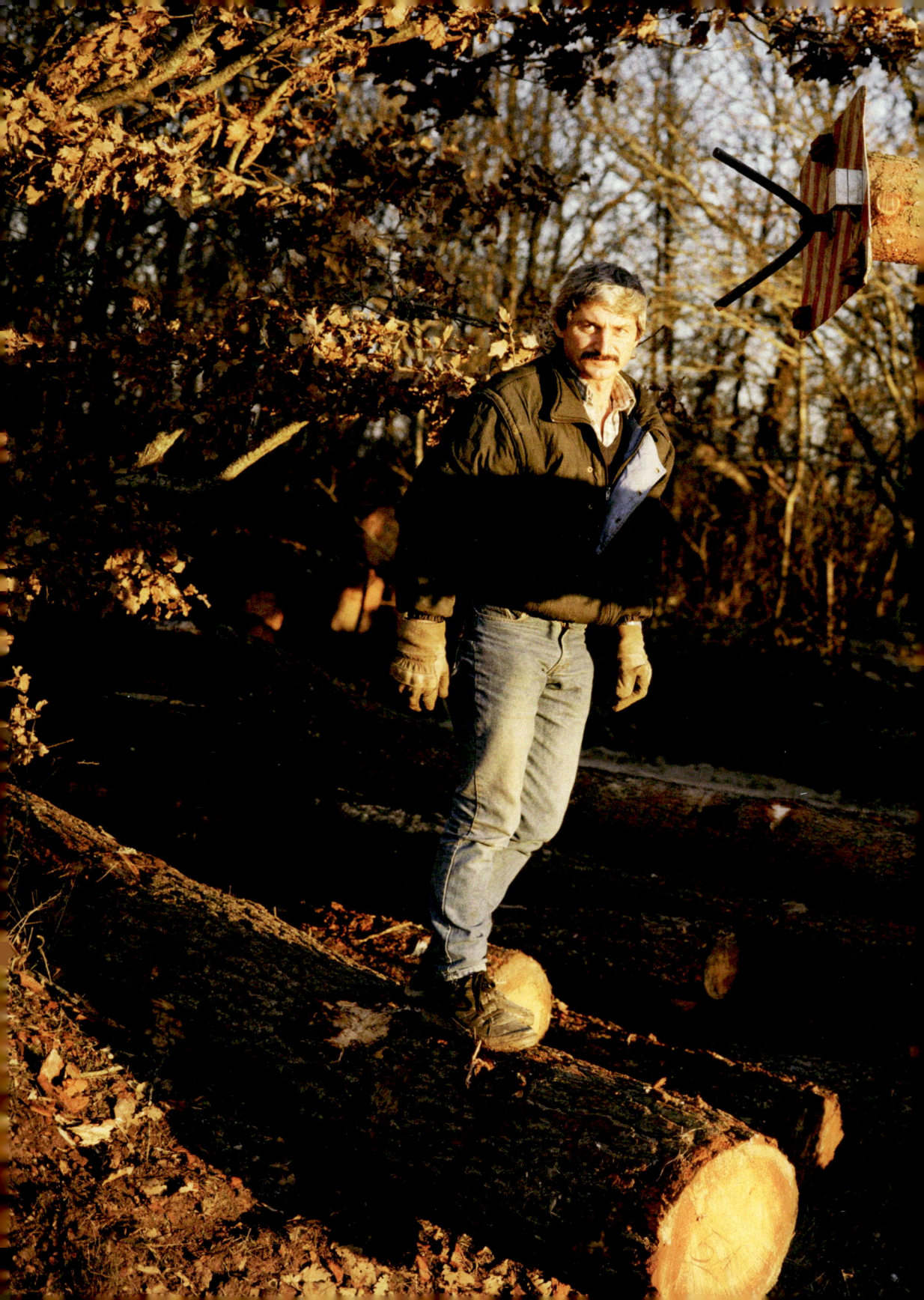

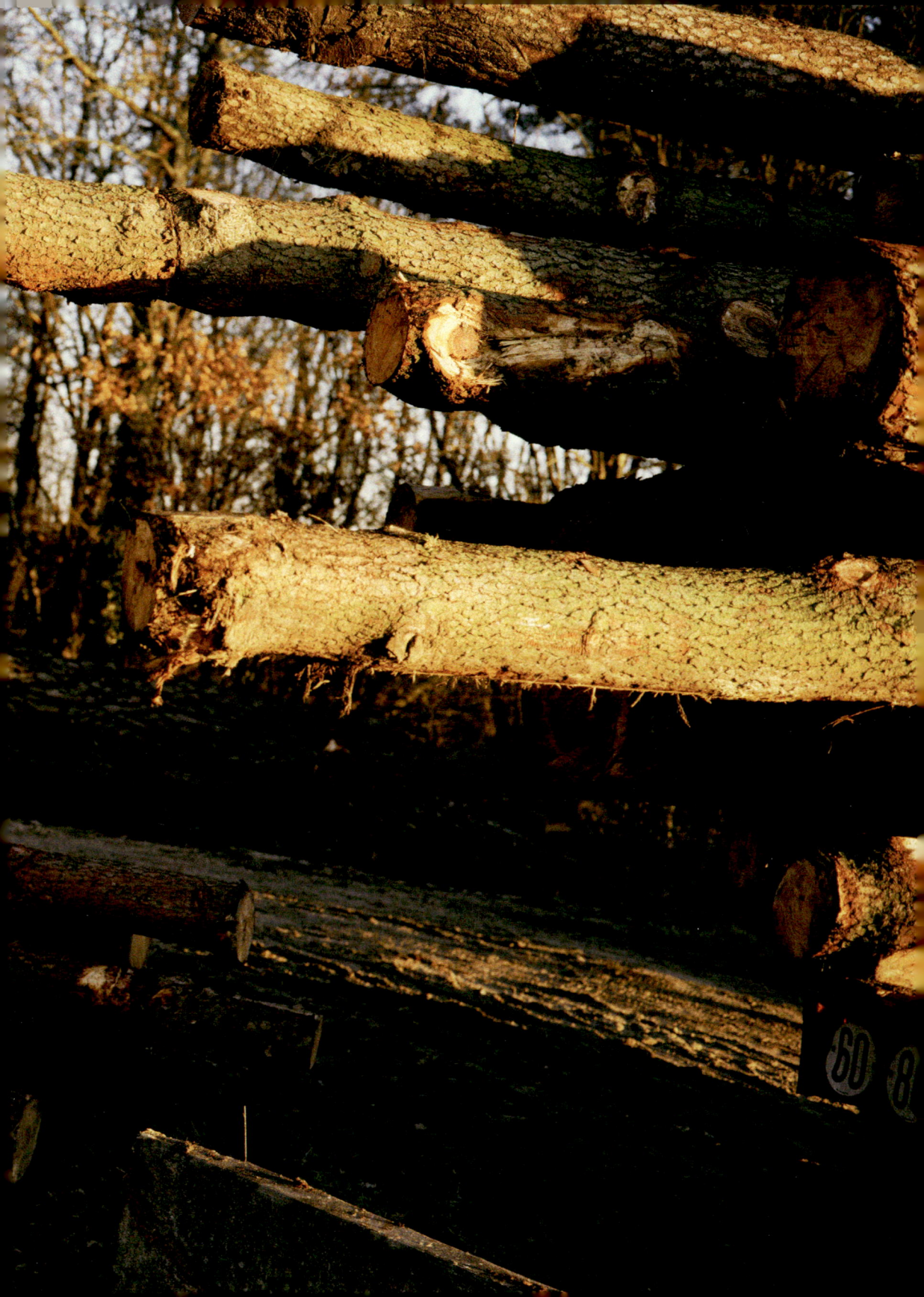

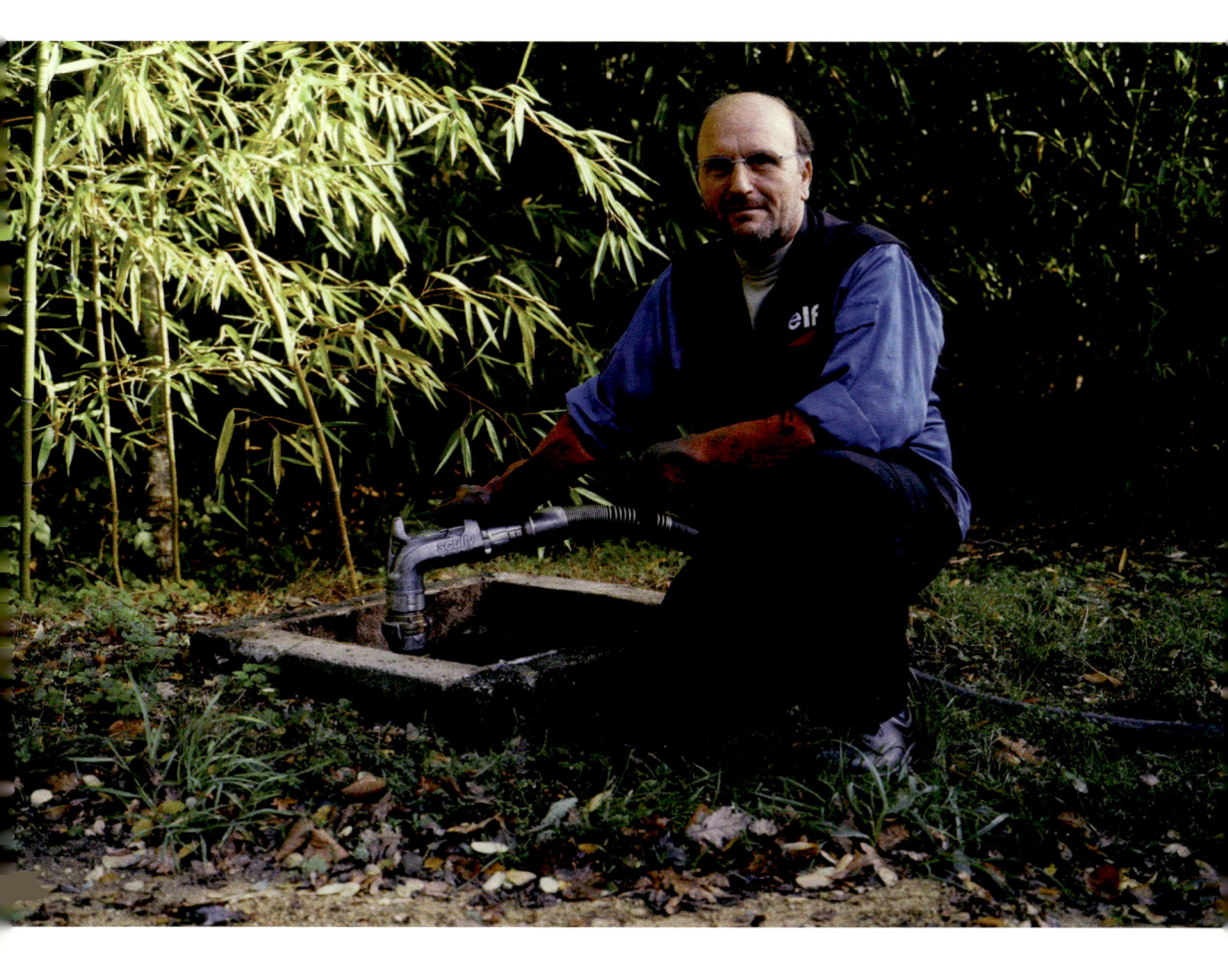

$$\vec{f}$$

$$\phi$$

$$f_s = f \cos(\phi)$$

$$\vec{f}$$

$$\vec{s}$$

$$W = \vec{f} \cdot \vec{s} = f_s\, s = f\, s \cos(\phi)$$

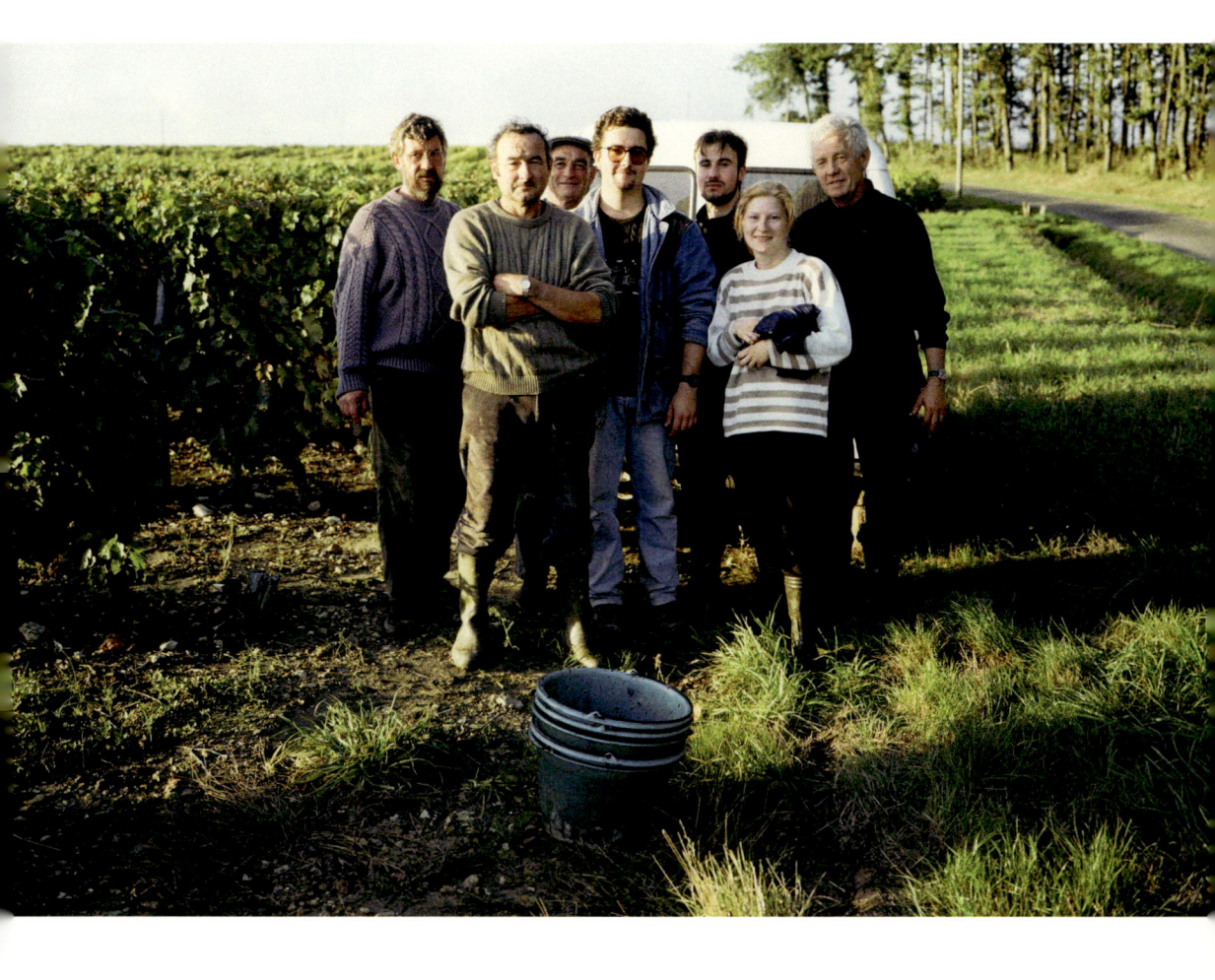

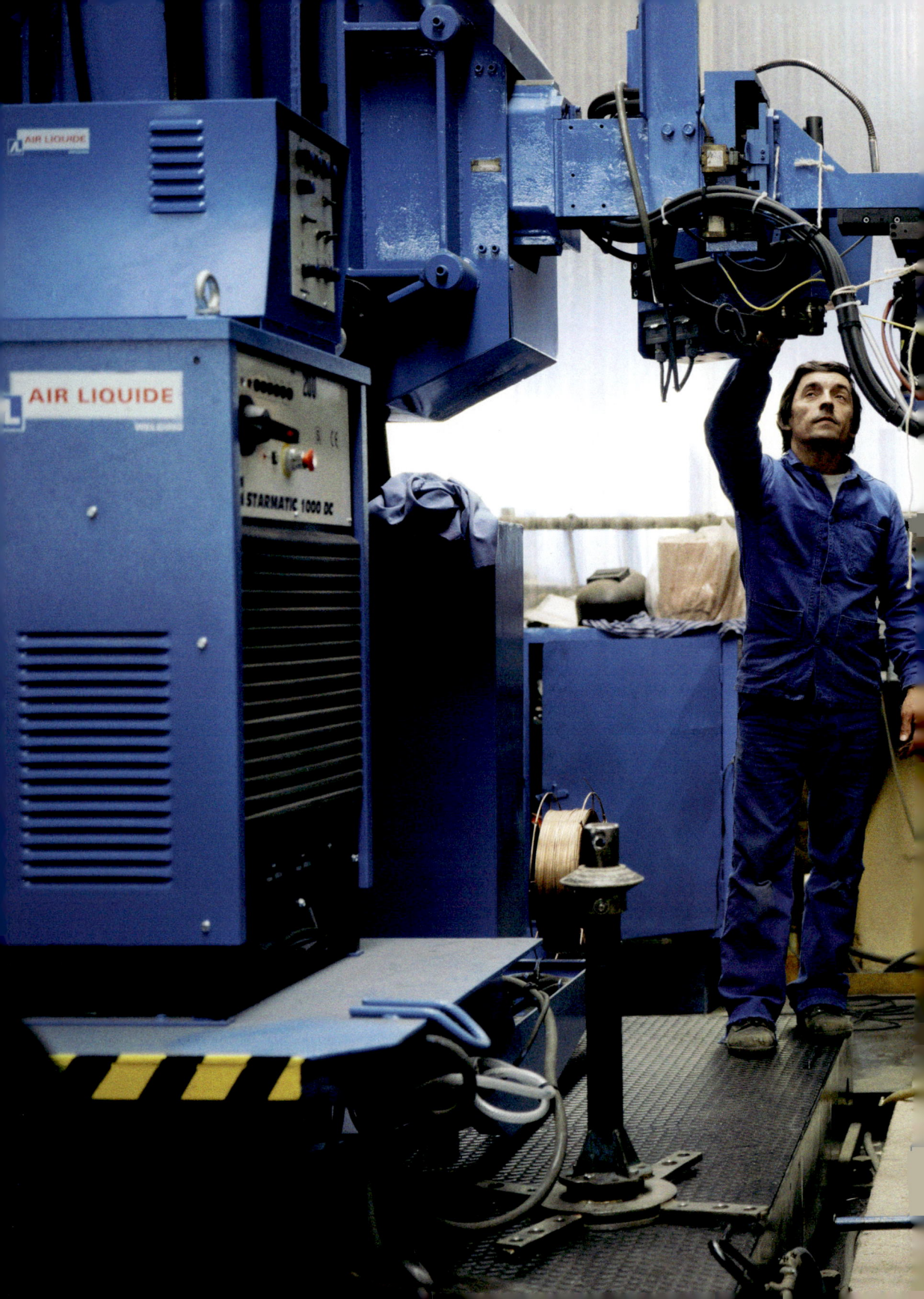

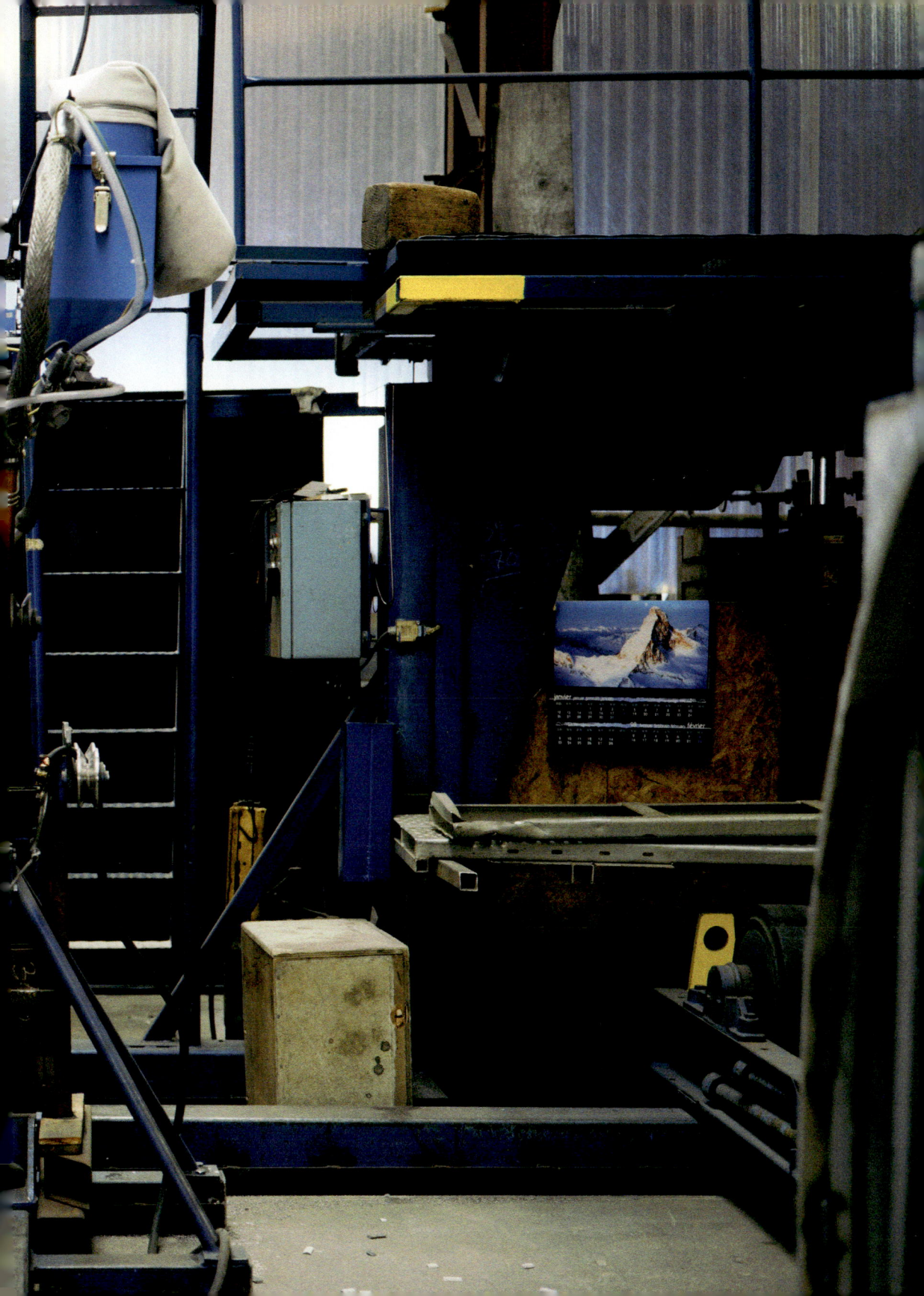

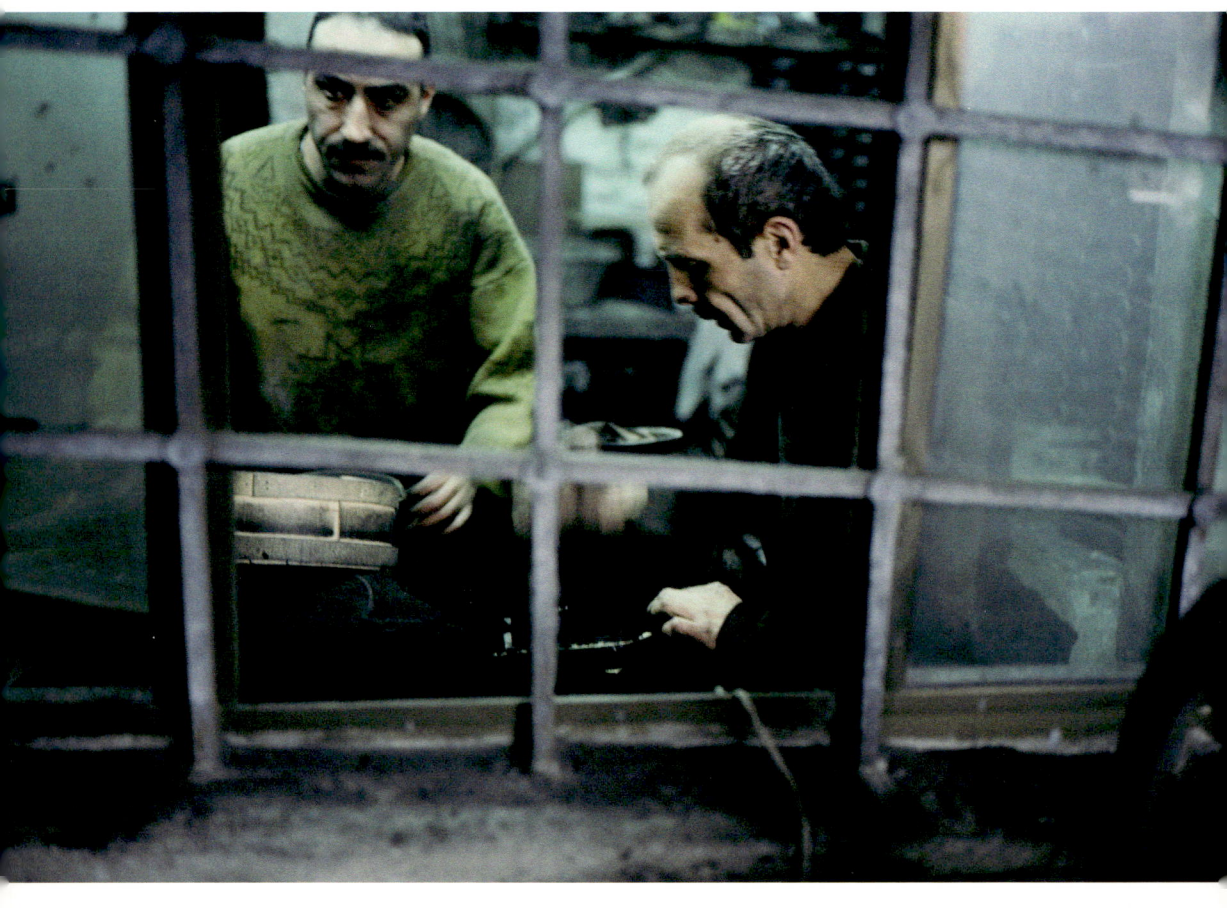

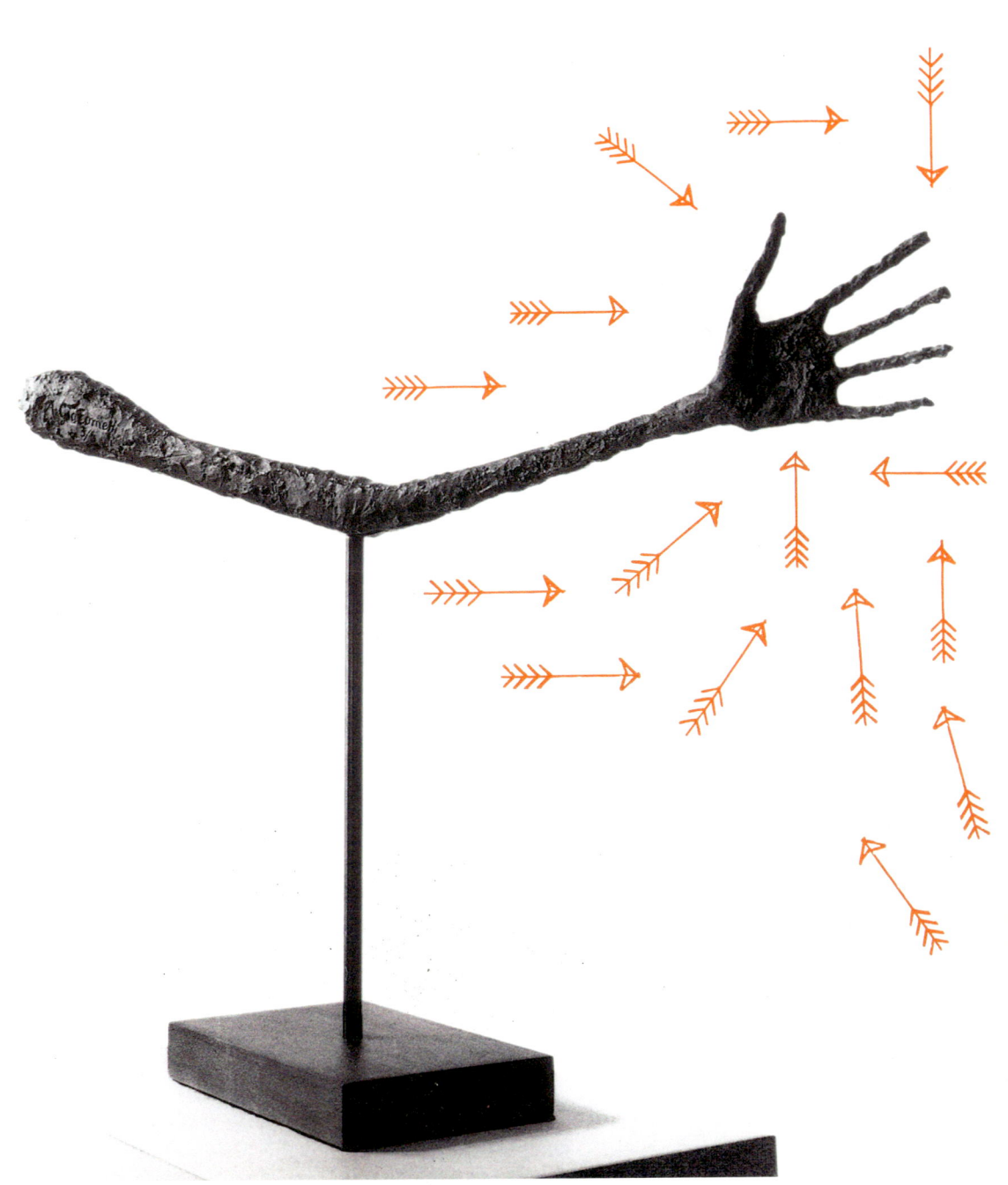

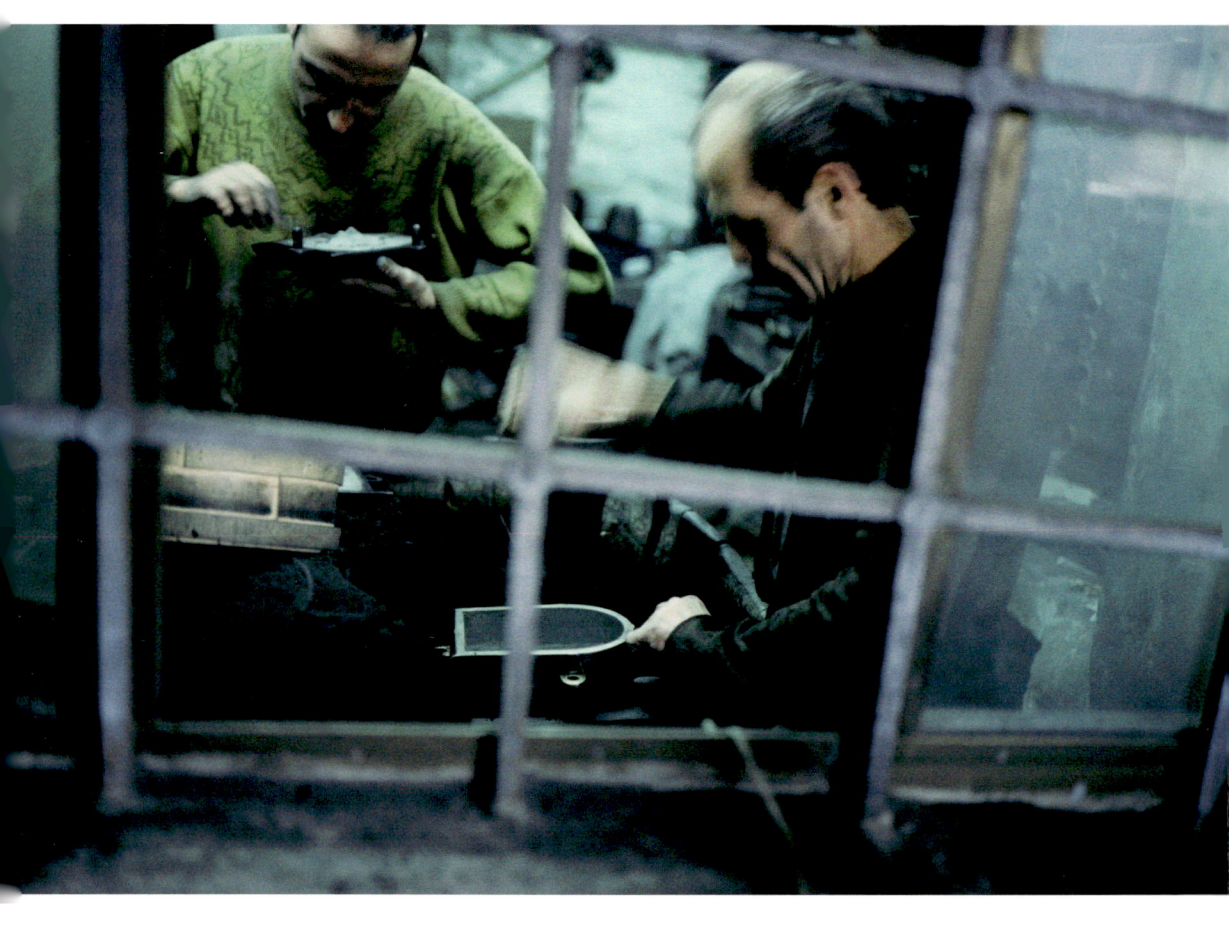

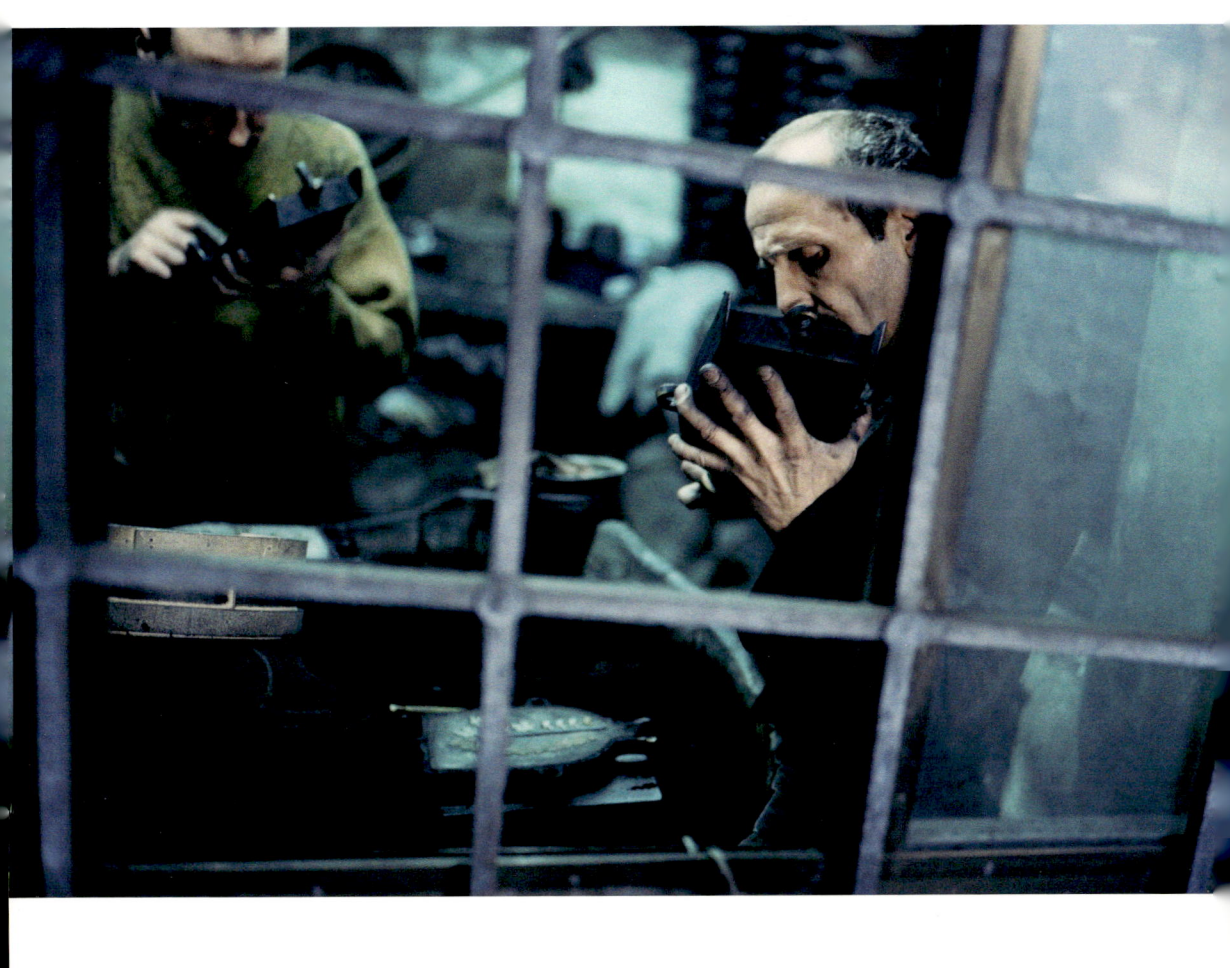

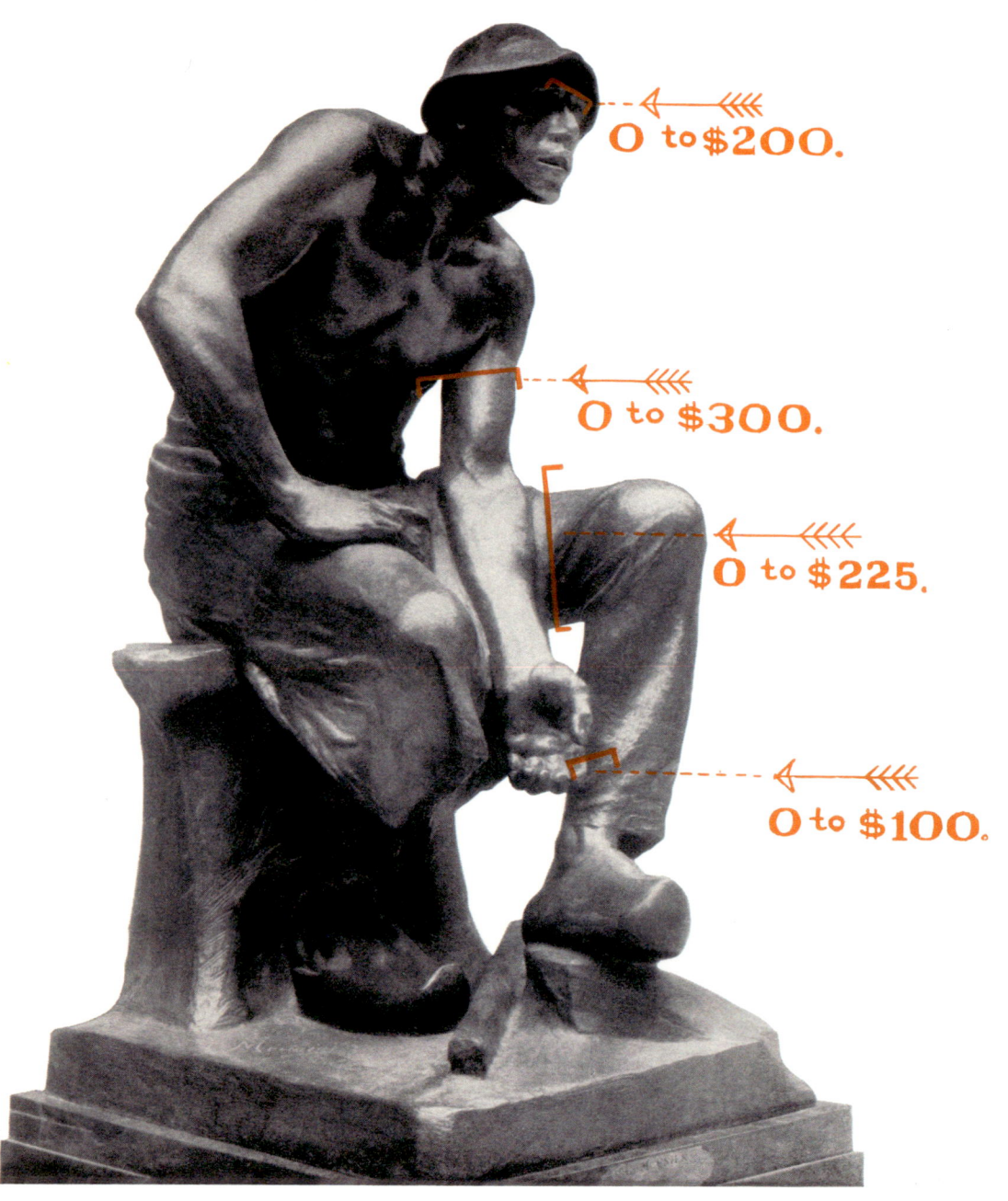

O to $200.

O to $300.

O to $225.

O to $100.

SHIPWRECK AND WORKERS
Allan Sekula

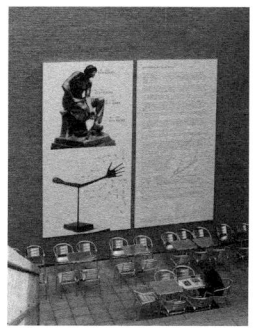

The cops are collecting their orange nets, looking to snare another group of unruly protesters like sardines. The Republican lady delegate standing outside Madison Square Garden, scouting out a safe place for lunch, announces with no little impatience that the president is a "hard worker". What this means exactly I try to guess. It is said as if she were his boss. Maybe he's not so bright, but he makes up for it with energy and zeal. A cheerful leader. A cheerleader. There's a job to be done, and he does it, and he gets everyone else to go along.

Imagine a monument to imperial labor for the 21st century: a cheerleader's megaphone and empty work boots, waiting for the next candidate in a business suit, ready to mingle, press the flesh, and share roasted fowl with the 'boots on the ground', a euphemism for those who do the dirty work, day in and day out. For a moment, their tasks are rescued from absurdity and violence by folksy but condescending populism.

By the mid-1920s, photomontage sounded the death knell of political monuments, at least in countries with a free press. Every monument and every politician aspiring to become a monument could be sentenced to the death of a few judicious paper cuts. No ceremony performed for the camera was safe from mockery.

Before the political cartoon entered the age of mechanical reproduction, monuments were still fundamentally intact. Monuments could answer and speak to other monuments: they were not yet mere vertical relics of exhausted bloodlines. A philosophical democrat from the artisan class could even imagine monuments that would implicitly answer the hauteur of the powerful, not with mockery, but with the dignity, gravity and energy of the laboring classes. This was the case with Constantin Meunier.

It is all the more remarkable that Meunier did this at the same time that industrial engineers were trying to rework the laboring body into an ever more efficient mechanism. He counters their pragmatic realism with an empiricism of his own.

With The *Puddler* (1884) Meunier responds both to the Cartesianism of Rodin's *Thinker* (1880) and to the pietism of *Millet's Angelus* (1857-1859). The seated ironworker is thinking, not praying. The disposition of his left arm provides a clue. Without looking, mouth agape in the heat from the smelting furnace, he lets the lactic acid of fatigue drain from his shoulder and elbow joint. *This is what I must do, in my repose, to recover and face the fire again.*

Just as both rider and horse know that the horse must drink to remain in motion.

It is surprising that one of the first sophisticated political photomontages, dating from 1909, took not King Leopold (a worthy target if there ever was one, especially in the last year of his life) but Meunier's *Puddler* as its subject.

The radical American lawyer, Crystal Eastman, painstakingly documents the miserly compensation doled out to the maimed railroad, steel-mill, and other industrial workers of Pittsburgh.[1] Her transformed *Puddler* is both St. Sebastian and a butcher's sectioned side of beef. The illustration reaches back to the Renaissance sources of social realism while pointing the way to the montages of John Heartfield and the statistical pictograms of the 1920s. For her bitter irony to strike home, and to maintain its distance from individual cases, her orange bookkeeper's overlay requires the somber typicality of an already-represented, elegiac figure.

Thus in practice she takes a middle stance in an ongoing debate about the relative value of images and statistics. Her fellow socialist, the German writer Kurt Tucholsky, who later collaborated with Heartfield, called passionately for "more photographs", and even claimed that "photographs of mutilated hands" are more convincing than "statistics, reports […] and provocative speeches". Eastman took a different tack, believing that "statistics are good stuff to start a revolution with".[2]

Eastman's acerbic statistical overlay of Meunier's sculpture predates his first (posthumous) American exhibition, at the Albright Museum in Buffalo, New York, in 1913, patronized by the barons of American steel making. Meunier enters America stage left in 1909, and exits stage right four years later, largely forgotten by a business civilization that takes abstract pride in 'hard work'. I'm surprised at how infrequently contemporary artists recognize his name.

It would be far-fetched to say that *Shipwreck* (1890), another of Meunier's sculptures, was a premonition of his son's death at sea, or of his own position in the history of art.

But would it be any less so to say his assembled workers remain today a premonition of what had already been imagined a century earlier, a universal republic? Or that the energy of this premonition still haunts the hand that becomes, through a feat of figurative abstraction, a wind vane or a fork?

[1] Eastman, Crystal, *Work Accidents and the Law* (*The Pittsburgh Survey*, vol. 2), New York: Charities Publication Committee, 1910, originally in: *Charities and the Commons*, vol. 21, No. 23, March 6th, 1909. The caption for the montage reads: "Valuations put on men in Pittsburgh in 1907". A table below gives the compensation details for 27 work accidents.

[2] Tucholsky, Kurt, 'Mehr photografien!', in: *Vorwärts*, June 28th, 1912, reprinted in Gesamtausgabe in: Bonitz, Antje *et al.* (eds), *Texte und Briefe/ Kurt Tucholsky*, Reinbek bei Hamburg: Rowohlt, 1996, vol. 1: 67-68. Eastman, Crystal, 'The Three Essentials for Accident Prevention', in: *American Academy of Political and Social Science Annals,* July-December, 1911, reprinted in: Cook, Blanche Wiesen (ed.), *Crystal Eastman on Women and Revolution,* Oxford: Oxford University Press, 1978: 280-290.

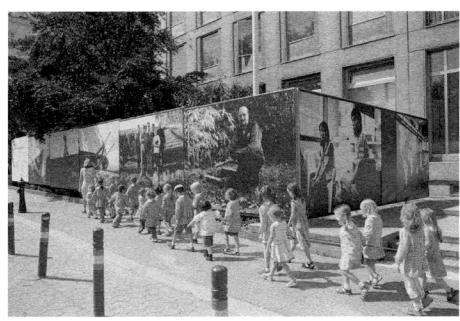 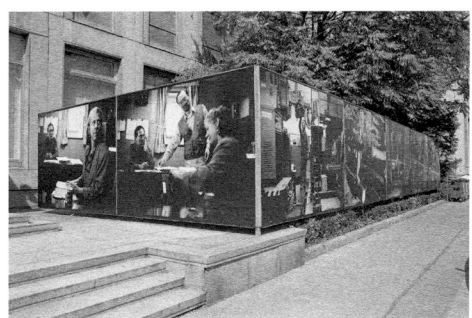

Images

p.185 *Shipwreck and Workers - Version 2 for Leuven* at The Stuk Arts Center, Leuven, Belgium, 2005

p.187 *Shipwreck and Workers,* Museum in Progress, Vienna, Austria, 2005

Sources for additional images

Alberto Giacometti, *La main*, 1947. Photograph by Mark Trivier, in *Alberto Giacometti*, (Basel: Editions Beyeler, 1991.)

"Definition of work in physics," adapted from http://www.ac.wwu.edu/~vawter/ PhysicsNet/Topics/Work/DefinitionWork.html

Production credits

Graphic design and German translation assistance: Ina Steiner

Project produced in cooperation with Museum in Progress, Vienna. (Coordination: Roman Berka and Brigitte Huck.)

Leuven production: *Meunier, a dialogue. Contemporary art meets Constantin Meunier in Leuven* (Coordination: Hilde Van Gelder, Lore Van Hees, Steven Vandervelden)

Color scans: A&I Hollywood. Mark Weiss.

Prints: Trevision, Grosshöflein, Austria.

THE LOTTERY OF THE SEA

Allan Sekula

179 minutes, color, sound. English, Spanish, Gallego with English subtitles. Camera, Writing, Voice: Allan Sekula. Editing: Elizabeth Hesik. The script that follows is for the introductory twenty-five minutes of the film.

The Lottery of the Sea takes its title from Adam Smith, who, in his famous *Inquiry into the Wealth of Nations* (1776) compared the life of the seafarer to gambling. Thus notions of risk were introduced by Smith through an allegory of the sea´s dangers, especially for those who did the hard work, and then, secondarily, for those who invested in ships and goods.

The film asks, is there a relationship between the most frightening and terrifying concept in economics, that of risk and the category of the sublime in aesthetics? We know that the sea a primordial source of sublimity, especially in the 18th century.

This film is an offbeat diary extending from the presumably "innocent" summer of 2001 through to the current "war on terror" all by way of a meandering, essayistic voyage from seaport to seaport, waterfront to waterfront, coast to coast.

What does it mean to be a maritime nation?
To rule the waves?
Or to harvest the sea?

An American submarine collides with a Japanese fisheries training ship. What does this suggest about the division of labor in the Pacific?

How do we remember the former emperor? As a general astride his horse? Or as a marine biologist peering through his microscope?

Panama decides whether to expand the width of its canal, over which it now exercises a certain qualified measure of sovereignty. *How is it that a scuba diver would be most prepared to question this great flushing of the jungle watershed?*

Galicia is presented with an unwanted gift of oil, with important questions following about the monomania of governments able only to conceptualize danger in one dimension. What can we learn about a people´s capacity for self-organization in the face of disaster and government indifference? *What do the oil-smeared fishermen of Bueu have to say?*

Barcelona turns anew to its seafront, producing a pseudo-public sphere and new real estate value to the north and even greater maritime logistical efficiency to the south. *What do the city´s invisible dockworkers have to say from their self-described "ghetto" about democracy?*

And in between we visit blizzards and demonstrations in New York, drifting prehistoric mastodons in Los Angeles, militant drummers and bemused African construction workers in Lisbon, millionaires or millionaire-impersonators (who knows for sure?) in Amsterdam and the stray dogs of Athens, all by way of thinking through seeing about the sea, the market, and democracy.

Prologue

Thick oil spilling.
Microtome slicing fish in wax.
Containers passing.

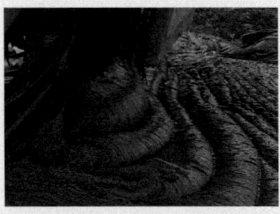 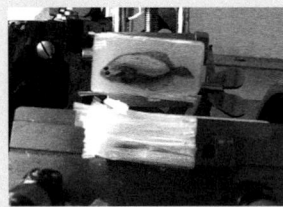 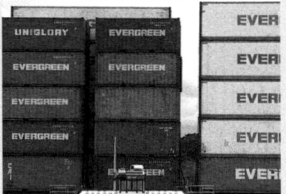

Soundtrack music:

Phil Ochs, "The Scorpion Departs and Never Returns" (1968).

Sailors climb the tree, up the terrible tree
Where are my shipmates have they sunk beneath the sea?
I do not know much, but I know this cannot be
It isn't really, it isn't really,
Tell me it isn't really.

Sounding bell is diving down the water green
Not a trace, not a toothbrush, not a cigarette was seen
Bubble ball is rising from a whisper or a scream
But I'm not screaming, no I'm not screaming,
Tell me I'm not screaming...

TITLE: YOKOHAMA JUNE 2001

Chinese seafarers buying used cameras and electronics at shipside.

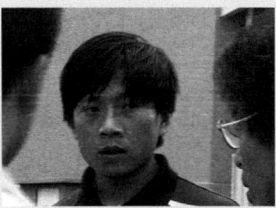

The informal economy in Japan...
used goods...
a little embarrassing for the Japanese...,
who leave these transactions
to the Mandarin-speaking petty traders
of Yokohama's Chinatown...

190

Chinese seafarers…
the latest volunteers for the bottom
of the global market in maritime wages.

When Adam Smith first spoke about risk,
he thought about the sea.

Could it be because risk is the most exciting
and terrifying concept in economics,
something like the sublime in aesthetics?

TITLE: THE LOTTERY OF THE SEA

Archival footage from 1920s: a heavy sea seen from deck, seafarers working rigging and handling life-boat, decks awash.

Every seafarer was a gambler,
a subscriber to the "lottery of the sea".

For enduring danger and hardship,
and for their skills,
the Scottish philosopher thought seafarers deserved to be well paid.
And yet their very mobility sunk their wages to the lowest levels.
True cosmopolitans,
they did not enjoy the competitive advantages of metropolitan workers.

Return to Chinese seafarers, haggling energetically, trading dollars for old cameras.

In seafarers,
Smith discovered the prototype
for a global market in labor.

And in merchant shipping,
he imagined the triumph of big business.
A fleet of twenty or thirty ships could,
in his words, "insure itself".
A great ship-owner could avoid
the optimistic follies of the lottery player.

Chinese seafarer struggles up gangway with huge stereo speakers

> The followers of Adam Smith can take heart.
> Inside every seafarer,
> a merchant is struggling to break free.

TITLE: ATHENS DECEMBER 2003

The ancient agora, with the temple of Hephaistos,
god of the forge and 'father' of Athens, in the background.

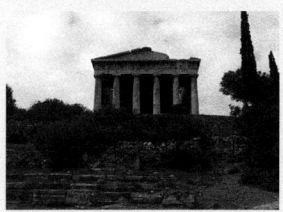

> The ancient *agora,*
> legendary birthplace of democracy.
> Stepping-stones of philosophy,
> market stalls of small traders,
> political platforms.

The flea market at Monastariki, a seated vendor, surrounded by boots, close-up of Greek adventure comics —a police dog sniffs at the body of a fallen woman, a rocket launches into space—, knick-knacks, model of Soviet fighter jet…

> The god of the forge chases the virgin goddess.
> The patroness of the city eludes his grasp.
> His ejaculate fertilizes the earth.
> A city of men springs forth from the soil:
> citizens without mothers.

… nautical souvenirs, an antique film projector, a painted mermaid, an antique accounting machine, made of brass.

> A race of ship-owners,
> venturing forth onto the sea,
> Slaves bending at the oars.

Graffito painting of sailing vessel with blood pouring from portholes.
Close-up of meat-grinder extruding chopped beef. Pink-gloved hands of butcher.

> **Ancient Athens and its port:**
> **walled-in,**
> **a continuous fortress against invaders.**
> **Women laughing and wailing inside the white walls.**

The central meat market: the Greek flag flies from a leg of lamb,
Sadistic horse-play between two meat vendors. Cleaver chops meat.
Hanging beef tongues, white stomachs, a pig's head, passing shoppers.

> **Two kinds of agoraphobe:**
> **Those who fear the market in the abstract,**
> **but love it in close proximity.**
> **And those who see it the other way around,**
> **from the corner office high above the street,**
> **or from behind the bullet-proof window of the speeding limousine.**
> **Confident in the numbers…**

Hanging placard depicting ewe and nursing lamb.

> **An unlikely pastoral among the red carvings.**
> **Our sister mammals.**

Extract from Never on Sunday. *Melina Mercouri plunges into Piraeus harbor, followed by boat-yard workers. Bazouki music.*

Subtitle: If you're not a slave, come on in…

Back to market crowd, worker with trash barrel makes his way through crowd.

> **The pseudo-disclosure of the agora:**
> **everything is fresh, but dead…**

Slicing lamb, butcher peels kiwi fruit against bloody apron, threatens camera with knife, flayed rabbits, wide-eyed girl.

Cut to fish market. A south Asian vendor displays a large octopus.

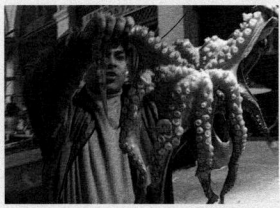

You like?

-It's beautiful.

It's beautiful.

Extract from Never on Sunday. *Taverna scene, Piraesus: Mercouri and Jules Dassin:*

You stay long in Greece?

-Maybe. I'm looking for something in Greece.

What?

-You won't laugh?

Why? You look for something funny?

-I came to Greece to… to find the truth.

Cleaning stainless-steel fish-market tables. Shoppers passing. Cut to hawsers creaking in Piraeus. Pan from Panamanian to Greek flag flying from large yacht. Tracking shot of cement ship, followed by decrepit cement plant.

The commodities we don't think about.
Heavy, omnipresent, uniform in composition,
but largely invisible.

Greek ships carry these unacknowledged goods:
cement, oil, coal, scrap metal,… steel.

But their Greekness
is attenuated and disguised.

Office buildings along the Piraeus waterfront: Panamanian Registry, Mediterranean Shipping. Male and female mannequins dressed in Greek naval uniforms.

The flag flying from the stern is Liberian, or Panamanian
–nations created by the United States–
or that of other desperately poor countries:
the Marshall Islands, Cambodia, even landlocked Bolivia…

All of this saves money, avoids regulation,
makes it harder to assign blame when accidents happen…

Toys in store window: Freddy Kruger menaces women in glass hemispheres, Arnold Schwarzenegger as Terminator, etc. Mechanical Santa gyrates like Elvis.

Soundtrack: orchestral rendition of "Jingle Bells".

American lawyers working for the shipping industry
invented this convenient system of disguises,
institutionalizing it after the second World War,
and helping the Greeks to rebuild their shattered merchant fleet
from the immense surplus left over
from the great convoys of the North Atlantic.

Blond woman on stilts dressed as Uncle Sam.
Music: Gene Krupa's band: "I am an American" (1940).

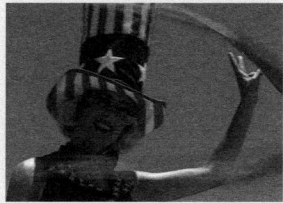

On the street
in a home
in a crowd
or alone
shout wherever you may be
I am an American
I am from the heart of me.

Container ships on horizon. Close-up of rain drops on blue railing.
Fishing boat passes behind aloe plants in foreground, trailed by a ravenous flock of gulls.

So now three years into "the war on terror"
the American Navy asserts its right
to board the thousands of ships
flying the Panamanian and Liberian flags,

Searching for weapons of mass destruction...
amidst the bags of tapioca and the giant rolls of newsprint...

Night. Man walking with possessions in plastic bag along Piraeus waterfront.

Anxiety and fear take charge,
and the port retreats into enforced invisibility,
no longer a theater of the world's connectedness.

Ferry preparing to depart. Crew shutting down vehicle ramp. Departure.

During the Olympic games,
Mexican reporters try to film Athens' port of Piraeus,
and are beaten by the police...

Wrong place,
wrong time,
wrong sport...

TITLE: US NAVAL BASE, YOKOSUKA, JUNE 2001.

One guided missile frigate ties up next to another. Japanese shipyard workers look on.

Two and a half years earlier:
the "war on terror"
has yet to be declared.

off camera voices:

I can see their securities working.

-They're checking on us, huh?

A old danger resurfaces:
war with China over Taiwan.

Japan has a stylish new prime minister
eager to purge the post-war constitution
of pacifist clauses.

A new right-wing American government
of dubious legitimacy
makes new friends
and looks for enemies.

Even Russia and Viet Nam
join up with the Americans
when naval exercises are conducted
in the south China Sea.

Accidents happen.
An American spy plane

flies provocatively close to the Chinese coast,
and collides with a defending interceptor.

The Navy press officer confesses:
"I miss the cold war.
I didn't want it to end".

View of shipyard. Workers pass on bicycles.
Bus-stop mural depicting American literary, artistic, musical figures. Slogan: "The day you stop reading is the day you stop learning".
Bicyclist. Destroyer's gun turret glides past. Close-ups of crudely painted caricatures on mural: "Allen Shepheard [sic], Stanley Krubruck [sic], Ansel Adams".

off camera voices:

    There's no "u"…

    -It's "i".

    …it's "i-c-k".

-The fact is you got Japanese radicals here.
They could fill a boat with explosives,
bring it down here to a naval base
and kaboom somebody.

Yeah.

-Yeah.

"*Musicians: John Coltrane, Louis Armstrong, B.B. King, Elvin Jones…*"

Cut to medium shot of entire bus shelter "[gr]eat Americans at your local library". Close-up: "Ansel Adams". Medium close-up: "Authors: John Steinbeck, Hemingway, Hawking [sic], Asimov".

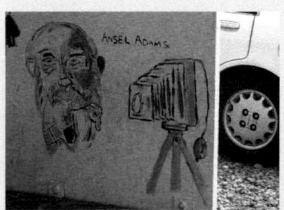

Slow zoom to close-up: "Hemingway, black hole".

You got radicals back in the States that could do that…

-What do you call it: propaganda of the deed?

Screams.
Yokohama carnival thrill ride plunges into abyss
in large pool of water. As spray clears,
all that remains is a hazy mist.

Film soundtrack: Destination Tokyo.

To me it's like going down in a sub.

Three crewmen at mess table. John Garfield in center.
Older submariner on left continues:

You shove off,
go deep under the sea,
when you come back up

you've got something inside
that's never been there before.

—the Irish and the Greeks:
born philosophers.

[John Garfield]
I got a philosophy too.
Every day a box of Cracker Jacks
with a prize in every package.

Carnival prize contest:
Winnie the Pooh stuffed bears circling on carrousel.
Slow zoom to close-up of "Made in China" label.
Raucous sound, electronic shouts and calls in Japanese,
in background.

Film soundtrack [Destination Tokyo]

Captain's voice [Cary Grant, off camera]:

I remember Mike's pride
when he bought the first pair of roller skates
for his little five-year-old boy.

They were the finest roller skates
money could buy.

Close-up of face of youngest crewman.
Cut to captain.

If Mike were here to put it into words right now,
that's just what he'd say:
More roller skates in this world,
including some for the next generation of Japanese kids.

TITLE: MISAKI FISHERIES HIGH SCHOOL. JUNE 2001.

Sea anchors hanging from classroom ceiling.

After the American submarine collides
with the Japanese fisheries training ship,
a friend remarks:

"Now we should call it the military-industrial-entertainment complex".

Nautical relief map of the Sea of Japan.

Destination Tokyo. View through periscope. View of periscope breaking surface. View through periscope of Mount Fuji, portentous music suggesting Oriental grandeur and despotism.

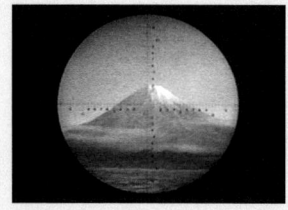

Cut back to relief map.

Off camera: radio distress call, through static.

Coast Guard, this is COMSUBPAC Pearl Harbor.
We have a vessel that has had a collision
approximately nine miles south of Diamond Head.

A commercial ship with a submarine
vessel has sunk.
People are in the water.

Model of a fisheries training ship, backlit in vitrine.

The submarine commander is showing off
for distinguished civilian guests.

Texas oil and gas executives
and their wives
crowd the conning tower.

Close-up of playful fisheries students in white uniforms and military-style caps, working at the rigging of their training boat. Boat is hoisted into water. Students board. Boat underway. Fishing boat passes in distance. Travelling shot of boat under full sail.

The submarine bursts upward from the deep,
slicing the undetected Japanese boat in two,
sending nine boys and men to their deaths.

During the cold war, a submarine commander
with Hollywood connections
proposes civilian junkets
aboard the top secret dreadnoughts of the deep.

The world of silence and lethal stealth
opens itself to the glare of PR.
The American commander,
a devout Christian,
wants to apologize in person to the families of the dead.

The Navy prefers more official and abstract apologies,
fearing perhaps the raw emotion of the encounter

Sandals of students, in a row on the dock.

Forced to resign,
the commander embarks on a new career
as an inspirational speaker.

Fish in tank. Baby fish preserved in wax. Case of glass microscope slides, with cellular cross-sections of fish in purple dye. Microtome sliding wax samples. Paintbrush holding thin cross sections.

The Japanese prime minister
failed to interrupt his round of golf

when informed of the disaster
and loses his job as a result.

The new prime minister
makes a point of visiting a shrine to Japanese war dead
currying favor with right-wing nationalists.

How is the late emperor to be remembered?

As a warrior astride his horse?
Or as a marine biologist bent over his microscope?

An elderly technician draws a sample for a tank in a glass pipette. Approach to microscope. View of swimming plankton.

Whatever the diplomatic protocols
or domestic pandering,
geopolitical relations
are governed by the sorrow and guilt that is not expressed.

The Americans offer no apology
for the atomic bombings
of Hiroshima and Nagasaki.
The Japanese do not apologize
for the massacre of Nanjing.

What does it mean to be a maritime nation?
To harvest the sea?
Or to rule the waves?

Adam Smith's division of labor on an oceanic scale.
One empire has defeated another.
American warships.
Japanese fishing boats.

The headmaster waves goodbye to the students,
sailing from the same dock
as did their doomed comrades
four months earlier.

How can the sea be both a killing field
and a mother who feeds us,
who must be nurtured in her turn?

TITLE: AUGUST 2003

Close-ups of passport.

The 19th-Century anarchists had a way of putting it:
"burn the documents!"

In my case it was more unwitting.
The documents almost drowned.

I twisted my back dodging a police baton on the Plaza Catalunya,
fell dead asleep a few hours later
only to find my passport floating on a small lake
cascading from the hotel bathtub.
Most of the inked entry and exit stamps were still legible,
except for those from South Africa and Russia,
countries that had recently undergone great sea changes.

Close-ups of Spanish entry document.

Now —three years later— I'm on my way back to Barcelona.

The entry paperwork has gotten more complicated.
Now the Spaniards address their visitors in five helpful languages.
Arabic and French for their former conquerors...
English for their former imperial rivals...

Workshop: looking at slides.

My workshop students, photographers and filmmakers.

Barcelona port headquarters. Press officer explains current state of port development to assembled group of students and guests. [in Castilian]:

**The whole urbanization project and the hotel
would be on the east side of the protected pier.**

**Among other things
the fishermen's area would be affected by the
new project.**

A woman guest poses a question.

**So the idea is that if tourists
take a cruise
they can stay in the area?**

**-Actually, the commercial area
will be separate from the residential.**

**Up to now, our problem has been
that cargo chips must arrive at this pier.**

**They must pass through this entrance,
which causes a lot of problems, etc.**

Filmmaker (off camera):

**So this is the land fill?
The dredging is to deepen this mouth?
You are taking immediately the land?**

Harbor tour.

Dredging, a grain slip moored at terminal. A chemical tanker. Scenes of the working port. Seafarers wave. Tugs maneuver a ship. The flag of China flies from a stern.

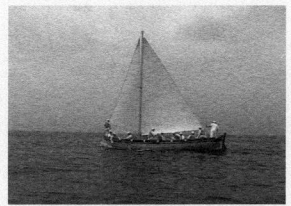 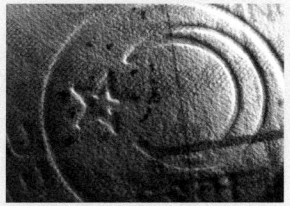 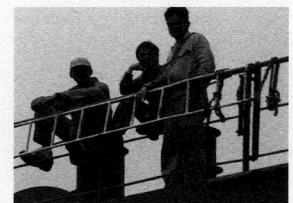

How do we respond to the new movement
calling globalization into question?

The World Bank is meeting in Barcelona.
Protestors are gathering from around Europe.

I suggest we take a break from finance capital,
and look at the physical world of circulating goods.

An antidote to the myth
of the instantaneous electronic circulation of capital
as if value were produced in the ether.

Barcelona, like Los Angeles,
has long turned its back to the working waterfront.

But my students have their own insights.
One young woman from a fishing family
better understands the market calls
of the Tokyo auctioneers of giant tuna
than does a visiting writer from Japan.

The secret international unity of trades and crafts.

[Tuna-fishing scenes from Riff Raff *(1934). James Cagney. The fishermen pause in their work and one of them addresses Muller, the Cagney character.]*

You'd be a big man if you'd listen.

-Listen to what?

Wages are not the working man's share of a commodity
he has produced.
Wages are the share of a commodity previously produced
of which the employer buys a certain amount of productive labor power.
That's right, isn't it?

-Huh? Oh, sure, sure.

All right.
The wage worker sells labor power to capital.
Why does he sell it?

-Why, because he's a sucker.
That's why.

Now look. Is work an active expression of a man's life?

-Yeah.

No.

-No, you dope!

There you are.
We need you Muller. You are a born leader.
You've got the power to sway the masses.
You could be the biggest man on the waterfront.

Malik suggests that more than anything
it is Islam that resists globalization
and that this turns on its notions of charity.

We argue.

Oakland Museum, Oakland CA, January 2003.

Elderly woman docent dressed as California Gold Rush miner of 1849 lectures schoolchildren on depicting travelers crossing what appears to be the Isthmus of Panama (or adventuring in Yucatan).

Docent:

> **OK, look at this picture and tell me what is wrong?**
>
> **-Oh, three horses…**
>
> **That's right. How many people?**
>
> **-Four.**
>
> **Not only are there four people and three horses**
> **but the artist who painted this was a Mexican man**
> **who never saw this landscape that he painted.**
> **His name was Arriola and he calls it "Tropical Landscape".**
> **When he first painted it there were no horses, no people.**
> **So he painted political figures,**
> **and then he could sell it,**
> **made it topical…**
> **But I do love it…**
> **I love counting the legs…**

Full moon rising through clouds.
Soundtrack: Azuero grito [shout]
resembling the sustained barking of dogs.

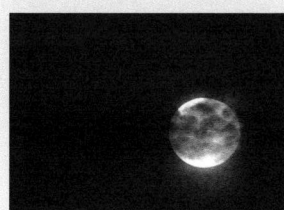

© Photographs:
Dirk Braeckman
Nick Hannes
Allan Sekula
Dieter Telemans
Luc Tuymans
Anne-Mie van Kerckhoven
Maarten Vanvolsem

© 2010 (2nd edition), 2006 Leuven University Press /
Universitaire Pers Leuven / Presses Universitaires de Louvain
Minderbroedersstraat 4, B-3000 Leuven (Belgium)

ISBN 978 90 5867 563 7
D/2006/1869/45
NUR: 651

Final editing: Jan Baetens, Jan Dirk Baetens, Sammy De Groote,
Rein Deslé and Hilde Van Gelder
Translations: Erik Eelbode, Rebecca Nuyts, Aarnoud Rommens
Proof reading: Paul Arblaster

Lay-out: Joke Klaassen

With the support of the Research Foundation - Flanders

Lieven Gevaert Research Centre
Arts Faculty K.U.Leuven
Blijde-Inkomststraat 21
B-3000 Leuven